The Literary Essays of John Heath-Stubbs

Also by John Heath-Stubbs from Carcanet

Collected Poems: 1943–1987
Selected Poems
Naming the Beasts
The Watchman's Flute
The Immolation of Aleph
Sweetapple Earth

Edited by John Heath-Stubbs

Thomas Gray: Selected Poems

Other books by A.T. Tolley

The Early Poetry of Stephen Spender: A Chronology
The Poetry of the Thirties
The Poetry of the Forties
My Proper Ground: A Study of the Work of Philip Larkin
    and its Development
Larkin at Work

Edited by A.T. Tolley

John Lehmann: A Tribute
Roy Fuller: A Tribute

The Literary Essays of John Heath-Stubbs

edited by A.T. Tolley

CARCANET

Published in Great Britain in 1998 by
Carcanet Press Limited
4th Floor, Conavon Court
12–16 Blackfriars Street
Manchester M3 5BQ

A CIP catalogue record for this book is available from the British Library.

ISBN 1 85754 352 1

The publisher acknowledges financial assistance from the Arts Council
of England.

This volume was produced by Carleton Production Centre, Ottawa, using
the TₑX typesetting system, with Adobe POSTSCRIPT Times Roman for
the text, and METAFONT Pandora for the titles.

Printed and bound in England by SRP Ltd, Exeter.

■ Contents

■ Acknowledgements

MY FIRST DEBT is to John Heath-Stubbs, who encouraged me to make this collection, and by whose permission these essays appear. I am also grateful to Michael Schmidt of Carcanet Press for his interest throughout the development of this book. Eddie Linden, a mutual friend of myself and John Heath-Stubbs, gave me early encouragement.

I am indebted to my wife, Glenda, for comment; to Lewis Ford for text transference; to Christina Thiele for preparing the text and for pointing out shortcomings; and to the staff of the Library at Carleton University, Ottawa. The University gave me a grant, without which the text could not have been prepared.

Danny Abse kindly found the text of the essay on Hart Crane, which he originally published. Shafik Megally provided valuable background information.

Acknowledgement is made of the following original publications of the texts in this book:

"Dryden and the Heroic Ideal" [from *Dryden's Mind and Art*, ed. B. King (Edinburgh, Edinburgh U.P., 1969)]

"Baroque Ceremony" [from *Cairo Studies in English* (1959)]

"Jonathan Swift" [Introduction to Crown Classics *Jonathan Swift: A Selection of Poems* (London: Grey Walls Press, 1948)]

"Pope" [Introduction to *Selected Poems of Alexander Pope* (London: Heinemann, 1964)]

"Thomas Gray" [Introduction to *Selected Poems of Thomas Gray* (Manchester: Carcanet, 1983)]

"George Crabbe and the Eighteenth Century" [from *Penguin New Writing* 25 (1945)]

"Wordsworth and Tradition" [from *Tribute to Wordsworth*, ed. M. Spark and D. Stanford (London: Wingate, 1950)]

"Landor's 'Gebir'" [from *PN Review* 38, 1984)]

"Shelley" [Introduction to Crown Classics *Shelley* (London: Grey Walls Press, 1948)]

"Poe" [from *PN Review* 61, 1988)]

"Tennyson" [Introduction to Crown Classics *Selected Poems of Alfred Lord Tennyson* (London: Grey Walls Press, 1948)]

"Ezra Pound: The Last Humanist" [from *Ezra Pound: A Collection of Essays to be Presented to Ezra Pound on his Sixty-fifth Birthday*, ed. P. Russell (London: Peter Nevill, 1950)]

"Structure and Source in Eliot's Major Poetry" [from *Agenda* 23 (1985)]

"Daughters of Memory: David Jones's *The Anathemata*" [from *Nine* 4 (1953)]

"Hart Crane" [from *Verso* 1 (1947)]

"Charles Williams" [London: Longman, for British Council (1955)]

"Cecil Day Lewis: A Real Poet After All" [from *The Tablet* 231 (1977)]

"Auden" [from *The Tablet* 230 (1976)]

"William Bell" [Introduction to *Mountains Beneath the Horizon* (London: Faber, 1950)]

"Tasso's *Gerusalemme Liberata* as Christian Epic" [from *Nine* 3 (1951)]

"Leopardi" [Introduction to *Leopardi: Selected Prose and Poetry*, ed. I. Origo and J. Heath-Stubbs (London: Oxford, 1966)]

"The Astrological Basis of Spenser's *Shephearde's Calendar*" [from *Urania and Cleo Confer*, ed. A. Kitson (London: Unwin, 1989)]

■ Introduction

JOHN HEATH-STUBBS's career as writer had its beginnings in the brilliant Oxford of the early nineteen-forties, when, over a span of a few years, Keith Douglas, Sidney Keyes, Drummond Allison, David Wright, Michael Hamburger, Williams Bell, Alan Ross, Philip Larkin, Kingsley Amis and John Wain were in residence. His poetic associations were with Sidney Keyes and Drummond Allison, both at The Queen's College; and it was in the ambience provided by their friendship— and particularly that of Sidney Keyes — that his style and tastes were formed. In 1941, Sidney Keyes and Michael Meyer edited *Eight Oxford Poets*, which included work by Douglas, Keyes, Heath-Stubbs and Allison. It was published by Herbert Read, then poetry editor at Routledge; and, shortly afterwards, Read published the first books by Keyes and by Heath-Stubbs — *The Iron Laurel* and *Wounded Thammus*.

In his introduction to *Eight Oxford Poets*, Keyes wrote:

> We seem to share a horror of the world's predicament, together with the feeling that we cannot save ourselves without some kind of spiritual readjustment, though the nature of that readjustment may take widely differing forms ... we are all ... Romantic writers ... and ... we have, on the whole, little sympathy with the Audenian school of poets.[1]

These words epitomise the changed cultural outlook to which the war had brought young writers, no longer drawn to the ameliorative enthusiasms that were part of the Left-wing literary ethos of the 'thirties, but faced with the cataclysm that the poets of the 'thirties had warned against. Heath-Stubbs was later to recall:

> For my part I was born a little too late, or too provincial in my education to have fallen under the spell of the early Auden. When I got to Oxford in 1939 he was definitely out of fashion with my friends and contemporaries. We were all for neo-symbolism or even the apocalyptic surreal of Dylan Thomas. I didn't even bother to read Auden very much at that time. (*Auden*)

[Titles in italics after quotations refer to the essays by Heath-Stubbs contained in this book.]

Keyes and Heath-Stubbs had a remarkable reciprocal formative influence on one another:

> I suppose in some sense we complemented each other. He was reading History. He had read the French Symbolists ... and he had read German poetry — Goethe and Schiller, who were quite unknown to me ... He was an enormous enthusiast for Rilke and for Hölderlin, whom I'd never heard of. I did my best to read Rilke; though I've never really been able to like him. Keyes was also ... better read in modern British and American literature than I was. I was really quite unaware that there was any modern literature ... later than Chesterton and Belloc and Shaw and Wells and, in poetry, the Georgians. It was Sidney Keyes very largely who introduced me to modern literature, in both prose and verse ... [2]

These years at Oxford saw not only the beginnings of Heath-Stubbs's career as a poet, but also the start of his writing about poetry. Michael Meyer, who edited the undergraduate periodical *Cherwell* from 1940 to 1941, recorded that he published only five poems by Heath-Stubbs, but included critical pieces by him in almost every issue; and later, when Heath-Stubbs's third collection of poems, *The Divided Ways*, appeared in 1946, Meyer "expressed the wish that he would write more literary criticism, which I so much admired."[3] Heath-Stubbs's first published literary essay seems to have been "The Poetry of John Gay", which appeared in *Cherwell* in February, 1941. The subject marked an enduring bent of his taste; and the essay was the first of hundreds of critical articles, introductions and reviews that Heath-Stubbs was to publish — the most notable of which make up this book.

When Keyes was killed in the Western desert in 1942, Heath-Stubbs turned almost as a duty to producing a book of critical history that would be a memorial to the opinions that he and Sidney Keyes had developed together.

> It was Sidney Keyes who introduced me to the work of Clare, Darley, and Beddoes, and to the serious work of Hood as opposed to his light verse, which I now think we underrated ... He said to me that somebody ought to write an overall study of the poets of this generation of the 1830's and the early 1840's; and the reason, in a way, that I started my book *The Darkling Plain*, which I wrote after I came down from Oxford, with chapters on these poets, was that it seemed to me almost a duty that had been laid upon me by Sidney Keyes.[4]

The Darkling Plain: A Study of the Later Fortunes of Romanticism in English Poetry from George Darley to W.B. Yeats was published in 1950. The authors discussed may today appear somewhat recherché: in 1950 the book must have seemed an eccentric cultivation of writers who were decidedly dated — Darley, Beddoes, the Pre-Raphaelites, Doughty. The awareness of Darley had been there in Keyes's poetry; and forty years later Heath-Stubbs could remember where Keyes bought the copy of Doughty that they read. Romantic poetry as a whole was still rather despised in 1940; but even today Doughty, with his epic of early Britain, must seem not to offer a very rewarding prospect. Just as Heath-Stubbs's own poetry may appear to some distinguished, but out of the main stream; so too do the aspects of English Romanticism defined by the authors included in *The Darkling Plain*. Yet it is a book of remarkable cogency and perceptiveness, revealing the inner life of much that is neglected — even though Heath-Stubbs has since turned his back on some of the works that he was then prepared to take seriously, such as Bridges' *The Testament of Beauty*.

In the introduction to *The Darkling Plain*, Heath-Stubbs said: "I have considered poetry as a species of mythology or significant dream. And for this reason I am more occupied with the implications of a poet's imagery, symbolically interpreted, than with his explicit 'philosophy of life'."[5] As he wrote to Michael Meyer concerning the response to poetry that he and Sidney Keyes shared: " we both had a capacity . . . for reading through to the heart of imagery . . . and finding significance which lay below the conscious level . . . "[6] That perception that a poem was to be experienced importantly in terms of its images was an abiding one for Heath-Stubbs. It is, of course, to be associated with the emphasis on the image as a cardinal device in modernist poetics — an emphasis that has been seen as having its origins in the poetics of the Romantic movement. It is not an emphasis that would have been made, for instance, by Heath-Stubbs's near contemporary, Philip Larkin; and not one that would be widely encountered today.

Another important early influence on Heath-Stubbs's tastes was Charles Williams. At the beginning of the war, Williams had moved to Oxford from London, with the Oxford University Press, for which he worked. A friend of C.S. Lewis, he was asked to lecture in the University. Heath-Stubbs attended those lectures, and found them sympathetic. In discussing the work of Williams, he related it to the changed attitudes that Sidney Keyes had articulated in *Eight Oxford Poets*:

> Younger poets became interested in mythological and religious symbolism, as a means of expressing areas of experience inaccessible to the intellect alone. Among some of these, Williams began to find readers. His influence is discernible in the work of Sidney Keyes and Vernon Watkins, and, in another way, in that of Anne Ridler and Norman Nicholson. (*Williams*)

Williams's approach to poetry was evidently very congenial to Heath-Stubbs and seems to have left its mark on his thinking:

> In a lecture which I heard him deliver at Oxford in 1943, Charles Williams distinguished five principal modes of the Romantic experience, or great images, which occur in poetry. They are: (a) The Religious experience itself . . . (b) The Image of woman . . . (c) The Image of Nature . . . (d) The Image of the City . . . (e) The experience of great art . . . (*Williams*)

Heath-Stubbs goes on to comment on these modes or images:

> In the first place, it will be seen that they are, psychologically, closely linked, especially as, in European poetry, Nature and the City are commonly personified as female figures. Dante's love for Beatrice was inextricably involved with his love for the city of Florence, and his ideal of the Empire. Wordsworth's attitude to nature is fundamentally that of a lover; he speaks of the great poem he planned, of which *The Prelude* was to be the first part, as "spousal verse". It is therefore impossible to treat of any one of these three great images in isolation. (*Williams*)

This mode of discussion, in which poetry is treated in terms of major images, and these major images are seen as recurrent and related throughout the history of poetry, was connected for Heath-Stubbs with a conception of literature as involving archetypal concerns and images — a view that found an earlier emergence in a book that he and Sidney Keyes had known at Oxford, Maud Bodkin's *Archetypal Patterns in Poetry*. This orientation to literature draws Heath-Stubbs back into pondering relationships with earlier philosophical and religious constructs that may today seem recondite — ponderings that reveal his learned intimacy with the details of the constructs he cites, as in his essay on "The Astrological Basis of Spenser's *Shephearde's Calendar*". When talking about Edgar Allan Poe, he mentions the encounter with Poe in the New York subway in Hart Crane's *The Bridge* as an emblem of the darker side of the American dream. He continues:

> In the pattern of Crane's poem the subway is an image of inferno, and that encounter belongs to a poetic tradition of similar encounters in or near the underworld. The origins of this tradition can be traced to Virgil's *Aeneid* and to Homer's *Odyssey* and even further back to the ancient Babylonian epic of Gilgamesh. It leads on to Dante's encounter with the spirit of Virgil in the dark wood, and to that of those two poets and the spirit of Dante's dead master Brunetto Latini in the *Inferno*; the tradition is continued later in Eliot's encounter with the "familiar compound ghost" (I think mainly W.B. Yeats, but Poe is also indicated) in the fire storm of the London blitz, over Bloomsbury. (*Poe*)

Few, in reading either Poe or Crane, would find the epic of Gilgamesh coming to mind; but the pattern of thought is entirely natural to Heath-Stubbs. It arises not merely from an acute awareness of what today would be termed "intertextuality": it involves a very living sense of a constant return in literature (and in life) to themes and images that recur because they embody for us spiritual confrontations and collocations that are eternal.

The vision of our civilisation and its cultural predicament that informs Heath-Stubbs's criticism is one in keeping with this approach to literature. Discussing the poetry of Leopardi, he speaks of "the loss to modern man of that mythopoeic view of the world whereby the Greeks were able to humanize the natural scene, and to feel at home in the universe" (*Leopardi*). And, speaking of the period in which Leopardi wrote — a period he sees as continuous with our own — he said:

> Characteristic of the whole movement was the poets' recognition of their alienation. As the nineteenth century dawned, this was borne in upon them by the new currents of political, philosophical, and scientific thought. Everywhere the old patterns of society were in the melting-pot, and long-established ideas were being challenged. The poets could no longer be certain of their role in society, nor sure of their audience. They were therefore forced to rely more and more on particular inspiration, fitful and transient though it might turn out to be, and less and less on exterior sanction and occasion. Since the traditional forms of religious belief seemed largely to have lost their significance, the poets constructed their own systems, taking their symbols from revived mythologies, or from their experience of erotic passion or of natural beauty ... Leopardi, perhaps more than any of his contemporaries, goes farthest in the exploration of his own alienation. It is this which makes him in some ways a more modern figure than they, a precursor of the existentialist thought of our own age. (*Leopardi*)

Heath-Stubbs's criticism is strongly marked by this concern with the passing of absolute certainty concerning the Christian world-view: a passing that dominated late nineteenth-century and early twentieth-century thinking and feeling in the work of poets as various as Hardy, Yeats, Eliot — and Charles Williams himself, though the latter two were Christians.

Heath-Stubbs was also a Christian. In his younger days he had gone through a period of religious questioning, which had led him, via the poetry of James Thomson (B.V.), to a study of Leopardi, a selection of whose poems he translated and published in 1946. Despite this, a preoccupation with religious questions is there throughout Heath-Stubbs's career as poet, and it manifests itself as the focal centre of the concerns that inform his best criticism. It goes along with a very detailed knowledge of Christian theology and ritual, and of their history, as in the comparatively early but very scholarly essay on Tasso, with its references to "Post-Tridentine Catholic theology, devotion and political aspirations" (*Tasso*).

The sense of things already outlined is related to Heath-Stubbs's idea of the intrinsic nature of poetry and of those who attain its highest achievements. He recalled an early conversation with the young Oxford poet, William Bell, who was killed climbing the Materhorn in 1948:

> 'Did I believe in the Muse?' It was an axiom with him that the Muse, who personified the psychologists' Unconscious, was the source of all real inspiration, and that every true poet must have an objective belief in her. I answered yes ... (*Bell*)

In discussing Auden many years later, Heath-Stubbs gave a related judgement:

> The highest and truest poets are creative and solitary visionaries who stand above and beyond the currents of their time. I believe that something of this quality did adhere to Eliot: to Auden it emphatically did not. (*Auden*)

As Yeats did, Heath-Stubbs seems to regard the Unconscious as the source of the images and visionary power of poetry.

His preoccupation with images that are found throughout the history of literature is associated with the central position that Heath-Stubbs gives to the epic poem:

> The history of this Epic tradition is to a large extent the history of European civilisation itself, and its continuity, at least down to the eighteenth century, was never broken ... The task of the Renaissance Epic poet was to re-interpret the ancient, pagan themes and images, in terms of his own Christian and Humanistic culture. (*Tasso*)

Heath-Stubbs himself is one of the few twentieth-century poets to attempt an epic with any success; and the decision to write a modern epic poem arose in part from the important cultural position that Heath-Stubbs accorded the epic.

Sidney Keyes had discovered Charles Williams's play *Thomas Cranmer of Canterbury*, and this led him and Heath-Stubbs to read Williams's poem *Taliessin through Logres*, a long poem based on Arthurian legend. This reinforced an interest that had been an abiding one for Heath-Stubbs, "The Matter of Britain".

> I'd always been fascinated by that subject. I had been planning an Arthurian poem ever since my undergraduate days. It was partly triggered off by Robert Graves's *Count Belisarius*, which is about a Roman

general in the time of Justinian, when the Byzantine Empire temporarily re-conquered Italy. In his preface to that novel, ... [Graves] says that, if King Arthur had been chronicled by a historian (as Belisarius was by Procopius) instead of by poets and minstrels, we might have a very different picture of a general trying to defend the last remnants of Roman civilization in England in the 6th century. This idea clicked.[7]

Heath-Stubbs continues with a comment that not only connects his interest in the Dark Ages with his vision of the present, but articulates a sense of our historical situation that underlies and connects many of his important attitudes to literature.

It was beginning to be a commonplace, in the 1930s and 40s, that we were perhaps living in a period when civilization was under threat, in a period not unanalogous to the last days of the Roman Empire. I still think there's some truth in that.[8]

It is this historical sense that permeates Heath-Stubbs's epic, *Artorius* (1973) with its anachronistic episodes of contemporary criticism that link its historical narrative to the present. The choice of subject was undoubtedly influenced by the work of Doughty and of Charles Williams; but it is a subject rooted in a mythology that is historical, yet historical largely in folk-memory. In this the choice reflects a related interest of Heath-Stubbs — folklore. In folklore, history becomes myth, the material of poetry; and the myths are passed on from generation to generation in an oral tradition, carrying with them the images that Heath-Stubbs dwells on in his criticism.

That preoccupation with images is something that Heath-Stubbs has in common with the Romantic poets; and he has said, in *The Darkling Plain*, that "The modern poet who deliberately rejects the Romantic tradition, rejects an experience through which the European consciousness has passed, and which has affected it profoundly."[9] It might be asked, then, how it is that, holding a view of poetry related to that held by the Romantics, Heath-Stubbs should have written so sympathetically about the poetry of the eighteenth century: more of the essays collected here are about Augustans than about Romantics. It was, after all, in the age of Dryden that the mythopoeic interpretations of the universe and man's place in it were dismissed by the voices of reason and science.

For Heath-Stubbs, the sense of order and tradition encountered in eighteenth-century poetry was undoubtedly congenial: his loving concern with the myths and ideas of the past goes along with an inherent conservatism. But, in his discussion of the Augustan period in English literature, Heath-Stubbs's historical perceptions merge with an

apprehension of a disturbing undercurrent in human nature, antagonistic
to reason, held in check in the Augustan period, but emerging powerfully
and centrally in Romantic poetry — an apprehension in keeping with
Heath-Stubbs's feeling that our own time had much in common with the
period that preceded the Dark Ages:

> The so-called Augustan Age of English literature represents one of those
> rare moments in history when perfection of style is achieved. This per-
> fection symbolizes the momentary triumph of civilization and the human
> intellect over that chaos which lies eternally around and within us ... Yet
> though chaos seemed to have been banished, the victory was not lightly
> won. The greatest geniuses of the age — Pope, its most absolute poet,
> Swift himself, and later, Johnson with his grave and profound melan-
> choly — are acutely conscious of the forces of unreason which continually
> threaten them ... The whole of the eighteenth century suffered from a
> deeprooted spiritual anxiety. It is surely no coincidence that madness
> overwhelmed Swift, Collins, Smart, and Cowper and threatened Johnson
> and Boswell ...
>
> In the work of Swift and Pope style is still strong enough to contain and
> limit chaos. But chaos is never far absent from their minds, and the
> consciousness of this gives to their work a kind of smouldering, nervous
> intensity, underlying its apparently calm surface ... (*Swift*)

Indeed, Heath-Stubbs frequently contends, as in the essay on Gray,
that "what we define as Romantic sensibility is in fact something that
was present throughout the eighteenth century, and the shift to Roman-
ticism proper was, in some respects, a shift of emphasis rather than a
revolutionary change" (*Gray*). The sense of this continuity underlies
Heath-Stubbs's discussion of the literature of the Augustan period.

Heath-Stubbs comes at the end of a period in English literary criticism
informed by the idea of a tradition inherent in a body of literature that
was at once past, and yet a living source for writers of the present. The
very idea of literary history emerged only in the late eighteenth century,
with the growing cultural dominance of vernacular literature, as opposed
to classical literature; and it was associated throughout Europe with a
sense of national cultural identity. *The Cambridge History of English
Literature* appeared at the turn of the century; and, in 1919, T.S. Eliot
wrote, in "Tradition and the Individual Talent", that anyone "who would
continue to be a poet beyond his twenty-fifth year" must "write ... with
a feeling that the whole of the literature of Europe has a simultaneous
existence and composes a simultaneous order".[10] As late as 1948, Anne
Ridler, a contemporary of Heath-Stubbs, could write that it was "Auden
(with, of course, dead poets, notably Sir Thomas Wyatt) who first made

me think I saw how to become" a poet.[11] The conjunction of Wyatt with Auden as living influences would not seem so natural today.

In the work of Heath-Stubbs, as both poet and critic, that sense of literary tradition involving a body of literature livingly available to us today is vibrantly present. In his poetry, as a cursory examination of titles alone will show, the literature of the past is an important inspiration, as are the images that inhabit it. One of the refreshing features of his criticism is his detailed and intimate knowledge of minor authors and their works, such as Blair's *The Grave*, and his readiness to give them intense attention. Since he began writing, there has arisen a greater awareness of the historical relativity of everything written, which has come to qualify our sense of the literature of the past, so that works seem sometimes to be approached as cultural symptoms rather than for their own sake. The unqualified immediacy of Heath-Stubbs's response to literature, learned but intensely engaged, is something no longer so frequently encountered; and it is for this immediacy that we must value his essays.

A.T. Tolley
Carleton University, Ottawa
December 1996

NOTES

1. S. Keyes, Introduction to *Eight Oxford Poets* (London: Routledge, 1941), vii.
2. "John Heath-Stubbs: An Interview" (with A.T. Tolley) *Aquarius* 17/18 (1986) 115–116.
3. M. Meyer, "John Heath-Stubbs in the Forties", *Aquarius* 10 (1978), 15.
4. "John Heath-Stubbs: An Interview" (with A.T. Tolley) 112.
5. J. Heath-Stubbs, *The Darkling Plain* (London: Eyre and Spottiswoode, 1950), xv.
6. Letter to Michael Meyer, Sept. 12, 1944; quoted in "John Heath-Stubbs in the Forties", 14.
7. "Clive Wilmer in conversation with John Heath-Stubbs" *PN Review* 19, 6 (1993) 52.
8. "Clive Wilmer in conversation with John Heath-Stubbs" 52.
9. *The Darkling Plain*, 179.
10. T.S. Eliot, "Tradition and the Individual Talent" in *Selected Essays* (London: Faber, 1951), 14.
11. A. Ridler, "A Question of Speech", *Focus* 3 (1948), 109.

A NOTE ON THE TEXT

The essays contained in this book were largely written as reviews or as contributions to books. The earliest is from 1945; the last, from 1989. They have the flavour of the periods in which they were composed; and nothing has been done to modify modes, mannerisms or references that today might seem old-fashioned. There has been no attempt to make uniform things such as spelling or punctuation. A few errors and misprints have been corrected, and quoted passages have been revised in places in keeping with standard texts.

A small number of minor changes have been made, with the permission of the author. These are of two kinds: in a few cases, references to the books whose reviews were the occasions of the essays have been removed; and, where there were footnotes that offered "asides" on the topic of an essay, they have been fed back into the text. One or two explanatory insertions have also been made at the request of the author, and those are set, for clarity, in square brackets. There are only a few essays where such changes have been made.

■ Related Reading

BY JOHN HEATH-STUBBS

Collected Poems (Manchester: Carcanet, 1988)

Hindsights (Autobiography) (London: Hodder and Stoughton, 1993)

The Darkling Plain (Criticism) (London, Eyre and Spottiswoode, 1950)

OTHER

Aquarius 10 (John Heath-Stubbs issue) 1978

A.T. Tolley, "John Heath-Stubbs" in *Dictionary of Literary Biography*, vol. 27, 138–149 (Detroit: Gale, 1984)

A.T. Tolley, *The Poetry of the Forties* (Manchester U.P., 1985)

J. Van Domlin, *John Heath-Stubbs: A Checklist* (Fontwell: Centaur Press, 1987)

INTERVIEWS

"John Heath-Stubbs: An Interview" (with A.T. Tolley). *Aquarius* 17/18 (1987) 112–120

"Clive Wilmer in Conversation with John Heath-Stubbs". *PN Review* 19, 6 (1993) 51–54

"Conversations III". *The Swansea Review* 16 (1996) 16–23

■ Dryden and the Heroic Ideal

T O REMARK on the extraordinary range and variety of Dryden's work is only to repeat what has been said time and time again. His acknowledged greatness is as a satirist, but he wrote with success in pretty well every form current in his time — heroic tragedy, comedy of manners, ode, elegy and song, polemical didactic verse, and narrative. But the last named of these is represented only by *Annus Mirabilis*, rather early on in his career, and by the translation of the *Aeneid*, and the *Fables* (likewise translations or adaptations) at the end of it. This is a little surprising. For it is to the ideal of Epic or Heroic verse (in his age the two terms were synonymous) that, I think, all his work really points. One might suggest that it is haunted by the epic poem which he never got around to writing. That this poem existed in his mind we know. Its subject was to be King Arthur, or the Black Prince's expedition to Spain to reinstate Pedro the Cruel as King of Castile.

Dryden indeed did write an opera on the subject of King Arthur, which we remember only for its lyrics, and more especially for Purcell's settings of them. If Dryden had written his Arthurian epic, it would doubtless have made more lively reading than the two that were written on that theme by his younger contemporary, Sir Richard Blackmore (though Blackmore has his moments). We do not, I think, regret a lost masterpiece — something to set beside *Paradise Lost*. But it is worth enquiring both why Dryden wanted to write an epic and why he did not in fact do so. And such an enquiry may, I suggest, throw some light both on the strength and the weaknesses of the poems that he actually did write.

The occasional nature of the greater part of Dryden's work has led to his sometimes being termed a verse journalist. Now it is undeniable that there went towards the making of many of his poems, especially the satires, an impulse which today would find its most natural outlet in some form of journalism. But the flair of a journalist and technical virtuosity alone are not enough to make a great poet. And a great poet Dryden certainly was. The fact is that he is a transitional figure. He has not yet really attained the Augustan view of society as a field for the exploration of the moral nature of man. This was to be the vision of Pope and of the eighteenth-century moralists and novelists. But he still carries with him something of that renaissance view which saw human society, and specifically the monarchical nation state, as ideally exemplifying the earthly realisation of a transcendent and cosmic order. What had once been imperial ritual had in his age passed into state ceremony. For Spenser and his contemporaries it was not absurd to impute to Elizabeth all the attributes of a goddess. Her court was that of an earthly Cynthia, surrounded by chaste nymphs and by heroes. In his baroque panegyrics Dryden is attempting to do the same sort of thing for Charles II and James II. The gap between ideal and reality was probably not actually any greater, but it was more patent. Dryden's age attempted to project its ideals in the Heroic mode: but its sensibility had now been invaded by a new, ironic and sceptical intelligence. And the latter was inevitably destructive of the former.

Annus Mirabilis may be considered, I think, as Dryden's first mature work. He was a slow developer, and although he was thirty-six at the date of its publication, it has a certain youthful verve and baroque extravagance about it, which is sometimes a little absurd but which is also endearing. The baroque wit of *Annus Mirabilis* is in the tradition of Cowley and Cleveland. It depends, in the metaphysical manner, on extended rhetorical figures often involving a union between the transcendent and the extremely mundane. The notorious passage, in which the Almighty extinguishes the flames of the Fire of London with a crystal pyramid, like a householder snuffing a candle, is an example, and so is that in which the Angel with the Flaming Sword descends to protect the powder magazines.

Dryden never wholly abandoned this kind of wit. In his maturer work it is more often apparent in his Pindaric poems. His adoption of the heroic couplet, in the Augustan form which he developed from Waller and Denham, had in itself a restraining influence. The closed couplet does not very readily admit of the extended trope. Hence its fitness for clarity of exposition and argument. Dryden calls *Annus Mirabilis* an Historical Poem, but it is clearly to be considered as a preliminary exercise in the epic manner by a poet who has wider ambitions in that field. Its subject matter is contemporary, the events of the year 1666 — the naval victory over the Dutch, and the Great fire of London. But clearly Dryden is doing more than writing a journalist's report on these; he is attempting to give them the wider and timeless context of epic poetry. In his prefatory letter to Sir Robert Howard he says:

I have call'd my poem *Historical*, not *Epick*, though both the Actions and the Actors are as much Heroick, as any Poem can contain. But since the Action is not properly one, nor that accomplish'd in the last successes, I have judg'd it too bold a Title for a few *Stanza's*, which are little more in number then a single *Iliad*, or the longest of the *Aeneids*. For this reason, (I mean not of length, but broken action, ti'd too severely to the Laws of History) I am apt to agree with those who rank *Lucan* rather among Historians in Verse, then Epique Poets: in whose room, if I am not deceiv'd, *Silius Italicus*, though a worse Writer, may more justly be admitted.

Annus Mirabilis then may be considered primarily as a Lucanian poem, though Dryden also acknowledges his debt to Virgil, especially in his epic similes. These latter, incidentally, are largely taken from animal life, and are often very lively; in them, Dryden writes as a naturalist and a member of the Royal Society. But the reference to Silius Italicus is also significant. He was the author of the *Punica*, an epic treatment of the Punic Wars. The point of the first part of *Annus Mirabilis* largely consists in an implicit identification of London with Rome, and of Holland with Carthage: "Our second Punic War." (The same comparison appears in Marvell's "Last Instructions to the Painter".) The poem is dedicated to the "Metropolis of Great Britain" and the City of London is in effect the hero and the unifying factor of the work. In the dedication it is addressed in quasi-religious terms: "You are now a Phoenix in her ashes, and, as far as humanity can approach, a great emblem of the suffering Deity." One of the best passages in *Annus Mirabilis* is that in which Dryden describes the repairing of the English fleet, after the first, apparently indecisive, encounter with the Dutch. Here the ship, the "London", is introduced with special emphasis. As the gift of the citizens to the King it typifies their loyalty, and by the recurrence of the phoenix image it becomes almost a symbol of the city itself, and prepares the way for the second part of the poem, dealing with the Great Fire:

> The goodly *London* in her gallant trim,
> (The *Phoenix* daughter of the vanish'd old:)
> Like a rich Bride does to the Ocean swim,
> And on her shadow rides in floating gold.

> Her Flag aloft spread ruffling to the wind,
> And sanguine Streamers seem the floud to fire:
> The Weaver charm'd with what his Loom design'd,
> Goes on to Sea, and knows not to retire.

> With roomy decks, her Guns of mighty strength,
> (Whose low-laid mouthes each mounting billow laves:)

Deep in her draught, and warlike in her length,
    She seems a Sea-wasp flying on the waves.

This martial Present, piously design'd,
    The Loyal City give their best-lov'd King:
And with a bounty ample as the wind,
    Built, fitted and maintain'd to aid him bring.

This passage is preceded by an extended simile in which the industry
of the dockyard workers is compared to that of the bees. The bee im-
age has a long tradition behind it, going back through the Middle Ages,
and suggesting not only industry but also the ideally ordered common-
wealth. But the introduction of the "London" leads on immediately to a
remarkable passage in which Dryden treats of the evolution of the art of
navigation from its primitive beginnings, and prophesies the progress of
modern scientific discovery:

By viewing Nature, Natures Hand-maid, Art,
    Makes mighty things from small beginnings grow:
Thus fishes first to shipping did impart
    Their tail the Rudder, and their head the Prow.

Some Log, perhaps, upon the waters swam
    An useless drift, which, rudely cut within,
And hollow'd, first a floating trough became,
    And cross some Riv'let passage did begin.

In shipping such as this, the *Irish Kern*,
    And untaught *Indian*, on the stream did glide:
Ere sharp-keel'd Boats to stem the floud did learn,
    Or fin-like Oars did spread from either side.
    . . . .

Of all who since have us'd the open Sea,
    Then the bold *English* none more fame have won:
Beyond the Year, and out of Heav'ns high-way,
    They make discoveries where they see no Sun.

But what so long in vain, and yet unknown,
    By poor man-kinds benighted wit is sought,
Shall in this Age to *Britain* first be shown,
    And hence be to admiring Nations taught.

The Ebbs of Tydes, and their mysterious flow,
    We, as Arts Elements shall understand:
And as by Line upon the Ocean go,
    Whose paths shall be familiar as the Land.

> Instructed ships shall sail to quick Commerce;
> > By which remotest Regions are alli'd:
> Which makes one City of the Universe,
> > Where some may gain, and all may be suppli'd.
>
> Then, we upon our Globes last verge shall go,
> > And view the Ocean leaning on the sky:
> From thence our rolling Neighbours we shall know,
> > And on the Lunar world securely pry.

Annus Mirabilis serves to remind us that Dryden has a foot in two worlds. One is the medieval-renaissance world, in which natural objects exist mainly to typify spiritual truths, and in which angelic intelligences intervene. The other is the modern scientific world in which objects are to be experimentally investigated, and subject to evolutionary change. That evolutionary ideas were in the air in Dryden's time, much earlier than is often supposed, can be shown from a passage in *The Hind and the Panther*, in which the doctrine of the fixity of species is put in question. Speaking of the wolf he says:

> The *Fox* and he came shuffl'd in the dark,
> If ever they were stow'd in *Noah's* ark:
> Perhaps not made; for all their barking train
> The Dog (a common species) will contain.
> And some wild currs, who from their masters ran,
> Abhorring the supremacy of man,
> In woods and caves the rebel-race began.

Dryden had already some years before embarked on his career as a writer for the theatre. His numerous plays present something of a problem for the critic. Hardly any of them is wholly without interest or merit, but they are an acquired taste. The Heroic Tragedy is a curious phenomenon. Basically it is a resumption and extension, modified by neo-classical influence, of the type established before the civil war by Fletcher and Massinger. Its relationship to the French classical tragedy of Corneille and Racine is rather remote. A closer contemporary European analogy is to be sought in the post-Monteverdian baroque Italian opera, as in the work of Cavalli and Chesti. Dryden himself in the Essay prefixed to *The Conquest of Granada* traces the origin of the form to Davenant's *The Siege of Rhodes*. This was written as an opera under the Commonwealth, when dramatic entertainments were banned, and rehandled as a play after the Restoration.

Dryden wrote for the stage because that still represented the field in which a writer could most readily earn his living. His natural bent was not essentially dramatic: but if this be so, it is astonishing that his plays should exhibit so much genuine vitality. What he seems to have aimed at, in the period of his early career in the theatre, was to make a virtue of necessity by transferring his epic aspirations to the dramatic form. It is clear from the rather euphoric prefatory essay to *The Conquest of Granada* that the acclaim of that play convinced him, if only temporarily, that he had succeeded:

> That an heroic play ought to be an imitation, in little, of an heroic poem and, consequently, that love and valour ought to be the subject of it.

Speaking of the character of Almanzor he says:

> The first image I had of him was from the Achilles of Homer, the next from Tasso's Rinaldo (who was a copy of the former), and the third from the Artaban of Monsieur Calprenede, who has imitated both.

Dryden's definition of the epic, therefore, includes not only the classical exemplars and the Italian Romantic Epic of the Renaissance, but the contemporary French Heroic Romances, considered as a species of prose epic. These once popular and now more or less unreadable forerunners of the psychological novel, their plots hinging on high-flown conflicts of love, honour, and virtue, represent one side of the seventeenth century's image of itself. The obverse is represented by the realism and cynicism of Restoration Comedy.

The central theme of *The Conquest of Granada* seems to me to consist in the juxtaposition of natural virtue, represented by Almanzor, and the corrupt and faction-ridden state of Granada under its ineffectual king, Boabdelin. But in fact Almanzor is more convincing when temporarily in defeat and placed in a pathetic situation. This occurs at the end of the first part of the play. He is compelled to resign Almahide to the king, and she to dismiss him:

ALMAHIDE. Adieu, then, O my soul's far better part!
    Your image sticks so close,
    That the blood follows from my rending heart.
    A last farewell!
    For, since the last must come, the rest are vain,
    Like gasps in death, which but prolong our pain.
    But, since the king is now a part of me,
    Cease from henceforth to be his enemy.
    Go now, for pity go! for, if you stay,
    I fear I shall have something still to say.
    Thus — I for ever shut you from my sight. (*Veils*)

ALMANZOR. Like one thrust out in a cold winter's night,
Yet shivering underneath your gate I stay;
One look — I cannot go before 'tis day. —
    (*She beckons him to be gone*)
Not one — Farewell: Whate'er my sufferings be
Within, I'll speak farewell as loud as she:
I will not be outdone in constancy. —
    (*She turns her back*)
Then like a dying conqueror I go;
At least I have looked last upon my foe.
I go — but if too heavily I move,
I walk encumbered with a weight of love.
Fain would I leave the thought of you behind,
But still, the more I cast you from my mind,
You dash, like water, back, when thrown against the wind. (*Exit*)

There is even a certain pathos in Almanzor's relapsing into his habitual
bombast ("I'll speak farewell as loud as she") as if he could not help it.
This bombast of Almanzor is of course frequently absurd, and invited
the burlesque of Drawcansir in *The Rehearsal*. But surely Dryden did
not intend it to be absurd. If he had there would have been no point
in the burlesque. But there is also an intentional element of ironic
humour — what Saintsbury has called "purple comedy" — in Dryden's
Heroic plays. One should consider the scenes in which the scheming
coquette Lyndaraxa appears. She belongs essentially to the world of
Restoration Comedy, and is first cousin to Congreve's Mrs. Marwood
and Vanbrugh's Lady Fancifull.

It is in relation to the scenes between the Emperor and the Empress in
Aureng-Zebe that Saintsbury used the phrase "purple comedy". This, the
last of Dryden's rhymed Heroic plays, is more restrained, and mitigates
the snip-snap of the heroic couplet by a freer use of enjambment. *Aureng-
Zebe* seems to me to have a greater coherence of theme than any of its
predecessors. The moral is the typically Drydenian one of the danger
of faction and disorder in the state. The Emperor, in allowing this to
come about, is guilty of a levity not unlike that of King Lear. Beside him
is placed the sinister Empress Nourmahal. She stands for unregulated
passion, which eventually issues in insanity. She has, of course, to run
stark mad not only in white satin but also in regular heroic couplets. But
the passage in which she does so is a not uninteresting example of the
tendency of the baroque to spill over into the surrealistic:

I burn, I more than burn; I am all fire.
See how my mouth and nostrils flame expire!

I'll not come near myself —
Now I'm a burning lake, it rolls and flows;
I'll rush, and pour it all upon my foes.
Pull, pull, that reverend piece of timber near:
Throw't on — 'tis dry — 'twill burn —
Ha, ha! how my old husband crackles there!
Keep him down, keep him down; turn him about:
I know him, — he'll but whiz, and go straight out.
Fan me, you winds: What, not one breath of air?
I'll burn them all, and yet have flames to spare.
Quench me: Pour on whole rivers. 'Tis in vain:
Morat stands there to drive them back again:
With those huge bellows in his hands, he blows
New fire into my head: My brain-pan glows.
See! see! there's Aureng-Zebe too takes his part;
But he blows all his fire into my heart.

Against these forces of disorder stands the heroic virtue of Aureng-Zebe himself, less flamboyant than that of Almanzor. It is contrasted again with the courage of Morat, in whom it is related to no moral principle but merely to that of self-seeking ambition. In this Morat is a kind of forerunner of Achitophel. One of the best scenes of the play is that in which Morat has got the heroine Indamora into his power. She has nothing to rely upon except her honour: but here this abstraction which everybody in these plays is always talking about suddenly comes before us as a real, positive and effective quality:

INDAMORA. How you confound desires of good and ill!
　　　　For true renown is still with virtue joined;
　　　　But lust of power lets loose the unbridled mind.
　　　　Yours is a soul irregularly great,
　　　　Which, wanting temper, yet abounds with heat,
　　　　So strong, yet so unequal pulses beat;
　　　　A sun, which does, through vapours, dimly shine;
　　　　What pity 'tis, you are not all divine!
　　　　New moulded, thorough lightened, and a breast
　　　　So pure, to bear the last severest test;
　　　　Fit to command an empire you should gain
　　　　By virtue, and without a blush to reign.

MORAT. You show me somewhat I ne'er learnt before;
　　　　But 'tis the distant prospect of a shore,
　　　　Doubtful in mists; which, like enchanted ground,
　　　　Flies from my sight, before 'tis fully found.

INDAMORA. Dare to be great, without a guilty crown;
    View it, and lay the bright temptation down:
    'Tis base to seize on all, because you may;
    That's empire, that, which I can give away:
    There's joy when to wild will you laws prescribe,
    When you bid Fortune carry back her bribe:
    A joy, which none but greatest minds can taste;
    A fame, which will to endless ages last.

MORAT. Renown, and fame, in vain, I courted long,
    And still pursued them, though directed wrong,
    In hazard, and in toils, I heard they lay;
    Sailed farther than the coast, but missed my way;
    Now you have given me virtue for my guide;
    And, with true honour, ballasted my pride.
    Unjust dominion I no more pursue;
    I quit all other claims, but those to you.

Dryden's characters have been called puppets. But, although Morat's conversion is rather sudden, we have here what is surely a convincing psychological picture of a man realising for the first time that the principle on which his life has hitherto been founded is wholly wrong.

After *Aureng-Zebe*, as everybody knows, Dryden grew "weary of his long-loved mistress, Rhyme" — that is, of course, as far as plays were concerned. With the abandonment of rhyme went to a large extent the abandonment of the idea of Heroic Drama, in the sense of transference to the stage of the principles of the Epic. The best of the later plays are therefore more truly tragic in conception. *All for Love* is "written in imitation of Shakespeare's style". This phrase, I think, refers to the adoption of blank verse. For the play is really very un-Shakespearean in conception. It is perhaps the only English Tragedy which can seriously be compared with the work of Corneille and Racine. What Dryden gives us here is a kind of mathematical demonstration of the balance of abstract forces. The symmetrical patterning of cross-relationships of love, honour, jealousy, and friendship is characteristic of Restoration Drama in general, comedy as well as tragedy. They give to the whole a structure which, if we imagine it spatially, is analogous to the balanced mathematical construction of Baroque architecture. In *All for Love* this principle is carried to the point where the whole meaning of the play depends upon it. Antony and Cleopatra stand for the values of love; Ventidius and Octavia for Roman virtue, which is however the value of a world well lost. Unlike Dryden's earlier heroes, Antony in defeat has allowed his heroic virtue to be wholly eclipsed by his passion, so that the two are now no longer compatible. Ventidius represents stoic virtue untouched by passion. He succeeds in temporarily arousing Antony and attempts to wean him away from Cleopatra to Octavia. Perhaps the most striking scene in the play is that in which Octavia and Cleopatra confront each other. The Restoration dramatists were fond of this kind of scene, which undoubtedly offered an opportunity for virtuoso acting by the actresses. But the scene in *All for Love* has more power than the similar one in Lee's *The Rival Queens*, which is probably its model. It is more than a mere slanging match, because Octavia and Cleopatra represent the two main conflicting forces of the drama.

The third force is friendship, represented by Antony's relationship to Dolabella. By a tragic twist Antony is brought to believe that Dolabella is about to betray him with Cleopatra. In repudiating her, he is divided from the one value still remaining to him, and his final destruction is thus made inevitable. Dryden's Cleopatra, much less complex than Shakespeare's, is a pattern of faithful devotion, and thus has no way of winning Antony back once he has ceased to believe in her. The stratagem of bringing to Antony a false report of her death, which leads to the final catastrophe, is not of her devising, but the ruse of her servant Alexas. In Alexas is concentrated all the Egyptian deviousness which was an integral part of the character of Shakespeare's Cleopatra. Alexas is a eunuch who has never loved; his cunning is of the head and not of the heart, and hence can be of no real service to Cleopatra nor withstand the inevitable workings of Fate.

It is not so easy, however, to determine what kind of love Antony and Cleopatra stand for in this play. It seems to change its nature according to whether we look at it from the point of view of Octavia and Ventidius or that of Antony and Cleopatra themselves. The first two of these characters stand for Rome with its connotation of Law. From their point of view Cleopatra is a seductress; at best Antony's love for her is Romantic Love — but that Romantic Love which is never consonant with marriage. But Cleopatra herself, in the moment before her death, claims the high title of wife, and abrogates to herself the Roman values. Her suicide is in the end not so much a romantic one, as that extreme assertion of virtue which Roman stoic tradition justified. This seems to imply that Love embodies a higher value with its own transcendent law.

But in the Prologue, Antony is, apparently, no better than "all the keeping Tonyes of the Pit". In that line the whole heroic structure of the play is abolished — and indeed this is often the case with Dryden's prologues and epilogues. Their values are those, presumably, of at least Part of the audience — a part which was not prepared to take heroic tragedy seriously. They went to the Theatre, one must suppose, for a temporary escape, to see characters motivated by ideals of Love and Honour which they did not envisage as being really relatable to actual contemporary life. Actual contemporary life was the subject of comedy, a school of manners. As a man of the world Dryden was probably in agreement with them: but not, I think, entirely so as a poet. It is precisely its ambiguity, or at least its double standard of values which makes *All for Love* a true tragedy, in a sense that this word does not really apply to the other Heroic Plays.

I have spoken of the element of ironic comedy in Dryden's Heroic tragedies. In comedy, as such, he was, as he himself admitted, less successful. *The Spanish Friar* and *Marriage à la Mode* are generally accounted the best, and the second of these is probably the more interesting to modern readers. As far as I can remember, it is the only one of Dryden's plays to have been given on the London stage in the last quarter of a century. There are two very loosely connected plots, the one, heroical-pastoral, in verse, and the other a typical piece of Restoration prose comedy. It is perhaps idle to look for any unity in it, but part of the theme of the verse plot is the contrast between pastoral innocence and the sophistication of courts, while that of the prose plot is the ironic discrepancy between the ideal of love or gallantry and the social reality of marriage. Furthermore, there is perhaps some parallelism between the way in which the characters of the verse plot change places in relation to the throne, and the swapping of partners in the prose plot, as in a dance set. A game of hide-and-seek and a masked ball are also features that set the tone of the play; for all the characters are in some sense victims of illusion and deception. There is some rather beautiful pastoral verse in the scene in which Leonidas and Palmyra remember their first innocent falling in love when they were supposed peasants. We may set against this idyll the cynicism of the song with which the play opens:

> Why should a foolish Marriage Vow,
>> Which long ago was made,
> Oblige us to each other now,
>> When Passion is decayed?
> We lov'd, and we lov'd, as long as we cou'd,
>> Till our love was lov'd out in us both;
> But our Marriage is dead, when the Pleasure is fled:
> 'Twas Pleasure first made it an Oath.

But this purely pragmatic view of marriage is not, after all, what is finally accepted — here, or elsewhere in Restoration comedy. Rhodophil must eventually go back to his Doralice, having escaped being cuckolded (though only just). And Palamede, at the injunction of his father, woos and wins Melantha whom he does not love. The irony is that Rhodophil really does have in Doralice a witty and charming wife, yet he is infatuated with Melantha. Palamede, who is obliged to marry the latter, sees her for what she really is — an affected *bourgeoise*, who apes the manners of the court and second-hand French fashions. The last interview between Palamede and Doralice is touching:

PALAMEDE. Yet, if we had but once enjoyed one another! but then once only is worse than not at all: It leaves a man with such a lingering after it.

DORALICE. For aught I know,'tis better that we have not; we might upon trial have liked each other less, as many a man and woman, that have loved as desperately as we, and yet, when they came to possession, have sighed and cried to themselves, Is this all?

PALAMEDE. Well, madam, I am convinced, that 'tis best for us not to have enjoyed; but, gad, the strongest reason is, because I can't help it.

DORALICE. The only way to keep us new to one another, is never to enjoy, as they keep grapes, by hanging them upon a line; they must touch nothing, if you would preserve them fresh.

PALAMEDE. But then they wither, and grow dry in the very keeping.

There is a great sadness underlying this. The ideal of romantic love is deeply felt, but felt to be unattainable.

When *Absalom and Achitophel* appeared in 1681 Dryden was fifty. This is certainly his most read and probably his finest and most characteristic work. The contemporary events which were its occasion provided Dryden with a subject with which he was really concerned. Growing up as he did during the Civil War period Dryden had come to believe in the necessity of a strong central monarchical authority, accepted as of divine right, and to hold in abhorrence violent mob rule and private opinion. For him, the attempt of Shaftesbury and the Whigs, with Puritan backing, to capitalise on the alleged Popish Plot, and to settle the succession on Monmouth instead of the lawful heir, threatened an outbreak of chaos and anarchy which was satanic in its nature.

Absalom and Achitophel is not mock-heroic, but, as Mr. Ian Jack correctly states, epic satire. Cowley's unfinished epic, *The Davideas*, had had as its subject-matter the career of King David. At a first glance, a hypothetical reader unacquainted with the events of the day might almost take *Absalom and Achitophel* to be another and better written book of Cowley's poem. Dryden had also read *Paradise Lost*. There are direct echoes of it in *Absalom and Achitophel*. The gap between the two poems is not so great as one might think (in spite of Dryden and Milton being on different political sides). Achitophel-Shaftesbury is a satanic figure; "Hell's dire agent". Like Morat (and like Milton's Satan) he is "irregularly great". (This phrase applied by Indamora to Morat has aesthetic and critical connotations. What might be said of a great but imperfect work of art is here used of a noble but morally faulty man. Nothing could illustrate better the way in which, in the neo-classical period, moral and aesthetic values were felt to be interdependent.) So, in a different way, is Zimri-Buckingham, the timeless type of the dangerously irresponsible intellectual, as Achitophel is of the unscrupulous power-driven politician. The characters of these are the best known passages in the poem. They are anthologisable and will stand on their own. It is quite legitimate to allow them to do so, for they belong to the widely practised seventeenth-century *genre* of character writing. But they gain immensely in significance in the context of the narrative of the poem. The passage in which Achitophel wins over Absalom is one of Dryden's best dramatic scenes, and should be compared with the temptation scene in *Paradise Lost*. In a sense Absalom-Monmouth bears the same relationship to his father the king, who as the Lord's Anointed is God's representative, as Adam does to God. The temptation which Achitophel presents to him is essentially the same as that which Satan presents to Eve. In both cases it is Proper Pride that is appealed to, in order to break the principle of Degree.

Absalom and Achitophel, as epic satire, is *sui generis*: but, in *Mac Flecknoe*, Dryden practically invented, as far as English literature is concerned, the mock-heroic poem. Spenser's Muiopotmos and Drayton's Nymphidia are earlier examples: but they are purely and delightfully exercises of fancy, and do not have the satiric content of the classical mock-heroic. Dryden seems to have conceived of the mock-heroic or burlesque as a kind of anti-image of the true heroic, as the following remarks from the prefatory letter to *Annus Mirabilis* may show:

> Such descriptions or images, well wrought, which I promise not for mine, are, as I have said, the adequate delight of heroick Poesie, for they beget admiration, which is its proper object; as the images of the Burlesque, which is contrary to this, by the same reason beget laughter; for the one shows Nature beautified, as in the picture of a fair Woman, which we all admire; the other shows her deformed, ... at which we cannot forbear to laugh, because it is a deviation from Nature.

The realm of Non-sense over which Shadwell presides is thus antithetical to Nature, the imitation of which is the object of all good writing. Shad-well is not only king over the realm of Nonsense, but also its Messiah or rather Anti-Christ. Flecknoe is his Elijah or John the Baptist. The near blasphemy of the passage in which this is implied is thus not wholly frivolous:

> Heywood and Shirley were but Types of thee,
> Thou last great Prophet of Tautology:
> Even I, a dunce of more renown than they,
> Was sent before but to prepare thy way:
> And coarsely clad in Norwich Drugget came
> To teach the Nations in thy greater name.

Mac Flecknoe provided the model for Pope's The Dunciad. The latter has the scope of a full-scale anti-epic. In it the Goddess of Dullness, the daughter of Chaos and old Night, threatens to destroy the whole Augustan order of reason and good sense through her "uncreating word". The best parts of it are perhaps Pope at his most truly serious. For although in his age the true Epic still remained in theory the goal to which the poet must strive, the mock-heroic more truly represented its characteristic spirit. The relation of the mock-epic to the true epic is therefore somewhat like the relation of comedy to tragedy, though it does not seem quite to have been conceived in those terms. Indeed, the mock-epic could not exist without the values of the true epic continuing to be taken, at least in theory, seriously. The mock-heroic is not a criticism of the epic, but of life. By magnifying trivialities to heroic proportions it shows them to be the more trivial. This is very obviously the method of The Rape of the Lock, for instance. But in so far as the age became increasingly concerned with practical reason, rather than with ideas, the neo-classical mock-heroic is a vital form, whereas the serious epic, after Milton, is not. It continued its theoretical existence till the end of the eighteenth century, realising itself in such works as Glover's Leonidas and Wilkie's Epigoniad. When it finally expired, the mock-heroic died with it. The "comic epic poem in prose" of Fielding, with its Cervantean derivation, was also related to the mock-heroic. It started one main stream of the English novel. The other began when Richardson transmuted the values of the Heroic Romance into those of bourgeois realism, and produced in Clarissa Harlow the only true tragedy of the eighteenth century.

Immediately after the passage quoted above from the preface to Annus Mirabilis, in which Dryden treats of the burlesque, he says:

> ... the same images serve equally for the Epique Poesie, and for the Historique and Panegyrique, which are branches of it ...

As panegyric writing we may class the "Heroic Stanzas on the Death of the Lord Protector", "Astraea Redux", and the "Threnodia Augustalis".

But the finest example is surely the "Ode to the Memory of Mrs. Anne Killigrew". It is of course nothing to the point that the accomplished lady was a very minor versifier. In this poem she is treated as a symbol of Poetry and the place it should occupy in the court, and of virgin purity:

> Thou youngest Virgin-Daughter of the Skies,
> Made in the last Promotion of the Blest;
> Whose Palmes, new pluckt from Paradise,
> In spreading Branches more sublimely rise,
> Rich with Immortal Green above the rest:
> Whether, adopted to some Neighbouring Star,
> Thou rol'st above us, in thy wand'ring Race,
> Or, in Procession fixt and regular,
> Mov'd with the Heavens Majestick Pace;
> Or, call'd to more Superiour Bliss,
> Thou tread'st, with Seraphims, the vast Abyss:
> What ever happy Region is thy place,
> Cease thy Celestial Song a little space;
> (Thou wilt have Time enough for Hymns Divine,
> Since Heav'ns Eternal Year is thine.)

This baroque heaven is on the model of the earthly court, and the promotion of the blest a kind of celestial honours list. The Deity Himself is a sort of *grand monarque*:

> And if no clust'ring Swarm of Bees
> On thy sweet Mouth distill'd their golden Dew,
> 'Twas that, such vulgar Miracles,
> Heav'n had not Leasure to renew . . .

The reference is to the legend that bees swarmed upon the cradle of Pindar, appropriate because this is a Pindaric poem. With all these images implying the relationship of poetry to an ideal order, Dryden poignantly contrasts the uses to which poetry has actually been put:

> O Gracious God! How far have we
> Prophan'd thy Heav'nly Gift of Poesy!
> Made prostitute and profligate the Muse,
> Debas'd to each obscene and impious use,
> Whose Harmony was first ordain'd *Above*,
> For Tongues of *Angels* and for *Hymns* of *Love*?
> O wretched We! why were we hurry'd down
> This lubrique and adult'rate age,
> (Nay, added fat Pollutions of our own)
> T'increase the steaming Ordures of the Stage?
> What can we say t'excuse our *Second Fall*?
> Let this thy *Vestal*, Heav'n, atone for all!

> Her *Arethusian* Stream remains unsoil'd,
> Unmixt with Forreign Filth, and undefil'd,
> Her Wit was more than Man, her Innocence a Child!

The very texture of words like "profligate", "prostitute", and "lubrique", with their clotted double consonants and lingual sounds, seem to enhance the emotion of contemptuous disgust. We almost picture Dryden picking his way through the garbage of Covent Garden.

The poem concludes with a vision of the Last Judgement and the General Resurrection. I do not think that there is any element of deliberate burlesque here. The literalistic picture of the reconstitution of the bodies of the dead, which must strike oddly to most modern readers, seems to have had a curious fascination for this period. It occurs in Cowley's ode "The Resurrection", and a little later in Young's "The Last Day". But what is noteworthy in Dryden's poem is the daring vindication of the special status of poets and poetry:

> The Sacred Poets first shall hear the Sound,
>   And formost from the Tomb shall bound:
> For they are cover'd with the lightest Ground
> And, streight, with in-born Vigour, on the Wing,
> Like mounting Larkes, to the New Morning sing.
> There *Thou*, sweet Saint, before the Quire shalt go,
> As Harbinger of Heav'n, the Way to show,
> The Way which thou so well hast learn'd below.

The figure of Anne Killigrew in this ode can be related to that of St Cecilia in the two cantata-odes which Dryden wrote for her festival. When Dryden came to write "Alexander's Feast" in 1697 he had forefeited his Laureateship and court favour. The celestial music of Saint Cecilia is by implication contrasted with the technical virtuosity of the court poet Timotheus. The irony of this poem has not, I think, often been noticed:

> A present Deity, they shout around:
> A present Deity, the vaulted Roofs rebound.
>   With ravish'd Ears
>   The Monarch hears,
>   Assumes the God,
>   Affects to nod,
> And seems to shake the Spheres.

The comic effect of the last three lines should be unmistakeable: Edward Young was wildly off the mark when, supposing Dryden used them to convey a feeling of dignity, he framed the whole of his long and disastrous "Ocean: an Ode" upon them. Alexander is a typical heroic figure — he had indeed been a central character in Lee's *The Rival Queens*, the most extravagant of all heroic tragedies. But here he is placed in a slightly absurd light, and he is also wicked. It is not he but Timotheus who guides the action of the poem, as he displays the power of music by arousing and allaying the various passions in the King. It should be noted that all these passions are really ignoble ones. Even Alexander's pity for the fallen Darius is a sentimental self-indulgence:

> With down-cast Looks the joyless Victor sate,
> Revolveing in his alter'd Soul
> The various Turns of Chance below;
> And, now and then, a Sigh he stole;
> And Tears began to flow.

It all ends up in an orgy of senseless destruction:

> The Princes applaud, with a furious Joy;
> And the King seyz'd a Flambeau, with Zeal to destroy;
> *Thais* led the Way,
> To light him to his Prey,
> And, like another *Hellen*, fir'd another *Troy*.

On this appalling scene Dryden suddenly drops the curtain, and invokes the Saint in whose honour the poem is really written. But there is irony even in the famous concluding lines:

> *He rais'd a Mortal to the Skies;*
> *She drew an Angel down.*

Timotheus only raised a mortal to the skies by flattering his self-conceit. After 1688 Dryden had good cause to say "put not your trust in princes". He had striven to support the idea of a divinely ordained monarchy in the persons of Charles II and James II, and had raised those mortals to the skies. But now that cause was lost, and England had become, and has remained ever since, effectively a republic.

In the foregoing pages I have tried to show how the baroque heroic ideal represented for Dryden the realisation in poetic terms of a transcendent order. But in his work it is continually struggling with an ironic and more modern spirit which is destructive of it. There is a kind of good-humoured serenity in his final work, *The Secular Masque*, written in the year of his death, 1700. It is a fitting farewell to the complex and turbulent seventeenth century. Diana represents the more extroverted age of the last years of Elizabeth and of James I, Mars the troubled times of Charles I and the Civil War, Venus the Restoration but

> *All, all of a piece throughout:*
> *Thy Chase had a Beast in View;*
> *Thy Wars brought nothing about;*
> *Thy Lovers were all untrue.*
> *'Tis well an Old Age is out,*
> *And time to begin a New.*

The new age did begin, and a new poet, Alexander Pope, was waiting in the wings. But, although he carried the Augustan ideals of style established by Dryden to greater perfection, he had in some ways a narrower range and a less masculine intellect than his illustrious master.

[1969]

■ Baroque Ceremony

A Study of Dryden's "Ode to the Memory of Mistress Anne Killigrew" (1686)

D R. JOHNSON considered Dryden's poem "To the Memory of Mrs Anne Killigrew" to be "undoubtedly the noblest Ode that our language ever has produced"; but this judgment has not generally been endorsed by later critics. Most recently the author of the section devoted to Dryden's poetry in the *Pelican Guide to English Literature* treats the Anne Killigrew Ode with scant respect, contrasting it unfavourably with the economy and directness of the "Elegy on the Death of Mr Oldham." Certainly, today, we cannot go all the way with Johnson. He had not, after all, read the "Intimations of Immortality," nor the "Nightingale" and the "Grecian Urn," nor "The Wreck of the Deutschland." The limitations of his critical perspective did not dispose him to look to Spenser's "Epithalamium" for a comparison; and "Lycidas," as he made quite clear in his "Life of Milton," he did not think highly of. Nevertheless, I believe that the Anne Killigrew Ode is a fine poem — one of the finest that Dryden wrote — and also particularly characteristic of his art, and of the temper of his age.

It is necessary to recognize the genre to which the Anne Killigrew Ode belongs, and the type of expression which the occasion of its writing was held to demand in Dryden's day. The poem is, first of all, a "Pindaric" Ode, while the lines on Oldham (in couplets) are an Elegy. The Great Ode, for which Pindar furnished the model, was taken by Neo-Classical critical theory as constituting, together with Epic and Tragedy, one of the major, serious species of poetry. The Elegy (and the funeral and amatory elegies were not clearly distinguished) was essentially a minor form — along with songs and sonnets, "a mere copy of verses." To put it in a way more congenial to our modes of thinking, the former are essentially public poetry. They embody the values on which the community at large places the highest estimate; and they have a ceremonial quality. At the Renaissance, ceremony (i.e. the symbolic embodiment of secular values) had tended more and more to take the place of ritual, the subsummation of all values into a framework of religious symbolism, which was characteristic of the Middle Ages. It is to this Renaissance tradition that Dryden's poem belongs, and it is, perhaps, the last truly valid example of its kind. Today when we think of ceremony, we envisage, perhaps, State pageantry — an empty show in which our personal feelings are not really engaged. The poetic equivalent would be such poems as Tennyson's "On the Death of the Duke of Wellington" or Laurence Binyon's "For the Fallen." But what we really value, on such occasions, is the "personal tribute," or the discreet obituary article by an intimate friend of the deceased. It is personal poems of love or grief by which we set the most store; these alone seem to us "sincere."

The Elegy on Oldham is sincere in our sense, and, indeed, it deserves the praise that has been given to it. "There is not one word more," says Professor Bonamy Dobree, in his introduction to the "Everyman" edition of Dryden's poems, "than the emotion justifies." Oldham was a young poet of promise, whose early death clearly moved Dryden — but Dryden the man of letters, Dryden the private citizen. Whether he really saw an equal promise in the verses of Anne Killigrew we may doubt. It does not really matter. She was a lady-in-waiting at the Court of James II, and Dryden was Poet Laureate of the same court. Her position, then, made her a symbol of the place that the arts — poetry and painting — have or should have in the Court, which is itself the focus of the community as a whole. For the arts Dryden did care deeply; and it is through this that his personal emotions are engaged and lifted up, so to speak, into the public ceremony, of which, as Laureate, he is the spokesman. It is in the same way that Milton's personal emotions, his intense sense of dedication to the poet's calling, are brought within the scope of "Lycidas," another poem written for a public, in this case an academic, occasion; although the actual death of Edward King was probably not any very acute personal blow to him. And again, Donne's private doubts find their place in his "Anniversaries," another occasional poem, which was perhaps one of Dryden's models here, as it certainly was for his "Eleonora."

It is to this class of poems that the Anne Killigrew Ode belongs, but Dryden stands at the end of the tradition. There were to be no more great odes till those of Gray and Collins, which, though superficially similar in form, are really purely aesthetic in inspiration, and those of the Romantics, in which the personal experience is caught up, not into a world of public ceremony, but into the exploration of the inner cosmos of symbols. The typical Laureate work of the eighteenth century was to be the vapid flattery of the Birthday Odes of Colley Cibber. For the Hanoverian Court no longer attempted to embody, as did that of the Stuarts, the Renaissance ideal of the Court as the cultural focus of the national life. And, even given the technical virtuosity of a Tennyson, later laureates, qua laureates, have not really done much better, if they have even tried to fulfil their function as public spokesmen.

But Dryden is not simply a Renaissance poet. He is also a man of the new, almost wholly secular age — the great Augustan satirist, and the Member of the Royal Society, interested in the new science, with its potential destructiveness to the traditional world view. Dryden's poetry in what he would have regarded as the major forms — his heroic tragedies, *Annus Mirabilis*, and his Odes — as distinct from his comedies, songs, epistles and satires, in fact incorporates in its imagery a great deal of the complexities of the metaphysicals — the combination, often tentative and half-paradoxical of conflicting, and even disturbing ideas. Yet the style — the "Grand Style" of Neo-Classicism — imposes a unity upon them. The triumph of his art in the Anne Killigrew Ode is the manner in which this is accomplished.

II

The imagery of the first stanza of the poem presents us with a picture from the traditional, mediaeval Christian cosmology. The spirit of Anne Killigrew is invoked "made in the last Promotion of the *Blest*." Heaven is courtly and hierarchical, calling the soul, which is a "probationer" here below, to its proper station in the celestial spheres of the Ptolemaic universe, either among the planets, or the fixed stars, or to tread "with Seraphims, the vast *Abyss*" — the limitless space which lies beyond the limited, spherical cosmos. It is the scheme of Dante's *Paradise*, but somehow, in Dryden, it has become, as it were, smaller, neater and more mechanical. But from this picture of a traditional, ordered universe, Dryden plunges immediately, in the second stanza, into contemporary speculations about the nature of the soul, which represent a complete break with mediaeval, scholastic theology. Anne Killigrew's soul came either through "traduction," or was "pre-existing." Traduction — the doctrine that souls are generated from souls at conception, just as bodies are from bodies, is in line with the view of the soul as a material substance, in its essence, perhaps, not necessarily immortal, and with the revived atomism of Hobbes. The doctrine of the preexistence of the soul, on the other hand, is Platonic. Consistent with it, if not necessarily implied in it, is the idea of transmigration, which Donne had played with in "The Progress of the Soul," and which Dryden here applies, provisionally, to Anne Killigrew. Neo-Platonism was very much in the air at the time, and the Cambridge Platonists were engaged in their attempted synthesis of Platonism and Christian doctrines. Platonism and atomism, inconsistent with each other and neither easily reconciled with orthodox theology, seem to have had a continuing and almost equal fascination for Dryden.

Here he leaves the question open, but, in a manner characteristic of metaphysical poetry, twists each of them into a compliment to Anne Killigrew's talents.

The point of view shifts again in the next stanza, though it becomes of increased complexity. Anne Killigrew's birth on earth was heralded by an auspicious conjunction of planets (Dryden uses the technical language of astrology) and by rejoicing among the angels in heaven —

> And if no clust'ring Swarm of Bees
> On thy sweet Mouth distill'd their golden Dew,
> 'Twas that, such vulgar Miracles,
> Heav'n had not Leisure to renew.

The reference here is to the birth of Pindar — appropriate, because Dryden is writing a "Pindaric" poem. But the image from classical legend is introduced only to be depreciated, "a vulgar miracle." Heaven (or God) is a *Grand Monarque*, who manages things after the grand, baroque manner. The angels rejoice at the birth of a poetess as at the birth of the Saviour, and there seems to be an actual reminiscence of Milton's "Nativity Hymn":

> And then if ever, Mortal Ears
> Had heard the Musick of the Spheres!

This, we may say, is almost, if not quite, blasphemy — and Dryden has often been arraigned for breaches of taste of a similar nature. If it is not quite blasphemy, it is by virtue of the high value which Dryden is able to establish, in the next stanza, for the idea of Poetry, for which the soul of Anne Killigrew, as we have said, has really become a symbol. It is the Renaissance, Neo-Platonic view of Poetry — the view of Sidney, Spenser and Milton as a heavenly gift, and the highest of all human sciences. It is a view scarcely to be found again, till we come to the Romantics. It is in the light of this view that Dryden is actually able to continue his already implied analogy, between Anne Killigrew and Christ, and offer the purity of her life and art to God as an atonement for the shortcomings of himself and his contemporaries.

The fourth stanza is, indeed, the most deeply personal passage in the poem. It is Dryden's obviously sincere confession of guilt in respect of the moral tendency of his works for the stage. Jeremy Collier's *Short View of the Immorality and Profaneness of the English Stage* did not in fact appear till 1698, twelve years later, but when it did Dryden, unlike Vanbrugh and others, made no attempt to defend himself, but admitted that he had offended. The imagery of this stanza, with its "fat pollutions," "steaming Ordures," its ruthless hammering home of the epithets "prostitute and profligate," "lubrique and adult'rate," brings before us a sense of physical revulsion, and makes the strongest possible contrast with the paradisical palms and celestial spheres of the rest of the poem. It anchors it, we may say, to earth, and even to Grub Street and Covent Garden (remembering the filthy condition of the London streets at this time). It looks forward to the imagery of Swift, to the Goddess Cloacina of *The Dunciad*, and brings home the bitter contradiction, clearly felt by Dryden himself, between the Renaissance idea of the poet, and the poet as hack. The changing economic relation of the writer to society in Dryden's day was already making this contradiction increasingly plain.

By contrast, the stanza following shows Dryden at his most delicate. It paints an idealized picture of Anne Killigrew as a figure of natural, innocent, untaught genius, and concludes with the exquisite lines:

> Ev'n Love (for Love sometimes her Muse exprest)
> Was but a *Lambent-flame* which play'd about her *Breast*:
> Light as the Vapours of a Morning Dream,
> So cold herself, whilst she such Warmth exprest,
> 'Twas *Cupid* bathing in *Diana's* stream.

Such organization of contrasting moods and themes within the framework of the Ode has, indeed, some analogy with the symphonic form in music. The sixth stanza may be termed the *scherzo*. Developing a favourite topic of contemporary criticism, the analogy of poetry and painting (cf. his preface to the translation of Du Fresnoy's *Art of Painting* published in 1695). Dryden pictures the innocent Anne Killigrew as a ruler of the contemporary kind, ordering the realm of Poetry, and annexing the neighbouring province of Painting:

> To the next Realm she stretcht her Sway
>   . . .
> (As Conquerors will never want Pretence,
>   When arm'd, to justifie the Offence),
> And the whole Fief, in right of Poetry she claim'd.

The conceit, extended through eighteen lines, becomes a miniature mock-heroic, comparable to *The Rape of the Lock*. The playful, innocent tone of the preceding stanza is continued, but at the same time we are conscious of Dryden the ironic satirist. The satire anticipates Swift's satire on contemporary European international politics in parts of *Gulliver's Travels*, so that Dryden the Royalist, smuggles, as it were, this criticism of the pretensions and methods of princes into this courtly poem, without in any way breaking up its essential unity.

Now follows, in the description of Anne Killigrew's painting, a passage whose octosyllabic movement is reminiscent of the landscape painting of Milton's "L'Allegro" and "Il Penseroso," as it anticipates one of the earliest and most successful of eighteenth-century landscape poems, Dyer's "Grongar Hill." What we have here is a classical landscape with mythological figures, suggestive of Poussin or Claude Lorraine. Again, in the next stanza, where the description of her painting is still continued, the movement alters once more, as James II, his Queen and their court, are imaged, in the grand manner, as Baroque, Heroic figures. At the same time, the somewhat grotesque conceit, in which Anne Killigrew's genius, "a ball of fire" —

> ... the further thrown,
> Still with a greater *Blaze* she shone ...

—nevertheless serves to remind us of Dryden's interest in physical science. Here again, we are met by the contrast between the Platonic aesthetic expounded in the passage on painting, and the very different scientific approach of the age.

The next stanza refers to Anne Killigrew's death, like that of her friend, Mrs. Katherine Philips, "the matchless Orinda" by smallpox. (Anne Killigrew died of this disease and not, as the *Oxford Companion to English Literature* mistakenly states, by drowning "while shooting London Bridge." The lady who suffered this somewhat sensational fate was in fact her aunt, who was a passenger in the barge of Henrietta Maria, Charles I's Queen, when the accident occurred. See George Ballard: *Memoirs of Several Ladies of Great Britain*, Oxford, 1752.) Here Dryden gives a softened form of a conceit he had disastrously and notoriously developed in his earliest published poems ("On the Death of Lord Hastings" printed in 1649). Speaking of the "cruel Destiny" Dryden says —

> O double Sacriledge on things Divine,
> To rob the Relique, and deface the Shrine!

—an image which reminds us of Dryden's still recent conversion to Roman Catholicism.

More successful, because more dramatic, is the next stanza, which pictures Anne Killigrew's "Warlike Brother on the Seas" offering vows for his safe return, unconscious of the disaster which has befallen him in his sister's death at home—but

> ... if thou ken'st from far,
> Among the *Pleiad's* a New-kindl'd Star,
> If any sparkles, than the rest, more bright,
> 'Tis she that shines in that propitious Light.

Here we have a frankly pagan conceit — the apotheosis of the heroine as a new star in the Heavens. But in placing Anne Killigrew in the light of a star, Dryden seeks, apparently, to reconcile it with the traditionally orthodox imagery of the first stanza of the poem. In so doing, he prepares the way for the concluding stanza, whose imagery is not only orthodoxly Christian, but biblical.

The image here is the traditional Christian picture of the Last Day and the General Resurrection — an image which must have impressed itself on Dryden's mind during his Puritan boyhood. Yet to our way of looking at things, at least, it is presented with a curious, materialistic literalness:

> When ratling Bones together fly
> From the four Corners of the Skie,
> When Sinews o're the Skeletons are spread . . .

At the same time the basic symbolism of the poem, and its real subject, the humanistic exaltation of poetry, is continued in the bold claim that —

> The Sacred Poets first shall hear the Sound,
>   And formost from the Tomb shall bound:
> For they are cover'd with the lightest Ground
> And streight, with in-born Vigour, on the Wing,
> Like mounting Larkes, to the New Morning sing.
> There *Thou*, sweet Saint, before the Quire shalt go...

This *grand finale* has often been praised above the rest of the poem. But its real effectiveness lies in the way in which many of the preceding themes, and apparently diverse points of view, are brought together and resolved in its grand Handelian music.

This poem, in fact, exemplifies a great many of the different aspects of Dryden's very varied genius. That Dryden was a good deal more than a poetic journalist, an opportunist, and a technical virtuoso, should, I think, be plain. Part of his greatness lies in the way in which so much of the richness and complexity of the earlier seventeenth century is preserved, while the additional tensions of his own age are held together, within the formal framework of Neo-Classical rhetoric.

[1959]

■ Swift

THE SO-CALLED Augustan Age of English literature represents one of those rare moments in history when perfection of style is achieved. This perfection symbolizes the momentary triumph of civilization and the human intellect over that chaos which lies eternally around and within us. The men of the eighteenth century found themselves in a world which had at last attained a breathing-space after the religious and political conflicts of the preceding age, when the forces of bigotry and fanaticism had been unloosed upon the world. Casting their gaze farther backwards they saw the Middle Ages only as a long night of superstition and ignorance, whose slumbers had been broken at last by the voice of Erasmus. Beyond that was the civilization of the ancient world: the Rome of Augustus and Virgil, of Horace and of Maecenas — a world in which they recognized their own counterpart and exemplar; and, more remote, with a radiance too bright, indeed, for their cool, reasonable understanding, was Athens. In the whole of the rest of the landscape of human history there was little else to be discerned but barbarism.

But now God had said, "Let Newton be!", and all was light. The laws of the Universe were revealed — simple, reasonable, beautiful — mathematical laws, which exemplified the all-embracing wisdom and foresight of the Supreme Being. Yet though chaos seemed to have been banished, the victory was not lightly won. The greatest geniuses of the age — Pope, its most absolute poet, Swift himself, and later, Johnson with his grave and profound melancholy — are acutely conscious of the forces of unreason which continually threaten them. It is these forces, and not really the forgotten hacks of Grub Street, who are seen marshalling behind the goddess Dullness at the end of *The Dunciad*:

> Thy hand, great Anarch! lets the curtain fall;
> And Universal Darkness buries All.

The whole of the eighteenth century suffered from a deep-rooted spiritual anxiety. It is surely no coincidence that madness overwhelmed Swift, Collins, Smart, and Cowper and threatened Johnson and Boswell. It was something very like madness, too, which drove Pope to weave his incredible spider-webs of intrigue and deception. In a milder form, the same malaise was the "white melancholy" of Gray, and that fashionable disease, "the spleen", which Matthew Green and the Countess of Winchelsea celebrated in verse.

At the end of the century chaos was to break loose once more. It expressed itself in the Gothic extravagances of the early Romantics, in the elegant satanism of the Hell-fire Club. It took on a new creative energy in the emotional religious outbursts of the Methodist and Evangelical revivals, claiming poor Cowper as one of its casualties. Finally, in the French Revolution and the Terror, it swept aside the eighteenth-century compromise for ever.

In the work of Swift and Pope style is still strong enough to contain and limit chaos. But chaos is never far absent from their minds, and the consciousness of this gives to their work a kind of smouldering, nervous intensity, underlying its apparently calm surface. Irony is the quality in which they excel, and it is a double-edged weapon. Take, for example, Swift's *A Modest Proposal*, in which he suggests that the poor may prevent their children from becoming a burden to them by selling them as food to the rich. How much more than simple sarcasm this is! As we read Swift's cool, reasoned prose, the careful computation of the exact sum which would be saved by such a scheme, the enumeration of the various advantages which would accrue to the whole community, how much do we not realize about society, and the real nature of the relations between rich and poor? Are they, stripped of our customary evasions, so different from this after all? But farther still below the surface there is a deeper and even more terrible irony. Who, reading these pages, can quite rid himself of the haunting suspicion that, deep down in his nature, Swift also shared that utter contempt for the Irish poor which by implication he imputes to his readers; and that a part of him, belonging not to the conscious intellectual self at all, but to the primeval savage which lurks in all of us, envisaged with pleasure the cannibalistic scheme which his real indignation and pity for the poor had created for itself as a satirical weapon?

The madness which finally overcame Swift was, almost certainly, of a wholly physical and organic origin — though modern psychology should make us beware of drawing too hard and fast a line between the physical and the psychological in such matters. But, in any case, it was the overturning of a mind absolutely hard, bright, and clear in its intellectual qualities. Happiness was once defined by Swift as the art of "being well deceived"; it was that deception which all his life he refused. His intellect could not compromise with the facts of the physical world —

hence his continual horror of the natural functions of the human body, its effluvia and its excrement. But the physical world, as always, had its revenge; and a bodily imbecility overthrew and blotted out that intellect in the end. In his continual dwelling on the facts of defecation there was an obsessive quality, a perverse love. At the end of *Gulliver's Travels*, refusing to accept humanity as it is, he degrades it to the status of the Yahoos, and finds his ideal, not in something surpassing the human, but in the brute, the horse.

Swift's verse is comparatively little read, but it is, as much as his prose, the expression of his personality — the enigmatic personality of a very unhappy, very great man. It may not appeal to the lover of romantic verse, or any, perhaps, but those who have learned to appreciate a certain dry elegance which is essentially a quality of classical poetry. Like his prose, it is of the Doric order, free from all unnecessary ornament, yet with an intellectual poetic fire of its own. Swift, in the light conversational octosyllabic couplet, attained a mastery comparable to that of his friend Pope in the more formal decasyllabic. Much of his verse is occasional, even ephemeral — but the force of his satire sometimes lifts it into a kind of macabre horror, and it becomes, as in the astonishing and terrible poem "On the Death of Dr. Swift", a veritable Dance of Death. But his characteristic tone is one of light and civilized raillery, the irony with which he strove to mask that savage indignation at life which habitually tore at his breast. "Cadenus and Vanessa" is as perfect in its way as Pope's *The Rape of the Lock*. In it, Swift strove, by disguising the affair in a framework of elaborate allegory, to wean Esther Vanhomrigh from the unfortunate passion which she had conceived for the man who had sought only to raise her to the status of an intellectual equal by the cultivation of her mind. But the poem was ineffective; poor Vanessa would not be warned, and died broken-hearted. With Stella alone, perhaps, did Swift succeed in establishing that intimate intellectual relationship which he sought. No one will ever know what was the real nature of the feeling between these two. Some have thought that they were secretly married. The Victorian sentimentalist, Thackeray, absurdly represented Swift as cold-bloodedly exploiting the tender devotion of Stella. Yeats, in his play *The Words upon the Window-pane*, makes Swift refuse to marry and beget children, because he foresees the chaos that is to come. Mr. Denis Johnston, in a brilliant radio programme, *Weep for Polyphemus*, first put forward, in 1938, the suggestion that Swift and Stella (Esther Johnson) were really uncle and niece, she being the natural daughter of Sir William Temple, and he the illegitimate son of the latter's father, Sir John; according to this hypothesis, the discovery of the presumed blood-relationship put a permanent bar to their association as lovers. But all we know is that their friendship was a lasting one. It endured for thirty-six years and was cut short only by Stella's death — a severe blow to Swift. Before he persuaded her and her companion, Mrs. Dingley, to come and live near him in Dublin, Swift corresponded regularly with them, putting down the most intimate account of his life in the *Journal to Stella*. That document remains, and with it the poems which Swift annually wrote for Stella's birthday. The latter, with their combination of unsentimental tenderness, wit, and good sense, are among his most perfect, most pleasing and most baffling productions. These two human souls keep their secret, as they move with a reserved smile in their formal dance. They refuse our questionings, and they do not require, perhaps, our pity.

[1948]

■ Pope

ALEXANDER POPE was born in London in 1688. His father, who was a linen-draper by trade, was the son of a clergyman of the Church of England, but had been converted in youth to Roman Catholicism. Not long after the poet's birth his father retired to Binfield in Windsor forest. As a Roman Catholic the young Pope was debarred from entering Public School or University. He was educated privately by priests, but also read widely for himself, especially in the Latin, English, French and Italian poets. His health was severely injured, whether by illness or accident is not certain, at the age of twelve, and Pope grew up stunted in stature and with a spinal curvature which rendered him hunch-backed. His poetic talents appeared very early, and were encouraged by his father. While still a child he wrote a play based on Homer's *Iliad*, to be acted by himself and his companions. Some of the Minor Poems date from his 'teens, while the *Pastorals*, his first published work, date from his sixteenth year. By this time Pope had already attracted the attention of several neighbouring gentry with literary tastes. Among these were the poet and critic Walsh (to whom the *Pastorals* were to be dedicated) and the old dramatist Wycherley. Pope's *Pastorals*, which had circulated in manuscript, came to the notice of the eminent London publisher and bookseller, Jacob Tonson, who printed them in his *Miscellany* for 1709. Pope now began to frequent London literary circles, and at first was drawn into that of Addison, whose meeting-place was Button's Coffee House. To this period belong such characteristic early poems as *An Essay on Criticism* (1711) and *The Rape of the Lock* (1712). *Windsor Forest* (1713), besides paying tribute to the countryside of Pope's boyhood, concluded with a passage prophesying a coming age of peace and prosperity as a result of the Peace of Utrecht, whereby Queen Anne's Tory ministry had ended the war with France. Addison and his friends were Whigs, but the sympathies of Pope, as a Roman Catholic, were inevitably with the Tories. It is not therefore surprising that he should move away from Addison's circle. He had already quarrelled with one of its members, Ambrose Philips, over the merits of their respective Pastorals.

Pope now formed a far stronger and more enduring friendship with the Tory wits, Swift and Bolingbroke. Together with Arbuthnot they founded The Scriblerus Club which also included Gay and the Irish poet Thomas Parnell. Its object was a concerted attack by means of satire and irony on pedantry and dull and bad writing of all kinds. From 1715 to 1720 Pope was almost exclusively occupied with his translation of Homer's *Iliad*. His embarking on this task represents, in more ways than one, a critical turning-point in his career. The profits he received from its sale by subscription were to render him financially independent for the rest of his life. But it was also a challenge to his endurance and self-discipline. A more mature and intellectually stronger poet was to emerge.

As for the translation itself, it is, in spite of several limitations, a major achievement. Pope's knowledge of Greek was in fact slight, and he relied considerably on earlier translations, both French and English (including Chapman's Elizabethan version). Nevertheless what he produced was a major Augustan poem in its own right. A poet so great and so universal as Homer needs reinterpreting and fresh translation for each succeeding age. To-day, no doubt, we seek qualities in Homer other than those which Pope and his generation most admired. We will find more modern — and probably much inferior — translations more illuminating. The Augustan polish of Pope will seem appropriate enough to us in those poems where he is dealing directly with his own time but transferred to heroic Greece it may strike us as incongruous. Nevertheless, his translation has a swiftness of pace and a rhetorical vigour which still make it eminently readable.

The *Iliad* translation was followed, between 1725 and 1726, by a version of the *Odyssey*. In the latter, Pope employed two minor poets, William Broome and Elijah Fenton, as his assistants in several of the books of the poem, but carefully revised and polished the material with which they provided him.

In 1719 Pope had secured the lease of a villa in Twickenham, where he continued to live till his death in 1744. He is buried in Twickenham church. In these later years Pope lived the life of an independent man of letters. He produced his edition of Shakespeare (1725), and composed such important original poems as the *Moral Essays* and *An Essay on Man* (1733–34) — these together forming the *Ethick Epistles* — *The Dunciad* (1728–43), and the *Imitations of Horace* (1734–38). These latter together with the wholly original "Epistle to Dr Arbuthnot" constitute perhaps his most mature and his finest work. Pope follows Horace closely, but substitutes contemporary allusions for those of the original, and frequently expands and adds to his material considerably. His assumption of the Horatian *persona* enables him effectively to appear as a detached moralist and commentator on his own age. This is partly because there was a more than superficial analogy between the Rome of Horace's time and the England of Pope's. Both were ages of prosperity and stability following on a period of prolonged civil disturbance and their literary ideals were also similar. In both cases what was aimed at was the polished imitation of generally recognized models of excellence, rather than originality of an absolute kind. Within this framework the poet was to express generally recognized and universal truths of human nature, in a language at once memorable and refined such as might most fittingly transmit those truths to succeeding generations. The term "Augustan", derived as it is from the Emperor under whom Horace wrote, is therefore quite fittingly used, in English literary parlance, for the age of Pope also.

Pope is then the greatest poet of this English Augustan age. Of his immediate literary contemporaries, only his friend Swift excelled him in intellectual and imaginative power; and in command of the technique of verse — especially of the rhymed couplet as a vehicle of satire and of reasoned argument — only his great predecessor and acknowledged master, Dryden, can be compared to him. The heroic couplet, indeed, Pope brought to perfection, and in his mature writings, seldom ventured to handle any other form; and when he did so venture (as in the "Ode for St. Cecilia's Day") he only partially succeeded. Those then who start with the presupposition that the heroic couplet is artificial and monotonous, or merely a vehicle for neat and polished epigram, will find their capacity for appreciating Pope's poetry severely limited. Yet in spite of the much greater appreciation and far more balanced criticism of Pope which has grown up over the last quarter of a century or so, this attitude, a hangover from nineteenth-century prejudice, is still far too common. It even tends to be accentuated by a distinctively modern development — our lazy reading habits. Under the impact of the ever-increasing volume of ephemeral popular journalistic and entertainment literature, intended not for reading but merely for skimming, we read too quickly, allowing the eye to run ahead of the ear and of the brain itself. Pope's verse should never be read in this way, but for preference out loud, at the speed of the natural speaking voice.

Full value should be given to the pauses, and the astonishingly subtle variety with which Pope introduces them into his verse. Pope's real mastery will then appear — a mastery over a limited but supremely delicate and sensitive instrument, like the clavichord and harpsichord of his own age which, when the ear of the listener has become accustomed to them, will often make the rhetoric of the nineteenth-century and modern piano seem ponderous by comparison. For Pope is far more than a pointed epigrammatist, and indeed, though many of his greatest triumphs were won in the field of satire, they are not his only triumphs. He can be splendidly rhetorical (as in his Homeric translations and parts of *An Essay on Man*) or easily conversational (as in his Horatian imitations and Familiar Epistles). He can make a sudden but perfectly natural transition from the fiercest satire to the personally tender (a good example of this is in the "Epistle to Dr. Arbuthnot", in the verses on Bufo and those immediately following on the death of Gay). His imagery is equally wide in its scope, it ranges from the Claude-like landscape painting of *Windsor Forest* to the Hogarthian grotesque realism of *The Dunciad*, from the exquisite sensuous realization of the artificial in *The Rape of the Lock* to the romantic wildness of *Eloisa to Abelard*.

But though we may readily admit the brilliance of Pope's writing, as well as a variety and range of tone not so often acknowledged, it may still be difficult to define the essential quality of his imagination — that in fact which makes him a great poet. The title, however, has often been denied to him. Matthew Arnold, indeed, went so far as to declare that both Dryden and Pope "are not classics of our poetry, they are classics of our prose" and found the work of the latter lacking in "high seriousness" and "an adequate poetic criticism of life". Yet this is hardly to take Pope on his own terms, nor on those of his own and his age's ideal of what poetry should be. For the Neo-classical age did take poetry seriously, and accorded to it an essentially moral, too often indeed, a didactic function. But the moral approach was one very different from that of Arnold or his Victorian contemporaries.

What this approach was may perhaps best be gathered from a statement of Pope himself, recorded by his friend Joseph Spence. "About fifteen," Pope told Spence, "I got acquainted with Mr. Walsh. He encouraged me much and used to tell me that there was one way left of excelling, for though we had several great poets, we never had any one great poet that was *correct* — and he desired me to make that my study and aim." This ideal of correctness is central to Pope and to his age, and it is a moral as much as an aesthetic ideal. Correctness meant adherence to the rules which criticism had deduced from the practice of the great poets of Classical antiquity and which these poets themselves had discovered in Nature. Nature was not so much the external nature of landscape (though the concept included that also) as human nature, the root quality of man's mind, everywhere and in all ages the same, modified only by accidental, local and temporal circumstances. To write correctly then was not to make oneself the slave of a set of arbitrary canons, but to make oneself free of universal truth. To neglect it was a moral offence, because it involved a falsification of values and a distortion of truth.

This frequently quoted statement of Pope on correctness must, therefore, be taken in conjunction with one rather less familiar, which follows shortly afterwards in the same conversation with Spence. "I am in no concern," Pope says, "whether people should say this is writ well or ill; but that it is writ with a good design. 'He has writ in the cause of virtue, and done something to mend people's morals' is the only commendation I long for." This moral concern is an essentially humanistic one. It directly parallels Swift's belief that his *Gulliver's Travels* would "marvellously mend the world". It is the duty of the imaginative writer to teach, by displaying the true nature of Man, and his relation to the Universal, and also by castigating in satire those follies and vices of his own time which are essentially deviations from Nature. Properly understood, a poetry thus inspired surely does not lack its own kind of high seriousness, and it is most certainly a criticism of life. Where it differs from that of the nineteenth century, as well as from that of our own day, is in its steady confidence that there is a clearly discernible, fixed and unchanging human nature, which furnishes the basis on which this criticism rests. In the nineteenth-century evolutionary historicism, and in our own day the social and psychological sciences, have largely undermined this belief. Hence for Arnold, and still more for us, criticism of life no longer rests on the universal light of an unchanging and readily discernible authority, but on that of subjective, questing, fitful and uncertain Romantic vision. So, far indeed from being no poet, Pope showed many of the characteristics of the poetical temperament (if we may allow that there is such a thing) in a singularly pure form. He was intensely devoted to his art, and furthermore made it almost the entire business of his life. This a remarkable combination of historical and personal circumstances both permitted and, as we may say, more or less compelled him to do. He was born of Roman Catholic parents in the year of the Glorious Revolution, which saw the deposition and flight of James II, and with it the death-blow to any hopes of a Roman Catholic ascendancy in England. The Papists, though they included some old families of culture and distinction (like Pope's friends, the Fermors and the Blounts), formed a despised and persecuted minority — the persecution taking the form of a series of petty and vindictive Penal Laws, which were not and could not be strictly enforced. They meant, however, that Roman Catholics spent their lives in an atmosphere of equivocation, subterfuge and evasion; and to this must be attributed some, at least, of the disingenuousness which undoubtedly sometimes marked Pope's character in later life even though recent research has done much to clear him from some of the worst imputations which have been made against him. It is true that the arguments of Pope's verse (especially in *An Essay on Man*) seem often to tend towards the universalism, naturalism and scepticism which formed part of the general intellectual atmosphere of his century. But he always remained formally loyal, at least, to the religion of his parents. This religion not only barred him from a Public School and University education, but also from any hope of ever attaining public office — whether that might offer the opportunity of actually exercising political power, or merely of a comfortable sinecure.

But these very circumstances enabled Pope as a boy to follow his own bent, and to engage in an intense and almost exclusive study of the English and Latin poets, and in his later years to devote himself entirely to literary composition. His enormously successful translation of Homer was the "five years labour" which made him financially independent. No longer having to rely on private or public patronage, he settled down in his villa at Twickenham, to play the congenial part of the detached Horatian observer and moralist.

Along with the social disabilities entailed on him by his religion, we must take into consideration Pope's stunted person and physical deformities (with consequent chronic ill-health). This increased his sensitiveness and irritability, as well as making him fatally vulnerable to personal attack — not excluding the threat of physical violence in an age that was not squeamish of it. One can hardly admire too much the courage of the man who, in spite of these handicaps, won his way (in the teeth of the continual attacks of his enemies) to a universally acknowledged literary pre-eminence, not only in the England of his day, but throughout civilized Europe. One must admire no less the note of urbane good-humour which sounds through his poetry as frequently as, and indeed, more frequently than that of spleen and bitterness. Yet the myth of Pope as a twisted monster of dwarfish malignity dies hard. It has, one supposes, a kind of sinister romantic appeal. It furnishes (like the similar myth of Swift as a misanthropic madman) a convenient excuse for ignoring the implications of his poetry when they are unflattering to the presuppositions of our own age. Yet a myth it largely is. Against the picture of Pope in his unrelenting warfare against Dennis, Addison and his circle, Bentley, and the Dunces generally, we must off-set that of the tender, affectionate and loyal friend, and the generous encourager of young poets of talent. Pope was undoubtedly that notorious species of animal which, when attacked, defends itself. But the attacks made upon him were often mean and brutal in the extreme. Furthermore, in singling out personalities as he did,

Pope was not prompted solely by motives of revenge. Departure from the canons of good taste and good sense were for him, as we have seen, moral offences. He used individuals as symbols of universal corruptions no less than did a greater poet, Dante, when he relegated some of his political opponents to the lowest circles of Hell. We, for whom these eighteenth-century feuds are forgotten history, may do well, in reading Pope, mentally to substitute for the proper names in his satire those of whatever literary or political figures of our own time may seem to us personally most fittingly to symbolize the particular type of perennial wickedness or foolishness Pope is aiming at.

Pope's poetical career falls rather markedly into two periods. Of the poems written before he was thirty, very few evince the satirical power with which he is chiefly associated. Of important early poems, only *An Essay on Criticism* is quite typically in the Neo-classical manner. The others such as the *Pastorals*, *Windsor Forest*, *The Rape of the Lock*, *Eloisa to Abelard* and the *Elegy to the Memory of an Unfortunate Lady* exhibit in varying degrees and in different ways a type of sensibility which anticipates that of the Romanticism of a later age, rather than that which is generally thought of as characteristic of the Neo-classical period. Such a cut-and-dried dichotomy between "Classicism" and "Romanticism" is, however, to a large extent misleading when we are considering the development of our literature. England never submitted as whole-heartedly to the Neo-classical rules as did France. The national temperament, as well as the established prestige of Shakespeare and the growing fame of Milton, precluded it. There is a strong undercurrent of melancholy, Gothicism, Primitivism, and other so-called Romantic qualities even in many Restoration writers — for example, in the tragedies of Otway and Lee, in Aphra Behn's novel *Oroonoko* and in some of Dryden's *Fables*. What is significant, however, is that it was only as he approached middle life that Pope "stooped to truth and moralised [his] song". The earlier verse is that of a brilliant and spirited youth. Beneath the strict convention (which may to us appear artificial, though to Pope's contemporaries it would not) there is much genuine feeling and even tenderness: note, for example, the sympathy for hunted animals and birds in *Windsor Forest* (Pope, in an article in Steele's *Guardian*, was one of the first to protest against the prevalent cruelty to animals which marked his age); and the half-amused, half-sad repining at the inevitable passing of youth and beauty, with their attendant frivolities, in Clarissa's speech at the end of *The Rape of the Lock*. The later work is that of an adult and morally concerned man.

Doubtless the intellectual discipline involved in the task of the Homeric translations, which form a kind of dividing wall between Pope's two creative periods, had something to do with this development. But more important, probably, was Pope's reaction to the changing historical situation of England. At the close of the reign of Queen Anne, Pope's Tory friends had been in power. Their great triumph, the Peace of Utrecht, seemed to Pope to promise a golden age of coming peace and prosperity. A Jacobite Restoration with the prospect of relief for the Roman Catholics, seemed still a possibility. The unexpected death of the Queen, and the coming of George I from Hanover, brought an end to all such hopes. Bolingbroke went into exile in France, while Swift ate his heart out in Ireland, his ambitions of political influence permanently frustrated. Though his Roman Catholic affiliations led Pope inevitably to associate himself with the Tories, he had no such political ambitions himself. But what happened to England under Hanoverian rule was in his eyes a progressive moral corruption. During Pope's later years the Whigs were in power, and the Tories in permanent and seemingly hopeless opposition. Walpole, though not a dictator in the modern sense, was for twenty years virtually absolute ruler of the country. He kept himself in power by his extremely skilful financial policy, by systematic corruption in both Houses of Parliament, and by control and censorship of the Press and of the Theatre. This in fact gave to England a much-needed period of stability, and increasing financial prosperity for the great City Merchants and the new Whig aristocracy. But in Pope's eyes there were "new Saturnian days of lead and gold". I hazard the guess that a close study of the credit and banking system in this period would throw much light on the imagery of Pope and of Swift — especially the latter's satire on projectors. But this task still awaits the emergence of a scholar combining a knowledge of economic history with literary imagination and sensibility. Suffice it to say that much of Pope's satire is to be read by no means as an outpouring of personal spite, but as a criticism, from a traditional humanist point of view, of the materialism of a commercial society. As such, it is by no means without significance for our own day.

One of the most important results which the changing economic structure of English society in the eighteenth century brought about was the emancipation of the writer from private patronage, and his emergence as a professional man of letters. Pope himself benefited by this change, making himself financially independent through the sale of his Homer by private subscription, and such important bookseller-publishers as Tonson and Lintot were always ready to give him good prices for whatever he wrote. A new middle-class reading public had in fact emerged, eager for instruction, information and entertainment. It was soon to find in the novel a form perfectly fitted to its tastes. Eventually, in the nineteenth and twentieth centuries, the novelist was to a large extent to put the poet out of business. This Pope could not foresee, but he was acutely aware of another aspect of the situation. This was the proliferation of a different sort of literature, largely journalistic in character, often indeed scandalous or sensational, designed not to uphold the traditional standards of excellence, but to sell as quickly and as widely as possible. This was duly poured forth by the literary underworld of Grub Street scribblers and profitably marketed by such unscrupulous publishers as Edmund Curle. It is true that a popular pamphlet literature of this kind had existed since Elizabethan times, but the eighteenth century really saw the beginnings of that expansion of mass sub-literature which in our own day has reached frightening proportions, and which is a real threat to genuine culture. It is this threat which forms the subject of Pope's great mock epic, *The Dunciad*, culminating in the powerful concluding passage in which the return of Chaos is prophesied. The vision here presented is dark indeed. As an analysis of the actual situation of eighteenth-century England it is a piece of rhetorical over-statement. But as a prophecy we may see it as having been largely fulfilled in our own time. As a poet, then, Pope is, I suggest, more than the mere spokesman of his age. That latter role he did, however, perform brilliantly, and at the time of his death was generally admitted to have done so. Very soon, however, signs of a reaction started to appear. This emerged with Joseph Warton's *Essay on the Genius and Writings of Pope* (1786).

Even Dr. Johnson in his magnificently balanced judgement in his Life of Pope (written, as Boswell tells us, *con amore*) is not so much delivering an accepted orthodoxy, as championing a cause already a little damaged. As the shift towards Romantic sensibility continued, the greatest of the Romantic critics such as Wordsworth, Coleridge, Hazlitt and De Quincey, were inclined to give Pope a place, albeit a high place, only in the second rank of poetry. He was held to be "artificial" rather than "natural". The outstanding exception in this generation is Byron, himself a major satirist, with his whole-hearted and enthusiastic championship of "the little Queen Anne master". In a letter to Murray, Byron wrote: "because his truths are so clear, it is asserted that he has no invention; and because he is always intelligible, it is taken for granted that he is the 'Poet of Reason', as if this was a reason for his being no poet. Taking passage for passage, I will undertake to cite more lines teeming with imagination from Pope than from any two living poets, be they who they may." In another letter he summed up his estimate of Pope as follows: "Those miserable mountebanks of the day, the poets, disgrace themselves and deny God, in running down Pope, the most faultless of

Poets, and almost of men. ... He is the moral poet of all civilization; and as such, let us hope that he will one day be the national poet of all mankind." It is true that Byron was partly using Pope as a stick to beat those poets among his contemporaries (especially Wordsworth) of whom he disapproved. But his rating of Pope is not such an extravagant overstatement as may at first sight appear. If Byron was largely blind to the profound insights which constitute the greatness of Wordsworth's poetry, he was right in maintaining that the concepts of great poetry and of reason were not mutually exclusive. More of a European than most of his English contemporaries, he senses in Pope those qualities which stand for the movement of humanistic enlightenment. This at best, made in the eighteenth century for a common culture, transcending national frontiers, and extending from Philadelphia and Dublin to Stockholm and St. Petersburg, if centred primarily on London and Paris.

Matthew Arnold's really rather offhand judgement, already referred to, set a new and unfortunate tone for Pope-criticism in the later nineteenth century, from which the twentieth was slow to emancipate itself. The studies of Lytton Strachey and Dame Edith Sitwell, written during the period of reaction against Victorianism which followed the First World War, read to-day somewhat like the efforts of literary dandies, self-consciously embracing an unpopular position. More substantial work, however, was to be done by such critics and scholars as Professor Bonamy Dobrée, Professor Geoffrey Tillotson, Mr. Norman Ault and Professor John Butt. To these we may add the highly individual, but imaginative and stimulating interpretation of Mr. G. Wilson Knight. The fresh and much more balanced and informed appreciation of Pope that has thus grown up, is typified by the magnificent Twickenham Edition of his writings. It is an edition fully worthy of a great poet.

For Pope's reputation to-day once more stands high—probably higher than it has for two centuries. Although the values of the twentieth century are very different from those of the eighteenth, we nevertheless need to make less of a historical adjustment of attitude than did our grandparents to appreciate his poetry. We have seen the harm which, carried to extremes, Romantic emotional self-indulgence can bring out, and are the more disposed to accept writing which, though passion is not banished from it, nevertheless remains cool, detached and ironic— yet at the same time morally committed. Furthermore, as we have already remarked, Pope's strenuous opposition in his maturer work to the corruption of standards brought about by the commercialization of literature remains of immense contemporary urgency. Pope is a poet who can be read and re-read with increasing pleasure. At first one is probably most taken with the brilliance of his wit and the immense technical skill of his versification. But as one gets to know his poetry better, and as one's own experience of life increases, one is more and more struck by the truth and accuracy — often the daring accuracy — of his insights into human nature and society. "The proper study of mankind," he wrote, "is Man." Of the study of Man, as a social being, his own poetry remains a magnificent exemplar. It is complemented, not abrogated, by the additional study which the great Romantics were to make of Man as the eternal solitary.

[1964]

■ Gray

T HOMAS GRAY (1716–1771) is probably the most considerable poet of the mid-eighteenth century — of the generation immediately succeeding that of Pope. But critical opinion has tended to vary as to his stature. For Matthew Arnold, Gray was possibly a major poet who "never spoke out". Arnold, who indeed had a certain temperamental and biographical affinity with Gray, tended sentimentally to identify with him and to see in him a forerunner of nineteenth-century Romantic attitudes. These attitudes Arnold found lacking in Pope, whose greatness he seriously underrated. Among the Romantics themselves, Wordsworth and Coleridge were inclined to down-grade Gray because, inter alia, of his heavily stylised poetic diction and to contrast him unfavourably with Collins. Collins was, indeed, a little in advance of Gray in the revival of lyrical forms in the eighteenth century and is, perhaps, the more original and forward-looking of the two. But he lacks Gray's strength and overall accomplishment. What we define as Romantic sensibility is in fact something that was present throughout the eighteenth century, and the shift to Romanticism proper was, in some respects, a shift of emphasis rather than a revolutionary change. Such a poem as Gray's "The Progress of Poesy" may seem to be Romantic in its idealisation of poetry as a vital force which goes hand in hand with the spirit of political liberty. But its concluding lines show Gray as firmly anchored to Augustan values. Speaking of the poet he says:

> Yet shall he mount, and keep his distant way
> Beyond the limits of a vulgar fate,
> Beneath the Good how far — but far above the Great.

By "the Good" we must understand the man of true benevolence — an Allen or an Allworthy, and by the Great, on the other hand, the great man in public life — Sir Robert Walpole for instance. Although the poet is "beyond the limits of a vulgar fate" his final place in the hierarchy defined by goodness and greatness is clear and basically unromantic.

Of the outward circumstances of Gray's life very little need be said. A Londoner by birth, and like Milton the son of a scrivener and moneylender, Gray went to Eton and then to Cambridge. Both at school and at the University he became the intimate of a circle of friends of considerably more affluence and social status than himself. These included Horace Walpole, George Selwyn and Richard West (whose early death was clearly a deep and lasting sorrow for Gray). In 1739 Gray and Walpole set out on a tour through France, Switzerland and Italy. In 1741 at Reggio they quarrelled and finished their travels separately. (They were reconciled after their return to England.) Walpole subsequently took the blame for this breach, and wrote:

> The quarrel between Gray and me arose from his being too serious a companion. I had just broke loose from the restraint of the University, with as much money as I could spend; and I was willing to indulge myself. Gray was for antiquities &c; while I was for perpetual balls and plays; — the fault was mine.

It is clear that there was a good deal of emotional tension between them, perhaps aggravated by the difference in their social backgrounds.

The rest of Gray's life was spent at Cambridge, where he resided first at Peterhouse and then at Pembroke College, and was appointed Professor of History and Modern Languages. Gray speaks in his letters of the "Leucocholy" or white melancholy which afflicted him. His sensitive, mildly depressive nature did not really fit him for the society of the hard-drinking Cambridge dons of his day, and he was, we know, the butt of undergraduate practical jokes. In spite of his very great learning he did not do much academically, beyond making notes for lectures not delivered, and a synopsis for a history of English poetry never written. As for his poetry, the entire corpus, in Greek and Latin as well as in English, is small. This poetry is, at first sight, wholly literary in inspiration — a poetry turned in upon itself, itself its own inspiration. But this is only a half-truth. What gives it its lasting appeal (as also with Gray's letters) is the sense, surely, that its formalities contain within themselves a deep undercurrent of emotions not made wholly explicit. These emotions were rooted, to a very great extent, in Gray's relationships with his friends — with West, with Walpole, and with Mason who became his biographer. But above all, in his letters to Charles Von Bonstetten (the young Swiss who visited Cambridge in Gray's later years) he comes near to speaking out, and speaking something very like the language of passion:

> My life now is but a conversation with your shadow — the known sound of your voice still rings in my ears — there, on the corner of the fender, you are standing, or tinkling on the pianoforte, or stretched at length on the sofa. Do you reflect, my dearest friend, that it is a week or eight days before I can receive a letter from you, and as much more before

you can have my answer; that all that time I am employed, with more than Herculean toil, in pushing the tedious hours along, and wishing to annihilate them; the more I strive, the heavier they move, and the longer they grow. I cannot bear this place, where I have spent many tedious years within less than a month since you left me.

And again:

It is impossible for me to dissemble with you; such as I am I expose my heart to your view, nor wish to conceal a single thought from your penetrating eyes.

There is nothing as direct as this anywhere in Gray's poems.

Among these poems it is "Elegy Written in a Country Churchyard" with which we must necessarily begin. Of this poem Johnson wrote, "Had Gray written often thus, it had been vain to blame, and useless to praise him." It was the universality of the sentiments which recommended this poem to Johnson (otherwise not altogether sympathetic either to the poetry or to the man) and which gained for Gray a European reputation. The poem for many has become hackneyed. Even in Gray's lifetime, and certainly throughout the nineteenth century, it was thought a suitable poem to be taught to the young that they might repeat it by heart. In that age it really was necessary, and often inevitable, that children should be early brought to come to terms with the idea of mortality. But the "Elegy" is a highly complex poem, and certainly today not readily to be apprehended by the very young. In one respect the poem belongs to a recognisable eighteenth-century genre — that of formal reflections on death. Earlier examples include Parnell's "A Night Piece on Death", Young's *Night Thoughts*, Blair's *The Grave*, and (in prose) Hervey's *Meditations among the Tombs*. But the word "elegy", in the eighteenth century, pointed rather to a connection with the tradition of amatory Latin poetry represented by Ovid, Propertius and Tibullus. The decasyllabic quatrain had first been used in English poetry as an epic metre — in D'Avenant's *Gondibert* and later, in Dryden's *Annus Mirabilis*. It was William Hammond (1710–42) who first used the quatrain for a series of love-elegies in imitation of Tibullus. Hammond's quatrains were printed, as were those of Gray, in the original edition of the "Elegy", continuously, with the alternate lines inset — thus suggesting, if only typographically, the alternation of hexameter and pentameter in the Latin elegiac metre. This connection with the Latin elegy should point us to the fact that Gray's poem is more than a generalised musing on death. The poem is a deeply personal statement. Gray began work on the poem in 1742. He had quarrelled with Walpole, and had been deprived, by death, of another close friend in Richard West. He was also stricken by his mother's death. He was a young man with few financial resources, whose future prospects seemed doubtful. Just as Milton, confronted with the early death of Edward King, was forced to question whether his own dedication to poetry was justified, so Gray's situation forces him to a similar questioning. The "Elegy" is full of echoes of "Lycidas", but it also points forward to another great poem of self-doubt and questioning, Wordsworth's "Resolution and Independence". The "Elegy" is sometimes claimed as a forerunner of Romanticism because of its use of natural imagery. The landscape of the poem is in fact quite generalised, and adds little to the already well-established Augustan tradition of rustic imagery. What is revolutionary in Gray's poem is his sense of common humanity with the dead who lie buried in the churchyard, and his projection of himself at the close of the poem as a solitary figure against a natural background:

> Haply some hoary-headed Swain may say,
>   'Oft have we seen him at the peep of dawn
> 'Brushing with hasty steps the dews away,
>   'To meet the sun upon the upland lawn:
>
> 'There at the foot of yonder nodding beech,
>   'That wreathes its old fantastic roots so high,
> 'His listless length at noontide wou'd he stretch,
>   'And pore upon the brook that babbles by.
>
> 'Hard by yon wood, now smiling as in scorn,
>   'Mutt'ring his wayward fancies he wou'd rove;
> 'Now drooping, woeful wan, like one forlorn,
>   'Or craz'd with care, or cross'd in hopeless love.'

The great solitaries that haunt Wordsworth's poetry, as well as Arnold's Scholar Gipsy, are implicit here, though Gray's figure is more stylised, and — the word need not be pejorative — more sentimentally conceived.

In approaching any poetry of the Augustan period the modern reader has to make certain adjustments. In particular, he has to accept the characteristic Augustan use of adjectival epithets, and the poets' employment of abstract nouns as apparently arbitrary personifications. With regard to the adjective, we have come to expect it sharply to particularise the noun it qualifies. But with Gray, and others of his generation, its function is rather to define the general and persistent quality of a thing. A passage which may at first sight seem otiose is often, in fact, quite firmly controlled in the light of this principle:

> For who, to dumb Forgetfulness a prey,
>   This pleasing anxious being e'er resign'd,

> Left the warm precincts of the chearful day,
> > Nor cast one longing, ling'ring look behind?

Each of these adjectives carries its full emotional charge, culminating in the oxymoron of "pleasing anxious being", and falling away in the "longing, ling'ring look" with which the quatrain closes. Similarly, in the first stanza of the "Elegy" the epithet "weary" in the third line not only defines the daily toil of the ploughman, but points to one of the key ideas of the whole poem—the toil which was the lot of the unremembered dead in the churchyard, and is also, by implication, the lot of mankind as a whole.

It is similar with the use of personifications, especially in the Odes. What at first sight may seem vague and pompous can turn out to have its own kind of precision when the nature of the rhetoric is properly understood. Let us take the following lines from "The Bard":

> Amazement in his van, with Flight combined,
> And Sorrow's faded form, and Solitude behind.

The subject is the warlike activities of Edward I. The sequence of abstract nouns plots quite accurately the impact of an invading army. It creates first "amazement" (in eighteenth-century English the word carries overtones of terror and shock). This is followed immediately by "flight", and what remains after the army is past is first "sorrow's faded form" (a generalised figure of mourning over the slain) and then "solitude" (i.e. the desolation of the devastated landscape). Later on in the same poem we have:

> Fair laughs the Morn, and soft the Zephyr blows,
> > While proudly riding o'er the azure realm
> In gallant trim the gilded Vessel goes;
> > Youth on the prow, and Pleasure at the helm;
> Regardless of the sweeping Whirlwind's sway,
> > That, hush'd in grim repose, expects his evening-prey.

The image is that of the Ship of State, presided over by the young king, Richard II. Youth, in the person of the King, is not at the helm (this line is often misquoted), but on the prow. It is Pleasure who is at the helm, capriciously steering the ship towards disaster.

"The Bard" and "The Progress of Poesy" are Gray's most ambitious and accomplished poems. They are attempts to reproduce in English the form and manner of the Greek Pindaric Ode. The odes of Pindar were composed to be performed by a choir of dancers, in honour of a victor at the games—the Olympic, Nemean, Pythian and Isthmian Games, those great national and religious occasions held at regular intervals in antiquity. The form of the poem consisted of a repeated sequence of strophe, anti-strophe, and epode. In the strophe and anti-strophe the dancers danced the same figure, while the epode was performed standing still, and therefore had a different metrical and melodic structure. Before Gray's time Ben Jonson in his "Ode to Sir Lucius Carey", and Congreve in his "Ode to the Queen", had attempted to give an English equivalent to this ancient form in terms of rhymed stanzas and stressed metres. But generally, from the time of Cowley onwards, so-called Pindaric odes in English had been written in what was really an irregularly rhymed free verse. In the hands of a master like Dryden this could be very effective, but in those of less accomplished poets was too often an excuse for diffuseness and formlessness. From the Restoration onwards it was the accepted medium for cantatas designed to be set to music, generally on some public occasion. Gray, in fact, uses this pseudo-Pindaric form for his "Ode for Music" (written for the installation of the Duke of Grafton as Chancellor of Cambridge University). This is a fine poem (finer than the Duke of Grafton, that "young man of lounging opinions", probably deserved). Coleridge indeed seems to have preferred this to Gray's regular Pindaric odes. These last, indeed, lack the quality of being rooted in a firm cultural and religious situation which characterised the odes of Pindar. The subject of Gray's two Pindaric odes is simply the celebration of the art of poetry itself, which Gray sees as indissolubly linked with the spirit of political and national liberty. "The Bard" shows the influence of Gray's studies in Old Norse and early Welsh verse, in which he had engaged in connection with his projected history of English poetry. The poem is deliberately obscure in an attempt to reproduce the manner of the prophecy of the *Voluspa* and the medieval writings attributed to Merlin. The ground covered in the Bard's Prophecy is largely that of Shakespeare's historical plays. The final vision of the triumphs of the Tudor age is masque-like in quality, and perhaps suggested by the witches showing to Macbeth of the future glories of Banquo's line. For the purposes of his poem Gray plays down the positive in the fortunes of the House of Lancaster — Henry V's victories. The uncomfortable fact that the advent of the Tudors, far from vindicating the Welsh tradition, led to the virtual extinction of Wales as a nation is equally irrelevant to Gray's poem.

"The Progress of Poesy" by contrast, is Greek rather than Gothic, and actually incorporates free translations of passages lifted straight from Pindar. Gray's ear for the music of English was almost perfect, giving rise to effects which look forward to the melodising of Tennyson. The latter poet particularly admired the lines about the Theban eagle (Pindar) —

Sailing with supreme dominion
Thro' the azure deep of air . . .

Equally remarkable is the quasi-balletic effect in the description of the
dancing Loves, with the shift from trochaic to iambic metres which
signalises the entry of Venus as prima ballerina:

With antic Sports, and blue-eyed Pleasures,
Frisking light in frolic measures;
Now pursuing, now retreating,
Now in circling troops they meet:
To brisk notes in cadence beating
Glance their many-twinkling feet.
Slow melting strains their Queen's approach declare:
Where'er she turns the Graces homage pay.
With arms sublime, that float upon the air,
In gliding state she wins her easy way:
O'er her warm cheek, and rising bosom, move
The bloom of young Desire, and purple light of Love.

Gray's imagination has also something of the quality of the allegorical
painting of his time. In the passage about Shakespeare he says:

Far from the sun and summer-gale,
In thy green lap was Nature's Darling laid,
What time, where lucid Avon stray'd,
To Him the mighty Mother did unveil
Her aweful face: The dauntless Child
Stretch'd forth his little arms, and smiled.
This pencil take (she said) whose colours clear
Richly paint the vernal year:
Thine too these golden keys, immortal Boy!
This can unlock the gates of Joy;
Of Horror that, and thrilling Fears,
Or ope the sacred source of sympathetic Tears.

Translated into prose terms this passage is a series of Augustan critical
commonplaces. Shakespeare is instructed by Nature. She presents him
with a pencil (paint brush) with which to paint her colours, and the keys of
the heart which unlock the springs of comedy (mirth) and tragedy (terror
and pity). Nevertheless Gray invests these with a genuinely mythopoeic
quality. These lines were doubtless remembered by Keats when, in *The
Fall of Hyperion*, the mighty mother, Moneta, unveils her aweful face,
white with the whiteness of leprosy or death, to the young poet.

Gray's shorter odes are modelled on those of Horace. Their range is considerable. The "Ode to Adversity" is the forerunner of Wordsworth's "Ode to Duty". The once very popular "On a Distant Prospect of Eton College" does not seem to me to ring quite true in its sentiments. I cannot think that the sensitive Gray found his schooldays in the extremely tough Eton of the early eighteenth century as idyllic as he would have us believe. The unfinished "On the Pleasures arising from Vicissitude" perhaps more prefigures the sensibility of the Romantics than any other poem of Gray:

> The meanest flowret of the vale,
> The simplest note that swells the gale,
> The common Sun, the air, the skies,
> To him are opening Paradise.

The "Ode on the Spring" has a delicate humour, akin to that which often appears in Gray's letters, in its evocation of the insect world. The invention of the microscope had made this world accessible to the eighteenth-century observers, and they found in it a microcosm that seemed curiously to mirror their own world. Gray was something of a naturalist, and even versified the Linnaean classification of insects in Latin hexameters. The same kind of lightness appears in the "Ode on the Death of a Favourite Cat". This is a miniature mock-heroic, in which we see with a kind of double vision — at one and the same time Horace Walpole's cat crouched on a china urn and a nymph in a conventional pastoral scene reclining by a fountain. The moral is really a mock-moral. If we were to take it too seriously, then Johnson's stricture, "if *what glistered* had been *gold*, the cat would not have gone into the water; and if she had, would not less have been drowned", would be irrefutable.

The sonnet on the death of West is one of the most deeply-felt of Gray's poems. It is remarkable as being (with the exception of one earlier example by Walsh) the only sonnet written in English from the time of Milton till the very end of the eighteenth century, when the revival of the form by Bowles and others heralded the beginning of the Romantic Movement. Nevertheless, this sonnet was severely criticised by Wordsworth on the score of its diction. It does not seem to me that Wordsworth's shafts always hit their mark. Thus the line, "And reddening Phoebus lifts his golden fire", seems to me to be a quite accurate account of what it describes. The sun, low on the horizon, is reddening, but its rays are reflected as golden light from the high-flying clouds of a fine spring morning. Another line to which Wordsworth took exception was, "The birds to warm their little loves complain", which seems to me to have both tenderness and point.

Gray's translations from Old Norse and Welsh poems were intended as illustrations for the early chapters of his projected history of English poetry. It may perhaps be instructive to set some lines from "The Descent of Odin" beside a more modern translation. This is Gray:

Uprose the King of Men with speed,
And saddled strait his coal-black steed;
Down the yawning steep he rode,
That leads to Hela's drear abode.
Him the Dog of Darkness spied,
His shaggy throat he open'd wide,
While from his jaws, with carnage fill'd,
Foam and human gore distill'd:
Hoarse he bays with hideous din,
Eyes that glow, and fangs, that grin;
And long pursues, with fruitless yell,
The Father of the powerful spell.

The passage from the Edda on which this is based is thus rendered by W.H. Auden and Paul B. Taylor (*The Elder Edda*, 1969):

Up rose Odin, unaging magician,
Harnessed Sleipnir, the eight-legged,
Sped down from Heaven to Hel's Deep.
The blood-dabbled Hound of Hel faced him,
Howling in frenzy at the Father of Runes.

It will be seen that Gray has rejected what his contemporaries would have termed the unnatural image of the eight-legged steed, but has otherwise considerably expanded and enhanced the "Gothic" element of gloom and horror. "The Descent of Odin" seems to have provided Blake with elements he used in Vala in his description of the descent of Urizen into the illusory world he has created.

Gray is more successful with the elegiac tone of Old Welsh poetry. He translated passages from the *Gododdin* of the sixth-century poet Aneurin, a heroic-elegiac poem commemorating those who fell at the Battle of Cattraeth (Catterick) against the Saxons. Here again is Gray:

To Cattraeth's vale in glitt'ring row
Thrice two hundred Warriors go;
Every Warrior's manly neck
Chains of regal honour deck,
Wreath'd in many a golden link:
From the golden cup they drink
Nectar, that the bees produce,
Or the grape's ecstatic juice.

Flush'd with mirth and hope they burn:
But none from Cattraeth's vale return,
Save Aeron brave, and Conan strong,
(Bursting thro' the bloody throng)
And I, the meanest of them all,
That live to weep, and sing their fall.

And here is the same passage, as translated by Anthony Conran in the *Penguin Book of Welsh Verse* (1967):

Men went to Cattraeth, they were famous.
According to dignified custom, that year
Their drink from gold cups was wine and mead.
Three and three score and three hundred, gold-torqued,
And after flowing mead, from those that charged
Only three by valour of battle escaped —
Aeron's two war-hounds and resolute Cynon,
And I from the bloodshed by grace of blest song.

Gray has here transformed something wild and primitive into Augustan terms, elegant and formal. The loss, of course, is great. Nevertheless, he does preserve something of the pathos of the original, and his lines touch the heart. It is this capacity to touch the heart which we find again and again in Gray's poetry, and it is by this that it endures.

[1983]

George Crabbe and the Eighteenth Century

THE ANTITHESIS between nineteenth-century Romanticism and eighteenth-century Classicism, particularly in regard to English literature, is an artificial one. It does not require a very wide acquaintance with the productions of the Augustan age to find those qualities of extravagance of sentiment and subject-matter, revolutionary unrest and intellectual adventurousness—the typical Romantic qualities—latent everywhere during the century which preceded the advent of Wordsworth and Coleridge; and not only in those writers whom the text-books have labelled "Pre-Romantics". If the Mediaeval subject-matter and the Gothic horror of Gray's "Bard", or his adaptions from the Norse, "The Fatal Sisters" and "The Descent of Odin", are "Romantic", what about the "Eloisa to Abelard" of Pope himself?

> The darksome pines that o'er yon' rocks reclin'd
> Wave high, and murmur to the hollow wind,
> The wandering streams that shine between the hills,
> The grots that echo to the tinkling rills,
> The dying gales that pant upon the trees,
> The lakes that quiver to the curling breeze;
> No more these scenes my meditation aid,
> Or lull to rest the visionary maid:
> But o'er the twilight groves, and dusky caves,
> Long-sounding isles, and intermingled graves,
> Black Melancholy sits, and round her throws
> A death-like silence, and a dead repose;
> Her gloomy presence saddens all the scene,
> Shades ev'ry flower, and darkens ev'ry green,
> Deepens the murmur of the falling floods,
> And breathes a browner horror on the woods.

What about—and now we travel backwards in time even beyond the age of Queen Anne—Dryden's *Fables*, in particular his "Theodore and Honoria", with its variant of the Wild Huntsman legend? And as for the Sentimental, it is already in full flood in the tragedies of Rowe and Otway, and the novels of Mrs. Behn. Indeed, in the "Heroic" style of

the Restoration period we see the beginnings of the Neo-gothic spring-
ing straight from the Metaphysical or Baroque: the revived Mediaeval
fashion from a manner which itself represented the last authentic ex-
pression of the Mediaeval imagination in artistic form. (There are some
noteworthy parallels in the English architecture of the same period.)

All this is now pretty generally admitted. But there is a danger in
laying too much stress on this Romanticism before the Romantics, and
in neglecting what was the genuine achievement of the writers of the
Augustan age; an achievement upon which they very properly prided,
themselves, particularly in their verse. This was the humanising and so-
cialising of the imagination, the conquest over the irrational and morally
disruptive elements in it, the control of strong passion in stronger form.
Pope, above all the rest, perfected in the Heroic Couplet a technical in-
strument which combined strength, subtlety and range to an astonishing
degree. It can only seem monotonous to an untrained ear, or to an eye and
tongue unskilled in the reading of verse. In the hands of a Dryden or a
Pope it is capable of almost every kind of music, and in each of the other
poets who followed in their footsteps it has its characteristic modulation,
different for each author, which the reader familiar with the poetry of this
period soon learns to distinguish. The sombre finality of Johnson:

> Year chases Year, Decay pursues Decay,
> Still drops some Joy from withering Life away;
> New Forms arise, and different Views engage,
> Superfluous lags the Vet'ran on the Stage,
> Till pitying Nature signs the last Release,
> And bids afflicted Worth retire to Peace.

The softer, slightly sentimental note of the Irishman, Goldsmith —

> The watchdog's voice that bayed the whispering wind,
> And the loud laugh that spoke the vacant mind . . .

— which note, indeed, he caught from his predecessor Parnell, that other
Irishman, the friend of Pope and Swift:

> So parting summer bids her flowery prime
> Attend the sun to dress some foreign clime,
> While withering seasons in succession, here,
> Strip the gay gardens, and deform the year.

Or, for contrast, take the breathless, overstrained rhetoric of the Wilkesite
agitator, Churchill:

> The time hath been, a boyish, blushing time,
> When modesty was scarcely held a crime;

> When the most wicked had some touch of grace,
> And trembled to meet virtue face to face;
> When those, who, in the cause of sin grown gray,
> Had served her without grudging day by day,
> Were yet so weak an awkward shame to feel,
> And strove that glorious service to conceal:
> We, better bred, and than our sires more wise,
> Such paltry narrowness of soul despise:
> To virtue every mean pretence disclaim,
> Lay bare our crime, and glory in our shame.

and the mild, provincial pleasantries of the *Table Talk* of his one-time fellow at Westminster, Cowper:

> Conscious of age, she recollects her youth,
> And tells, not always with an eye to truth,
> Who spann'd her waist, and who, where'er he came,
> Scrawled upon glass Miss Bridget's lovely name,
> Who stole her slipper, filled it with tokay,
> And drank the little bumper every day.

To have created an organic tradition which had room for all these possibilities was the real triumph of eighteenth-century poetry. It was necessary, doubtless, that Romanticism should finally disrupt that tradition, but it is a mistake to assume that it was wholly bankrupt by the closing years of the century. George Crabbe as a young man enjoyed the patronage of Burke, and submitted his work to the correction and criticism of Johnson. Yet he was to outlive Byron, Shelley and Keats by nearly a decade, and was still producing some of his best and most characteristic work up to the time of his death. But his poetry is wholly a logical development of the central Augustan tradition, and its frequent power and originality are a striking testimony to that tradition's vigour.

I wish particularly to stress the essentially Augustan nature of Crabbe's poetry because I believe that its reputation has suffered as a result of that criticism which has adopted a purely historical estimate of his work, and has sought to exhibit him as a forerunner of the Romantics, together with his three strikingly diverse contemporaries, Cowper, Burns and Blake. In the case of the first of these such a treatment may, perhaps, to some extent be justified, but in his alone. Burns stands at the end of a respectable eighteenth-century tradition of Scottish vernacular verse — itself the resumption of a much older tradition that had scarcely died. As for Blake, so far from forerunning anybody, he outruns the Romantics, and most of our contemporaries, too. Crabbe has been made a precursor of Wordsworth, and even of Tennyson, but his Naturalism is of a different order to theirs, and he shows his strength precisely where each of them is weakest. Or he has been treated mainly as a landscape poet, and his occasional pieces of natural description have, by the anthologists, been torn from their proper context, where alone, as I hope to show, their true poetic significance is apparent.

Crabbe's early poem, *The Village*, is, indeed, mainly a descriptive piece, basically a satire, almost a parody — a counterblast to the incipient Romanticism of Goldsmith's *Deserted Village*. Its documentary value is considerable — and we must remember that the meanness and squalor which Crabbe found in the lives of the peasantry, and the waste and neglect which he saw in the condition of the land itself, represented neither more nor less than the truth. It is, however, the underlying moral attitude which makes the poetry of *The Village*. Crabbe's treatment of his subject is fundamentally classical; he judges the life and conditions of the village as falling short of an organically conceived, functional ideal. Natural beauty, for him, is represented, as it was for Virgil, by the fruitful, systematically cultivated landscape. Crabbe was, as it happened, a keen amateur naturalist and botanist. And just as he has a sharp eye to record the different types of humanity under varying economic conditions, so likewise he is an accurate observer of what modern biologists would term the ecology of the natural scene:

> Lo! where the heath, with withering brake grown o'er,
> Lends the light turf that warms the neighbouring poor;
> From thence a length of burning sand appears,
> Where the thin harvest waves its wither'd ears;
> Rank weeds, that every art and care defy,
> Reign o'er the land, and rob the blighted rye:
> There thistles stretch their prickly arms afar,
> And to the ragged infant threaten war;
> There poppies nodding, mock the hope of toil;
> There the blue bugloss paints the sterile soil;
> Hardy and high, above the slender sheaf,
> The slimy mallow waves her silky leaf;
> O'er the young shoot the charlock throws a shade,
> And clasping tares cling round the sickly blade;
> With mingled tints the rocky coasts abound,
> And a sad splendour vainly shines around.

Note that this heath, and the various flowering plants which are here described, might equally well be regarded as romantically beautiful. But they are described not for the sake of their own wild life, but are humanised and erected into figures of guilt. Crabbe goes on to compare the scene to —

> ... the nymph whom wretched arts adorn,
> Betray'd by man, then left for man to scorn ...

He, indeed, imputes a "moral life" to natural objects, but it is the reverse of that which Wordsworth found in them, since it is seen as the consequence, not the source, of man's feelings of social morality.

The Village was published only a few years before the outbreak of the French Revolution, but in spite of its exposure of the miseries of the poor and the veil with which polite sentimentality strove to cover them, its basic inspiration has nothing in common with that which animated the Revolutionary Romantics of the succeeding generations. Crabbe's ideal throughout his life appears to have been that of the settled agrarian community which was in fact rapidly passing away. If he praises the benevolent landlord who watches over the welfare of his tenants, his pity for the sufferings of the latter in other cases is always checked by reproaches against their want of industry, thrift and sobriety. He draws his values from the past, but it was by such means that he was able to supply himself with that strong framework of moral and human standards which gives its remarkable consistency to his later work.

We have seen that Crabbe's imaginative attitude to landscape is to be sharply distinguished from that of Wordsworth and the other Romantics. For these last it is Nature that is truly alive, a quasi-divine Power. The human personality is, in a sense, less than Nature, and partly, at any rate under the conditions of civilisation and intellectual maturity, alienated from her. For Crabbe, on the other hand, it is the human personality which acts upon an essentially lifeless and featureless Nature. The poem entitled "The Lover's Journey" is composed as an obvious set-piece to illustrate this point of view:

> It is the Soul that sees; the outward eyes
> Present the object, but the Mind descries;
> And thence delight, disgust, or cool indiff'rence rise;
> When minds are joyful, then we look around,
> And what is seen is all on fairy ground;
> Again they sicken, and on every view
> Cast their own dull and melancholy hue;
> Or, if absorb'd by their peculiar cares,
> The vacant eye on viewless matter glares,
> Our feelings still upon our views attend,
> And their own natures to the objects lend;
> Sorrow and joy are in their influence sure,

> Long as the passion reigns, th' effects endure;
> But Love in minds his various changes makes,
> And clothes each object with the change he takes;
> His light and shade on every view he throws,
> And on each object, what he feels, bestows.

Thus the poem begins and continues to illustrate the text by describing the journey of a lover who rides to and from the appointed meeting with his mistress, and thus views the same landscape twice altered by the differing emotions to which he is successively subject. The psychological point of view of Crabbe's is directly in the eighteenth-century tradition. He is putting into practice in his poetry the theories of the imagination developed towards the beginning of the century by Addison and Shaftsbury, and expounded in his not inconsiderable philosophical poem, *The Pleasures of the Imagination* by Mark Akenside. These theories, to be sure, were also the *framework* upon which the Romantics built up their statement of the relation of Man and Nature — or, rather, the inadequate tools by means of which they sought to explain certain powerful personal intuitions, which pointed the way to a different and profounder conception of the relation of the individual to his environment. But for Crabbe these theories were not inadequate, because he had not passed into that more spacious world bounded by the dimensions of the Romantics. Hence his poetry is at home in the world of individual human beings, as is that of Dryden or Pope, and the prose of the great line of eighteenth-century novelists from Richardson and Fielding to Crabbe's contemporary, Jane Austen. That of the Romantics, with the partial exception of Byron, is not.

The best of Crabbe's sketches, both of individuals and of classes in *The Village* and *The Parish Register*, descend directly from the satiric character-portrait of Dryden and Pope. But as Crabbe's art develops he largely abandons the satirical method, with its element of conscious distortion, and makes his portraits rounder and fuller. His extraordinary eye for detail — the eye of a man trained in medicine or of the field naturalist — gives to his pictures a documentary value quite apart from their poetic merit. Critics have, I think, in general paid him his due in respect of the former, but have failed to recognise the latter. For it is the poet who gives to the cataloguing of individual idiosyncracies the significance whereby his characters take on something of the same quality as Chaucer's. Here, for instance, is the gently ironic conclusion of his portrait of the Vicar from *The Borough*:

> The rich approved — of them in awe he stood;
> The poor admired — they all believed him good;

The old and serious of his habits spoke;
The frank and youthful loved his pleasant joke;
Mothers approved a safe contented guest,
And daughters one who back'd each small request:
In him his flock found nothing to condemn;
Him sectaries liked — he never troubled them;
No trifles fail'd his yielding mind to please,
And all his passions sunk in early ease;
Nor one so old has left this world of sin,
More like the being that he enter'd in.

It is indeed a mistake to think of Crabbe as mainly a descriptive genre-painter of the eighteenth-century peasantry. From *The Parish Register* onwards the narrative element plays a larger and larger part in his work. Moreover, in his later poems he no longer confines himself to what his own age would have termed "the labouring poor", but draws his characters from among the provincial middle classes, the prosperous farmers, and even the country gentry. At the same time his preoccupation becomes increasingly psychological and less strictly moral or social.

The original satirical impulse of Crabbe develops in his later years into something wider, a more human sense of irony. Many of his tales are little comedies of manners which might conceivably have been written in prose by Jane Austen, had she cultivated the short story instead of the full-length novel, and had she possessed the rather wider acquaintance with the vagaries of human nature in different classes which Crabbe's calling as a country clergyman provided him with. That she greatly admired Crabbe's work is well known, and she is reported once to have let the remark fall that she ought to have been married to him. It might, one feels, have been an excellent match. But it is when Crabbe's irony takes on a tragic tone that he shows himself the more remarkable and original poet. The story of Edward Shore furnishes us an example of this tragic irony. The hero is represented as a free thinker — and that for Crabbe and most of his audience meant not so much the assertion of an intellectual freedom as the denial of the moral laws whereby the society of the day was held together, and with which religion, for the eighteenth-century Protestant, had become almost entirely identified. But Edward Shore himself denies this, and places his reliance upon the individual Reason. He possesses a friend, older than himself and of sceptical principles; the wife of this friend he seduces, meanly abusing his trust. The incident brings disgrace and remorse in its train, and going from bad to worse, Edward Shore finds himself at last in the Debtors' Prison. From this situation he is, after a time, released; but the shock of discovering that this is through the kind offices of that very friend whom he had wronged is too much for him. His brain gives way, and he becomes first a maniac and then a harmless idiot:

> Harmless at length th' unhappy man was found,
> The spirit settled, but the reason drown'd;
> And all the dreadful tempest died away,
> To the dull stilness of the misty day.

In outline this may seem at first sight a crude enough cautionary tale, but its psychological subtlety becomes more and more apparent as we examine it closer. Edward Shore relies on his reason to preserve his virtue, but as soon as he is tempted he falls a victim to his passions. He cannot persevere in villainy, but the consciousness of a guilt he will not openly admit to leads to his material as well as his moral ruin. But it is the sheer irrationality of what follows that finally defeats him. His friend, by his action of generous forgiveness, displays a side of human nature which the scepticism to which they both subscribed had failed to take into account. Finally. Shore, who had deified his own Reason, finds himself deprived of that very faculty, and becomes the companion and the butt of children:

> Rarely from town, nor then unwatch'd, he goes
> In darker mood, as if to hide his woes;
> Returning soon, he with impatience seeks
> His youthful friends, and shouts, and sings, and speaks;
> Speaks a wild speech with action all as wild —
> The children's leader, and himself a child;
> He spins their top, or, at their bidding, bends
> His back, while o'er it leap his laughing friends;
> Simple and weak, he acts the boy once more,
> And heedless children call him Silly Shore.

The tale of the two brothers, the Shelleys, of whom one, the outwardly virtuous, is a gamekeeper, while the other, more reckless and lovable, seeks independence and is forced by his poverty into poaching, and in the conflict which ends only with the death of both of them, has in it the material of tragedy in its simplest and most primitive form. The tragedy centres upon the figure of the gamekeeper's wife, who nevertheless loves the poacher. The description of her journey by night, in an attempt to avert the tragedy, is another good example of Crabbe's psychological treatment of descriptive passages:

> She heard strange noises, and the shapes she saw
> Of fancied beings bound her soul in awe.

> The moon was risen, and she sometimes shone
> Through thick white clouds, that flew tumultuous on,
> Padding beneath her with an eagle's speed,
> That her soft light imprison'd and then freed;
> The fitful glimmering through the hedgerow green
> Gave a strange beauty to the changing scene;
> And roaring winds and rushing waters lent
> Their mingled voice that to the spirit went.

The brief comment —

> Two lives of men, of valiant brothers, lost!
> Enough, my lord, do hares and pheasants cost?

put into the mouth of one of the keepers when the bodies are discovered is perhaps the most effective piece of social criticism in the whole of Crabbe's work.

Perhaps one of the most deservedly famous of all Crabbe's descriptive passages is the following, which is taken from the story of Peter Grimes:

> When tides were neap, and, in the sultry day,
> Through the tall bounding mud-banks made their way,
> Which on each side rose swelling, and below
> The dark warm flood ran silently and slow;
> There anchoring, Peter chose from man to hide,
> There hang his head, and view the lazy tide
> In its hot slimy channel slowly glide;
> Where the small eels that left the deeper way
> For the warm shore, within the shallows play;
> Where gaping muscles, left upon the mud,
> Slope their slow passage to the fallen flood;
> Here dull and hopeless he'd lie down and trace
> How sidelong crabs had scrawl'd their crooked race;
> Or sadly listen to the tuneless cry
> Of fishing gull or clanging golden-eye;
> What time the sea-birds to the marsh would come,
> And the loud bittern, from the bull-rush home,
> Gave from the salt-ditch side the bellowing boom:
> He nursed the feelings these dull scenes produce,
> And loved to stop beside the opening sluice;
> Where the small stream, confined in narrow bound,
> Ran with a dull, unvarying, sadd'ning sound,
> Where all, presented to the eye or ear,
> Oppress'd the soul with misery, grief, and fear.

This has a strange, dark, brooding melancholy about it such as we some-times find in the work of Tennyson (also a poet of the East Coast, with its "glooming flats"). It is indeed not far off from the dream landscape of the later poet's "Mariana", where everything that is seen is coloured by the presence of the wasted, passion-starved life which is that of the lonely inhabitant of the Moated Grange. In Crabbe's poem, however, it is the guilt-ridden mind of the drunken, sadistic fisherman which here projects itself. He is soon to be overtaken by madness and haunted by the ghosts of the father he has defied and the unfortunate boys he has murdered. It is to be noted how the continually repeated images of slime and polluted waters constantly suggest the pathological state of the festering mind of Peter Grimes.

It is easy to scoff at this element in Crabbe's work as crude melodrama. It represents rather the seeping back into consciousness of all that the eighteenth century strove to suppress, yet which had nevertheless played a part in its most characteristic poetry. It is there in the phantasmagoria of *The Dunciad* (especially the fourth book) and in the distorted figures which crowd the Cave of Spleen in *The Rape of the Lock*:

> Unnumber'd throngs on ev'ry side are seen,
> Of Bodies chang'd to various Forms by *Spleen*.
> Here living *Teapots* stand, one Arm held out,
> One bent; the Handle this, and that the Spout:
> A Pipkin there, like *Homer's Tripod* walks;
> Here sighs a Jar, and there a Goose-pye talks;
> Men prove with Child, as pow'rful Fancy works,
> And Maids turned Bottels, call aloud for Corks.

as it is in the savagery of Swift, the sadness of Johnson. The Romantic movement was to face this element; and in so doing gave it truly poetic form and transformed it into something else. But in the closing decades of the eighteenth century it breaks through the surface both of life and of poetry like a stream of amorphous lava. Hence the enthusiasm of Smart and the Methodists, the visionary hysteria of Blake, the mania of Collins and Cowper. And in the solid, rugged surface of Crabbe's poetry there are also fissures. *Peter Grimes* is one of them; and the comparatively early poem "Sir Eustace Gray" is, perhaps, more than a mere fissure. Rather it is a pot-hole through which we look down at the seething and bubbling sea of fire, which, we are astonished to realise, was beneath our feet all the time.

Like so many of Crabbe's tragic poems, it deals with the subject of sudden shock and conversion. Sir Eustace Gray has been reduced to madness partly through misfortune, partly through the consciousness of guilt and religious enthusiasm. The most famous passages in the poem are those in which he describes his possession by devils —

They placed me where those streamers play,
    Those nimble beams of brilliant light;
It would the stoutest heart dismay,
    To see, to feel, that dreadful sight:
So swift, so pure, so cold, so bright,
    They pierced my frame with icy wound;
And all that half-year's polar night,
    Those dancing streamers wrapp'd me round.

Like some of the poetry of Coleridge and Francis Thompson, and the prose of De Quincey, these passages are famous as owing their inspiration to the author's use of opium. But the whole poem shows a facet of Crabbe's poetic character which is hinted at more frequently in other passages of his work than is generally realised. We see how closely his strong moral bent is linked with an extraordinary capacity for rendering poetically a particular mental state of oppressive guilt and anxiety.

I hope I have been able to show that Crabbe is more than a commonplace moralist whose verse is occasionally enlivened by passages of descriptive writing. He has suffered by comparison with the great Romantic writers who were the younger contemporaries of his long life. He is to be judged not according to the standard by which these wrote, but in relation to the Augustan tradition which they destroyed. From that standpoint, indeed, he was their superior; and Byron, whose own verse retained much of the vigour and catholic quality, if little of the formal perfection of the eighteenth century, rated him above almost all of them. (True, with that lack of consistent judgment which tempts even his loyalest admirers to lose patience with him, Byron rated equally high — or even a little higher — the elegant vacuity of Samuel Rogers.) In the next generation it was Edward Fitzgerald who alone, among the Victorians, carried on the Augustan tradition of grace and urbanity in poetic expression, who was the great champion of Crabbe. The latter's poetry would (prophesied Fitzgerald) outlast Browning. Browning is not in fashion in the twentieth century, but I suppose there are few who would go all the way with Fitzgerald on that point. Nevertheless, Crabbe seems to wear remarkably well.

[1945]

■ Wordsworth and Tradition

We speak of Wordsworth, and rightly, as the greatest of the English Romantic poets. But the term "Romantic", as applied to a group or school of writers of the early nineteenth century, belongs, not to Wordsworth's own vocabulary, but to that of later critics and historians of literature. It is a useful label; but had Wordsworth known of it, and foreseen our use of it, I doubt if he would have been altogether happy in accepting our application of it to himself. The *Lyrical Ballads*, with the Preface to the Second Edition of 1800, were a manifesto, and we may regard them as having revolutionised the current conception of poetry. But neither Wordsworth nor Coleridge saw themselves as innovators, or as making a break with past traditions of poetry. Their appeal, rather, was to what they regarded as the true principles of poetic tradition, which had underlain the practice of all the great poets of the past — the Greeks, Chaucer, Shakespeare, Milton, and the anonymous authors of the old ballads. What they rejected were certain later developments of the poetry of the eighteenth century, which they regarded as corruptions of tradition. On the one hand there was the decadence of the limited classicism of the Augustans, with its stylisations of diction and its artificial restrictions of subject-matter. Wordsworth's dislike of these aspects of Augustanism lead him, perhaps, to do less than justice to the achievements of Dryden, of Pope, and of Gray. But he was equally, if not more, in reaction against other aspects of late eighteenth-century writing, which literary historians have classed (along with his own work and that of Coleridge) as "Romantic" or "Pre-Romantic". He protested against the "frantic" Gothic novels of the day, against the imitations of German *Sturm und Drang* literature, and later, against the lack of real observation of nature which he detected in Macpherson's *Ossian*.

Against such affectations Wordsworth and Coleridge appealed to the truth of Nature and of the human Imagination. These two truths, for them, were essentially one, though for Wordsworth, the emphasis is on Nature, for Coleridge, on the Imagination. In the period of their most fruitful collaboration, Coleridge's metaphysical conception of the Imagination as the shaping force of the Universe, and Wordsworth's intuitions, received from his earliest years, of Nature herself as a living and a life-giving force, seemed to justify and reinforce one another. But in reality there was a fundamental divergence between their respective ways of looking at the world. This divergence was only to become apparent when, with advancing years, each was faced with the problem of how they were to continue to write poetry when the emotional impulses from which that poetry sprang became less and less frequent and less intense. That crisis is recorded by Wordsworth in his "Ode: Intimations of Immortality". In this poem he sees himself as cut off from the Nature that had once inspired him, but he does not doubt that she still retains her life and her power; that:

> There was a time when meadow, grove, and stream,
> The earth, and every common sight,
>> To me did seem
>> Apparelled in celestial light,
> The glory and the freshness of a dream.
> It is not now as it hath been of yore; —
>> Turn wheresoe'er I may,
>> By night or day,
> The things which I have seen I now can see no more.
>
>> The Rainbow comes and goes,
>> And lovely is the Rose,
>> The Moon doth with delight
> Look round her when the heavens are bare,
>> Waters on a starry night
>> Are beautiful and fair;
>> The sunshine is a glorious birth;
>> But yet I know, where'er I go,
> That there hath past away a glory from the earth.

Coleridge's "Dejection" is his reply to Wordsworth's "Ode". In its original draft Wordsworth was actually addressed in it by name; only after the quarrel which sprang between them did Coleridge alter these passages so as to eliminate mention of Wordsworth. Coleridge, like Wordsworth, feels that he can no longer receive the imaginative stimulus from Nature that he once did. But for him, the vital source from which he is cut off is his own subjective Imagination. The beauty which he had realised in Nature was only a dramatisation of his human emotions:

> O Lady! we receive but what we give,
> And in our life alone does Nature live:
> Ours is her wedding-garment, ours her shroud!
>> And would we ought behold, of higher worth,

> Than that inanimate cold world allowed
> To the poor loveless ever-anxious crowd,
>   Ah! from the soul itself must issue forth
> A light, a glory, a fair luminous cloud
>   Enveloping the Earth —
> And from the soul itself must there be sent
>   A sweet and potent voice, of its own birth,
>   Of all sweet sounds the life and element!

This stanza expresses Coleridge's Idealist attitude, defined by his studies in contemporary German philosophy. The attitude is typical of nineteenth-century (and later) thinking on aesthetic matters. It heralds one of the fundamental splits in the wholeness of culture, which was to lead to a progressive weakening, especially in the succeeding Victorian Age. In this age, the practical activities of Science were dominated by Materialism, speculative philosophy by Idealism. Poetry and the arts in general were torn between the two — all of them being departmentalised, to their mutual loss. Under the influence of materialism, Victorian poetry felt itself obliged to inculcate scientific, or utilitarian moral truth — as in much of Tennyson; or became preoccupied by minute and lifeless description of nature (Tennyson again), or a kind of painstaking historical-costume accuracy (as often in Browning). But the influence of an Idealist philosophy on poetry was hardly less harmful. The latter became subjective, formless, intellectually undisciplined, and abstracted from life into a world of dream and reverie. We see the beginnings of this already in Coleridge's own poetry (such as "Christabel" and "Kubla Khan"). The tendency is more marked in the work of Shelley and Keats (whose "Lamia" is itself an allegory of the unresolved conflict between Idealism and Materialism). By the end of the century, with the Pre-Raphaelites, and still more the Aesthetes of the 'nineties, poetry had become something completely divorced from the practical business of life — something namby-pamby and a little shameful.

But Wordsworth's experience of Nature, in his most creative poetry, was neither that of the materialist or the idealist. She was neither a dead, mechanical cosmos, nor an imaginative projection of the human mind, but an organic, self-existent reality, from which the human mind itself drew its own power and life. We may best designate his fundamental attitude as Realism — using that term rather in its medieval, scholastic sense (not in its later nineteenth-century sense, which is practically synonymous with Materialism). The comparative failure of Wordsworth's later poetry was largely due to his allowing this Realism to fall to the level of mere Materialism — attempting to draw a prudential moral lesson from external Nature, instead of accepting the whole of her potentialities, for evil as well as for good. It was this which shocked Blake, when, after reading *The Excursion*, he said: "I see in Wordsworth the Natural Man rising up against the Spiritual Man continually, and then he is no Poet but a Heathen Philosopher at Enmity against all true Poetry or Inspiration." But at his best Wordsworth's conception of the Universe has a wholeness which it shares with the work of the older poets down to the later part of the seventeenth century. The Cartesian revolution did much to destroy this sense of wholeness, and it is almost lost to English poetry after Wordsworth's time, till it was restored by Hopkins, and, perhaps, by some of our contemporaries.

The sources of this sense of wholeness in Wordsworth are to be looked for, I think, in his countryman's background, with its traditional patterns of life, and its pieties. Wordsworth was not a peasant, like John Clare. But he came of solid North Country yeoman stock, whose way of life was not so far remote from that of the peasantry. He has often been accused of idealising, even of sentimentalising, the Cumberland peasantry who play such a prominent part, especially in his early poetry. Perhaps this was sometimes the case; but he often evinces an extremely shrewd insight into the less amiable qualities of the peasant— his meanness, his grasping hunger for land and small property. In "The Last of the Flock" he tells of the encounter with a farmer, who had once been wealthy, but is now carrying the last of the sheep he had owned to be sold. The man tells his own story, and how he was forced gradually to diminish his flock to save his wife and children from starvation:

> Sir! 'twas a precious flock to me,
> As dear as my own children be;
> For daily with my growing store
> I loved my children more and more.
> Alas! it was an evil time;
> God cursed me in my sore distress;
> I prayed, yet every day I thought
> I loved my children less;
> And every week, and every day,
> My flock it seemed to melt away.

The starkness with which these lines present the extent to which even the most natural of human affections are influenced by our material economic circumstances is in its way quite terrifying.

The religious background of Wordsworth's upbringing was that of an old-fashioned eighteenth-century High Churchmanship, rooted largely in the works of such seventeenth-century divines as Jeremy Taylor. But in the period of his most creative writing he had ceased to believe in the religion of his childhood. His real religion was that worship of Nature which finds expression in his poetry. This faith of his is often called Pantheism; but it would be more correct to use the term "Pan-entheism". This latter term implies, not the reduction of all things in the Universe to aspects of the Divine (which would be Pantheism properly so-called), but the doctrine that God dwells in and informs all created things, though he is transcendent as well. This latter doctrine is strictly compatible, as more extreme Pantheism is not, with orthodox Christian thought. Indeed, Miss Edith Bathoe, in her book, *The Later Wordsworth*, has pointed out that the famous passage in "Tintern Abbey" —

> a sense sublime
> Of something far more deeply interfused,
> Whose dwelling is the light of setting suns,
> And the round ocean and the living air,
> And the blue sky, and in the mind of man;
> A motion and a spirit, that impels
> All thinking things, all objects of all thought,
> And rolls through all things.

— closely echoes a passage in one of Jeremy Taylor's sermons, which, in its turn, is based on St. Athanasius.

It might be said, in fact, that Wordsworth unconsciously transferred much of the sacramental thinking, which formed part of his traditional Christian background, to his attitude to Nature. For him, the Cumberland hills, and other objects of natural beauty, become vehicles of Grace, in the place of the Sacraments of the Church; almost, indeed, they become incarnations of the Divine. It is to the Christian mystical poets of the seventeenth century — such as Henry Vaughan (whose work he knew) and Thomas Traherne — and to the Christian Platonist Henry More, that we must go for the closest parallels to Wordsworth's religious attitude to Nature.

If we understand rightly this relation of Wordsworth to an organic tradition going back to the seventeenth century, it may be possible to take a juster view of his political development than some of his critics and biographers have done. Wordsworth has too often been represented as a youthful revolutionary who turned his back on his early libertarian ideas, and sought refuge in a reactionary Toryism. The episode of Annette Vallon, a French girl of Royalist sympathies, is, ever since it was unearthed a generation ago, usually dragged in here. It can, of course, be made to prove anything you please; but there is really no evidence that his love for Annette was of anything but passing significance in Wordsworth's development. Wordsworth's sympathies, it must be remembered, were with the Girondins, not the extremist party of the French Revolution. They represented the old, independent Republican tradition of the eighteenth century, whereas the Jacobins were much more like reformers and revolutionaries of the modern type. The Toryism to which Wordsworth later retired, was less an expression of reaction than an affirmation of the traditional pattern of society, based on land-holding, with its sense of the mutual obligations existing between landlord and tenant. It stood out against the encroachment on individual liberty of the Whig industrialists of the time. In his later years, Wordsworth retained his belief in the virtues of the free peasantry, and detested the policy of enclosures which was destroying the conditions which made a free peasantry possible. Though opposed to all ideas of violent revolution, he is recorded, at this period, to have expressed a large measure of sympathy with the aims of the Chartists.

Wordsworth's espousal of political traditionalism went hand in hand with a return to orthodox Christianity. *The Ecclesiastical Sonnets* express an ideal of the Church of England which forms one of the links between the old High Church tradition and the revived Catholicism of the Oxford Movement — whose Romantic theology owed not a little to Wordsworth's inspiration. These sonnets contain some not unworthy examples of his work, besides the wonderful "Mutability" — one of the finest sonnets he ever wrote. The decline in Wordsworth's later work has been very much exaggerated. It is undeniably cold — but it never sinks to the banality and vulgarity of which most of the Victorians, from Tennyson to Swinburne, were capable at their worst. But it is chiefly disappointing because it fails to develop the magnificent achievement of his earlier years. *The Prelude* remains a prelude only, without adequate afterpiece.

The truth of the matter seems to be that Wordsworth's Realistic conception of the Universe was born out of an older, organic and traditionalist pattern of society, which the Industrial Revolution swept away. A beautiful and little-known sonnet, written likewise in his later years, shows how Wordsworth was conscious that even the type of traditional religious faith with which he was most familiar belonged to a past order of things:

> Oft have I seen, ere Time had ploughed my cheek,
> Matrons and Sires — who, punctual to the call
> Of their loved Church, on fast or festival
> Through the long year the house of Prayer would seek:
> By Christmas snows, by visitation bleak
> Of Easter winds, unscared, from hut or hall

They came to lowly bench or sculptured stall,
But with one fervour of devotion meek.
I see the places where they once were known,
And ask, surrounded even by kneeling crowds,
Is ancient Piety forever flown?
Alas! even then they seemed like fleecy clouds
That, struggling through the western sky, have won
Their pensive light from a departed sun!

There is a sense in which the closing lines of this poem might be applied
to Wordsworth himself. It is possible to see him as the last of the giants —
the last truly great poet whose sense of things was a unity; who was, in
fact, a full man.

[1950]

◼ Landor's *Gebir*

WALTER SAVAGE LANDOR's *Gebir*, first published in 1798, is an extraordinary poem, difficult to place in relation to the history of English poetry in general. Landor was to become the principal representative in English literature of that classicizing movement in art, architecture and literature, which, in Europe as a whole, accompanied the movement we call Romanticism. That such a classical movement existed is not generally recognized, I believe, by literary critics aud historians, though its existence in the visual arts — in the paintings of David, the drawings of Flaxman and the architecture of the brothers Adam, to mention only a few instances — is acknowledged. In poetry this new classicism is not just a continuation of the Augustanism of the early eighteenth century, founded as that was on Roman models. The new classicism looked rather to Greece. In England its beginnings are perhaps to be found in the verse of Gray, Collins and (more especially) Mark Akenside. Landor does in fact mention Akenside in the preface to *Gebir* as providing a model for his blank verse, along with "The poet of our Republic" (Milton). The third name that he cites, William Armstrong, author of that curious poem *The Art of Preserving Health*, possibly recommended himself to Landor by his Epicurean philosophy.

But in a European context, we should think of other names — notably Andre Chénier in France, some aspects at least of the work of Goethe and Schiller in Germany, and Leopardi in Italy. The poetry of these men, I suggest, has features in common which are not Romantic. In the case of Landor and Chénier, at least, there is a relation between this kind of classicism and that aristocratic republicanism which crystallized in revolutionary France in the Girondin party, and it was as a Girondin that Chénier, the only real poet the French Revolution produced, was guillotined.

Gebir is, in fact, a short epic on the Vergilian model, aud one of the few poems in English since *Paradise Lost* which does anything to develop the epic tradition. The style is severely classical (it was first written in Latin, and published as *Gebirus*) and sometimes so abrupt as to be obscure. The poem is full of that sharp concreteness of imagery which in our century recommended Landor to Ezra Pound. But instead of being based on one of the great mythical, legendary or historical themes which cry out for epic treatment, Landor has based his poem on an obscure pseudo-oriental romance which he found in a circulating library. (Its author was Clara Reeve (1729–1807), best known for *The Old English Baron*, sometimes claimed as the first historical novel.) Oriental romances were popular reading through-out the eighteenth century and, for the most part, like the contemporary "Gothick" novels, trivial enough. They provided a kind of escape from Augustan rationalism, pursuing the fantastic and the picturesque wonders to be found in popular Arabian or Persian literature. The greatest of them, William Beckford's *Vathek*, retains vitality through the extraordinary extravagance of its imagery, reflecting as it does something of the extravagance of the author's own life, and something also of his personal guilt-feelings. In the coming Romantic Movement other poets besides Landor were to exploit this kind of material for verse narratives. Landor's friend Southey used Arabian material in *Thalaba the Destroyer* and Hindu material in *The Curse of Kehama* — both poems are now completely unreadable. Thomas Moore's *Lalla Rookh*, a series of oriental narratives set in a prose framework, was a best-seller in its day. But perhaps the greatest poem which this fashion produced was Coleridge's "Kubla Khan", basically a fragment of a similar oriental romance.

Gebir in spite of its source does not at all exploit this fashionable oriental colouring. Gebir, King of Iberia, has invaded Egypt — but this is clearly not the Egypt which was part of Moslem Arab civilization, but an ancient Egypt of some unspecified archaic period. In 1798 Napoleon was engaged in his Egyptian campaign, and as we shall see, this is extremely relevant to an understanding of Landor's poem. Napoleon's Egyptian adventure, in fact, was to bring about the beginning of serious archaeological discovery in Egypt, and to re-create for the European imagination the reality of Pharaonic civilization. But this was in the future. For Landor, as for the writers who had preceded him, nothing was known of ancient Egypt except what had been reported by Greek and Roman authors. It is this archaic-classical vision of Egypt, a land vaguely envisaged as of extreme antiquity and the home of ancient sorcery, which informs Landor's poem.

Landor's *Gebir* is not, of course, an allegory. Nevertheless, following the precedent of Vergil, it is full of references, partly by way of prophecy, to the historical events of Landor's own time. It is these references, I think, which make *Gebir* a true epic poem of lasting interest, and not just a piece of pseudo-oriental fantasy. The poem has two parallel narrative threads. One is concerned with Gebir himself, his martial exploits and his marriage to Charoba, the Queen of Egypt. The ending of the poem is tragic, since Gebir is destroyed at the very moment of his marriage by the evil machinations of the jealous Dalica, the Queen's nurse and a sorceress. The other narrative is concerned with the adventures of Gebir's brother, the shepherd Tamar, and his marriage with a nymph, perhaps the spirit of Liberty, who arises mysteriously from the sea. The moral meaning of the poem may perhaps be that Gebir, the man of violence, and descendant of a line of guilty kings is doomed, while from the peace-loving Tamar the future deliverer of mankind is to be descended.

This deliverer is, in fact, Napoleon Bonaparte. In 1797 he had established himself in his Italian campaign as an apparent champion of liberty and is hence a hero for the youthful Landor, whose strong republican sympathies (never to be abandoned) are expressed throughout the poem with a degree of frankness which might well have got the author into trouble.

In Book III of the poem, Gebir makes a descent to the underworld guided by Aroar. [The name "Aroar" could perhaps be read as a partial anagram of the true surname of Voltaire, "Arouet"; though, at a later date, Landor speaks disparagingly of Voltaire.] This very impressive piece of writing is modelled on Aeneas's descent to Avernus in Book VI of the *Aeneid*, but also, I think, owes something to Dante. Whereas Aeneas is shown the future glories of Rome and of his descendants, Gebir is treated to a vision of his predecessors, Iberian Kings of Gades, in torment for the crimes they have committed during their lifetimes. These figures typify English Kings seen from the point of view of Landor's implacable republicanism. The first is described as follows:

> 'What wretch
> Is that with eyebrows white, and slanting brow?
> Listen! him yonder, who bound down supine,
> Shrinks, yelling, from that sword there, engine-hung,
> He too amongst my ancestors? I hate
> The despot, but the dastard I despise.
> Was he our countryman?' 'Alas, O King!
> Iberia bore him, but the breed accurst!
> Inclement winds blew blighting from north-east.'
> 'He was a Warrior then, nor fear'd the Gods?'
> 'Gebir he fear'd the Demons, not the Gods:
> Though them, indeed, his daily face adored.
> And was no warrior; yet the thousand lives
> Squandered, as stones to exercise a sling!
> And the tame cruelty, the cold caprice —
> Oh madness of mankind! addrest, adored!'

This is a savage picture of the still-living George III, in whose name England had been plunged into war with France and a reactionary government established at home obsessed with fears of revolutionary violence, ("sword there, engine hung", is the guillotine). The reference to his fear of demons, I think, glances cruelly at the king's insanity. The next figure to be introduced is apparently William III, generally considered by the Whigs as deliverer and champion of liberty, but not by Landor:

> Behold the giant next him; how his feet
> Plunge flound'ring mid the marshes, yellow-flower'd
> His restless head just reaching to the rocks.
> His bosom tossing with black weeds besmear'd
> How writhes he 'twixt the continent and isle.
> What tyrant with more insolence e'er claim'd
> Dominion? when, from th' heart of Usury
> Rose more intense the pale-flam'd thirst for gold?
> And call'd forsooth. *Deliver*!

The marshes here are an allusion to William's Dutch origin, just as George III's ancestors have been blown by inclement winds from Germany. It should be remembered that the Bank of England was founded during the reign of William III, and the introduction of Dutch credit and banking systems gave a strong impulse to the development of capitalism.

The sound of sensuous music heralds the appearance of the third of Gebir's doomed ancestors, in whom we recognize Charles II who notoriously accepted a pension from Louis XIV in consideration of pursuing policies agreeable to the French Monarch:

> 'Hearest thou not the harp's gay simpering air,
> And merriment afar! mark the wretch accurst
> Who sold his people to a rival king.
> Self-yoked they stood, two ages unredeem'd'

The climax of this passage is a vision of a headless king. This is, of course, Charles I — but Landor intends his readers to recall the fate that had more lately overtaken Louis XVI of France:

> 'O Horror! what pale visage rises there!
> Speak, Aroar — me, perhaps mine eyes deceive,
> Inured not, yet methinks they still descry
> Such crimson haze as sometimes drowns the moon.
> What is yon awful sight? why thus appears
> That space between the purple and the crown?'

A second group of historical allusions is found later on in the poem, in the vision which the nymph shows her newly-espoused Tamar in Book VI.

After viewing Cyprus and Crete we come to this passage:

> 'Look yonder,' cried the Nymph, without reply,
> 'Look yonder!' Tamar look'd and saw two isles
> Where the waves whiten'd on the desert shore.
> Then she continued, 'That which intervenes
> Scarcely the Nymphs themselves have known from Fame:
> But mark the furthest; there shall once arise,
> From Tamar shall rise, 'tis Fate's decree,
> A mortal man above all mortal praise.'

The two isles referred to must be Sardinia and Corsica respectively, and the "Mortal man above all mortal praise" is therefore, as we have already indicated, Napoleon.

The climax of this vision is a prophetic view of Republican France. This includes an interesting and quite explicit reference to the new calendar which had been introduced in 1796, and in which fresh names for the months (Thermidor, Brumaire, Florial and the rest) were substituted for the traditional Roman names:

> Time, Time himself throws off his mottly garb
> Figur'd with monstrous men and monstrous gods,
> And in pure vesture enters their pure fanes,
> A proud partaker of their festivals.
> Captivity led captive, War o'erthrown,
> They shall o'er Europe, shall o'er Earth extend
> Empire that seas alone and skies confine,
> And glory that shall strike the crystal stars.

Among poets of the present century, Yeats, Pound and Eliot all greatly respected Landor's work. But, in recent years there has been a tendency to dismiss him as a mere *belle-lettrist* in regard to his prose writings, while the anthologists have generally represented his verse only by short epigrams. But a careful reading of the *Imaginary Conversations* will reveal more than mere surface polish. They contain genuine dramatic insights, both tragic and comic, as well as a consistency of philosophical and political thinking: in the one case Stoic-Epicurean humanism, in the other conservative-radical republicanism. Among Landor's poems, not only *Gebir* bears witness to its author's powers of constructing a work on a relatively large scale. But this early poem alone, perhaps, contains within its rigid classical conventions a certain wildness and almost prophetic power. It is as if Landor here joins hands with that one of his contemporaries who in other respects might seem to stand at the furthest remove from him — the William Blake of the Prophetic Books.

[1984]

■ Shelley

IN 1870, WILLIAM MICHAEL ROSSETTI in the preface to a collected edition of Shelley's poems, could, without hesitation, link his name with those of Shakespeare and Milton as one of the three supreme embodiments of the English poetic genius. Shelley's was the voice of youthful, romantic, revolutionary lyricism. In his lifetime he was ostracised as an atheist and a dangerously subversive rebel; after his death his political poems were enthusiastically circulated among the Chartists and the intellectuals of the discontented masses of the hungry 'forties. But the prosperous stability of the mid and later Victorian age appeared to banish once more the threat of revolution. Readers of poetry learned to delight in the half feminine, dreamy charm of his verse, while his wild prophecies of a world regenerate seemed to be about to find their justification through the current faith in the steady progress of scientific and humanitarian enlightenment.

The times have changed, and we live once more in a revolutionary age — but it is an age no longer youthful in spirit. It is not surprising, therefore, that Shelley's reputation has suffered a partial eclipse. We have learned to be sceptical of idealism and of romanticism; and the poets themselves have come to distrust poetry. Under the impersonal scrutiny of an intellectual criticism much of Shelley's work simply crumbles away. His musical charm is often merely specious, covering a demonstrable vagueness of thought and imagery, even a total lack of true meaning. Particularly is this the case with that portion of his work — his shorter lyrics — on which his reputation seemed once most securely to rest. Long before though, Matthew Arnold had warned readers of Shelley that they would find here only "a gallery of his failures". In the face of the strictures of Mr. Eliot, or such analysis as Dr. Leavis has applied to some of the poems, there is little that can be said. Such pieces as "When the lamp is shattered" or "Music, when soft voices die", for all their long-standing popularity with the anthologists, are really intellectually indefensible. They are so in a way that cannot be alleged of the slightest and most casual lyric of Shakespeare, or of a host of minor Elizabethan and Caroline poets. Shelley's admirers, feeling themselves still swayed by a

deep-lying sympathy for his ideals and his character, have been com-
pelled, like Mr. Herbert Read, to undertake a defence which is psycho-
logical in its approach — a vindication of him as a personality rather than
as a poet.

It is this personality, indeed, which first of all engages us. For even
if he is not, after all, one of the greatest of English poets, he is still one
of the queerest and most strikingly individual. This baronet's heir, and
descendant of an old Sussex family, the wild-eyed, tall, round-shouldered
youth with the shrill, somewhat discordant voice, was the very type of
the eccentric aristocratic rebel. "Mad Shelley" he was called in his Eton
schooldays; from University College, Oxford (where his brief residence
is now commemorated by a memorial of singular hideousness) he was —
quite properly — sent down for an atheistic pamphlet which, with his
characteristic thoroughness, he had sent to each of the bishops of the
Church of England, as well as to the heads of the University. Singularly
diverse elements of thought jostled against one another in his growing
mind — a love of scientific theory and experiment, Godwinian ideas of
political justice, Rousseau's cult of feeling, Platonism, Hellenism, and a
"Gothic" delight in ghosts and demonology, the bizarre and the horrible.
His hatred of cruelty and oppression was sincere and uncompromising.
If we are tempted to impute to his excursions into political propaganda
an adolescent lack of realism, we forget how actual were the injustices
which Shelley challenged. The solutions which he advocated, however
little chance they might stand of adoption, in his own time or since, were
fundamentally righteous. His ideas on marriage were less practicable —
given the normal nature of man and woman; nor did they prevent him
from behaving, on occasion, like an insufferable prig. His first wife,
Harriet Westbrook, with whom he chivalrously eloped to rescue her from
an unhappy existence in a boarding-school, committed suicide when he
left her for Godwin's daughter Mary. The latter, an intellectual, managed
to keep him, in spite of Emilia Viviani, Jane Williams, and others. As
with his fellow Romantics, Landor, Byron, and Beddoes, England could
not hold him. His years of self-banishment in Italy were happy and
productive enough. But his death, which occurred when he was thirty,
as the result of a boating accident in a storm at sea off Leghorn in 1822,
was perhaps a half suicide. His friends, Byron among them, cremated
him in the high pagan style upon the sea-shore, because the authorities
would not permit the transport of his body to the Protestant cemetery at
Rome, where his ashes now rest.

The note of strangeness sounds all through the poetry of Shelley, from
the opening of *Queen Mab*, with its haunting evocation of the spirits of

Sleep and Death, to *The Triumph of Life*, where Rousseau, the type of
the poet whom Life has overcome, appears, withered and monstrous:

> I turned, and knew
> (O Heaven, have mercy on such wretchedness!)
>
> That what I thought was an old root which grew
> To strange distortion out of the hill side,
> Was indeed one of those deluded crew,
>
> And that the grass, which methought hung so wide
> And white, was but his thin discoloured hair,
> And that the holes he vainly sought to hide,
>
> Were or had been eyes: . . .

His world is largely a dream-world — a universe of archetypal and archaic
symbols. The Tower of intellectual contemplation, the Cave of death and
re-birth, the enchanted Chariot and Boat of the spirit, the Serpent as the
type of wisdom and good — these recurring images of his poetry are
among such symbols.

Much that is extravagant — dreamlike or nightmarelike — in Shelley's
poetry may be traced to the influence of the "Gothic" novels which were
amongst his favourite reading as a boy. But he stands also deliberately
and self-consciously in the succession of the great poets of the European
tradition of the past. He lacked a classical discipline, but his sympathy
with the Greek poets, and with those of the Renaissance, was instinctive.
The list of those masters to whom he sought to assimilate himself, by
translation or close imitation, is instructive. It includes the authors of the
Homeric Hymns, Aeschylus, the Euripides of the *Cyclops*, Aristophanes
(in *The Cloud* as well as *Swellfoot*), Plato, Moschus (whose *Lament
for Bion* is one of the models for *Adonais*), Virgil (who in his *Fourth
Eclogue* told how "the world's great age begins anew"), Dante, Petrarch,,
the Jacobean tragedians, and, as lyrical dramatists, Calderon and Goethe.
Diverse as these authors are, in all of them we discern a tendency for
the lyrical to become the truly metaphysical, and to lift itself into the
over-world of myth and symbol. This faculty Shelley also possessed,
but in his brief life he never attained, except by flashes, to that mature
and disciplined intellectuality, that union of thought and feeling, which
alone could give a wider validity to his vision. Perhaps he alone of the
poets of his day, with his enthusiasm for and understanding of science
(whose theories are practically transmitted in *The Cloud* and the last act
of *Prometheus Unbound*) combined with his Hellenism, his Platonism,
and his Romanticism, could have achieved a synthesis which would have

given a true imaginative validity to the nineteenth-century myth of Evolution. Such a synthesis might have made Shelley comparable to Dante, who brought together in his Comedy the diverse elements of Mediaeval science and theology, religious mysticism, and the cult of Courtly Love. Goethe alone of the writers of his time, in the second part of *Faust*, came near to the comprehensiveness of Dante; but Goethe, unlike Shelley, ignored the most significant event of the age, the French Revolution. It is perhaps the lack of any really organic religious feeling (as distinct from a vague pantheistic or idealistic intuition) that we feel most in Shelley; this alone might have provided the point around which the diverse objects of his intellectual and emotional preoccupations could crystallize.

Shelley, then, falls short of being a great metaphysical poet. His work remains a collection of beautiful fragments — fragments often with a greater potency of suggestion than the more aesthetically satisfying achievements of other poets. He is at his weakest in direct rhetorical statement of ideas; most a poet, when he succeeds in invoking them by more indirect means. In this respect he may be called, properly speaking, a symbolist, and he is, indeed, the forerunner of the Symbolist movement of the later part of the century. Poe, the immediate begetter of the French Symbolists, was, if we consider his verse as distinct from his prose, little more than a somewhat crude imitator of certain features of Shelley's work. One cannot help wondering whether Verlaine and probably Mallarmé also, did not learn something from Shelley's lyrics. Yeats admired him from his earliest years, and in an interesting essay deduced a "philosophy" from his poetry which was really an attempt at an interpretation of his symbols. More recently, Boris Pasternak has drawn a parallel between Shelley and the Russian Symbolist Blok.

It is this aspect of his work, perhaps, that is most likely to appeal to the modern reader. Shelley is a poet of the archetypal dream-world, or sometimes, of waking reverie against the background of bright Italian landscape. We are beginning today to understand something of the true significance of our dreams. Perhaps in the light of this understanding we will be able to listen once more to the spirit which speaks in the dream-poetry of Shelley, telling of universal liberty and a world redeemed through love.

[1948]

■ Poe

It is a pleasure for me to visit again this great city of New York and an even greater pleasure, as well as a privilege, to have been asked to speak in this beautiful cathedral of yours. The subject of Edgar Allan Poe has been assigned to me and this is fortunate, for among all the poets who are commemorated here, it is Poe alone of whom I can claim to have more than a superficial knowledge. Perhaps you are thinking that that is because I am an Englishman, for I believe it has sometimes been said that Poe occupies an anomalous place in the American tradition, that his influence has been greater in Europe than in his own country, and that his reputation outside the United States is excessive. I do not subscribe to this view of Edgar Allan Poe. I think that no other country but America could have produced this writer. It is perhaps true that he was the first American poet to have a wide-reaching influence outside the land of his birth. As for his *Tales of Mystery and Imagination*, they have always been popular in England. Indeed, when one first comes across them as a schoolboy, and not in class, at the age of nine or ten, one is not conscious that one is reading "literature", for they are simply exciting and frightening stories, like the detective stories of Sherlock Holmes, or on a lower level, the stuff one reads in horror comics. But as a poet, in the narrower sense of the word, Poe's influence has been stronger on the continent of Europe than in Great Britain. That influence was first of all on Baudelaire and then on the French Symbolists who were his successors, but it extended as far afield as Russia. It was a Russian composer, Rachmaninov, who set Poe's poem "The Bells" as a cantata.

Now from the point of view of the English-speaking reader, Poe's verse, with the exception of only a very few lyrics, must be approached with reserve. Its metrical skill too often seems mechanical, its imagery too narrow, too repetitive, too divorced from actual waking life. To some extent, these deficiencies disappear in translation. It is noteworthy, for example, that the French poet, Stephane Mallarmé, chose to render Poe's poem "The Raven" in prose. There are two, or possibly three, poets

---

(Originally given as a lecture at the Cathedral of St. John the Divine, New York City, on the occasion of the oration of a memorial to Poe in the Poet's Corner of the Cathedral.)

of the English-speaking world whose continental European reputation may sometimes seem to the English-speaking reader to be perversely exaggerated. The first of these poets is Lord Byron. The second is Poe, and the third, a rather more doubtful case, I think, is Oscar Wilde. All three of them, with all their brilliance, do show these deficiencies of taste, which I suggest may well get overlooked in translation. All three are in some respects derivative poets. Byron and Wilde were both victims of persecution by their societies, on account of the scandal of their private lives, and the European reader may well consider them to be martyrs to that well-known phenomenon, English — might I say Anglo-Saxon? — hypocrisy. Poe likewise was in some respects an outcast from his society. His life was a kind of nightmare and so was his death: that his body was found on a park bench where he had been abandoned by an election mob who had used him as a dummy voter, had, one is tempted to say, a kind of symbolic quality. It was Byron who became, as it were, the godfather of the first phase of European romanticism. That was the phase which saw the poet as a splendid individualist, a heroic rebel, a flouter of conventions. And Poe is the godfather of the later phase of the same movement, when the poet is thought of as an arcane craftsman, a master of magical incantation, and an interpreter of marginal and shadowy experience.

But Poe is an American poet, and he would not, I venture to state, have attained to international importance had he not been American. Let us compare him with the English poet, Thomas Lovell Beddoes. Beddoes was Poe's almost exact contemporary. He was also an eccentric and a poet *maudit*. His career ended in self-imposed exile in Germany and ultimately in suicide. He operates in much the same field of sensibility as Poe. His poetry is full of the imagery of death, of ghosts and graveyards and skeletons, and he has the same black humour as Poe. His most ambitious piece of writing, on which he continued to work through the years and which was never published during his lifetime, was a pseudo-Jacobean drama with the significant title of *Death's Jest Book*. Now it seems to me that by any objective criteria of criticism, Beddoes was a much better poet than Poe. His imagery is not only more original but has greater definition. His musical ear is finer and much more subtle than Poe's. He came of a distinguished intellectual family and with his medical training, had a strong grasp of the science of his day. This interest in science he shared with Poe, as did both with their common master, Shelley. But who outside the English-speaking world, possibly indeed outside England, has heard of Beddoes? Little of his work was printed during his lifetime and much indeed remained unpublished for the next two generations. During the 1930s and 1940s, when critics and poets were reassessing the whole tradition of English poetry, there was a strong interest in Beddoes' work, but I think this has largely died down today. Against the extraordinary rich flowering of English romantic poetry from Blake, Wordsworth and Coleridge, through to Byron, Shelley and Keats, Beddoes stands only as a minor, eccentric writer. But Poe's achievement was to bring an absolutely new note into the American tradition, that was also to catch the ear of the world at large.

American writers, unlike those of Britain or other European countries, have had to construct their own mythology, to raise a pantheon of symbolic figures from their past, and to this pantheon Poe belongs. But it is the dark side of the American imagination, the nightmare which underlies the American dream, which he represents. "And why do I often meet your visage here / Your eyes like agate lanterns?" So wrote Hart Crane, when in his great poem *The Bridge* he encounters the ghost of Poe in a New York subway. In the pattern of Crane's poem the subway is an image of inferno, and that encounter belongs to a poetic tradition of similar encounters in or near the underworld. The origins of this tradition can be traced to Virgil's *Aeneid* and to Homer's *Odyssey* and even further back to the ancient Babylonian epic of Gilgamesh. It leads on to Dante's encounter with the spirit of Virgil in the dark wood, and to that of those two poets and the spirit of Dante's dead master Brunetto Latini in the *Inferno*; the tradition is continued later in Eliot's encounter with the "familiar compound ghost" (I think mainly W.B. Yeats, but Poe is also indicated) in the fire storm of the London blitz, over Bloomsbury.

Poe was proud to call himself a Bostonian, but the fact that he was born in that city was almost an accident, contingent on the calling of his parents as strolling actors. It is, of course, to the South, to Virginia, that he really belongs. But we must not forget his spell in New York as an editor and his schooldays in England. Other later journeys to Europe, even, it has been alleged, as far afield as Russia, are ill-authenticated. But Poe certainly did attend private schools in England, particularly one in what is now the north London suburb of Stoke Newington. This school forms the setting for his story "William Wilson". Stoke Newington, incidentally, has an interesting connection with two notable writers of the eighteenth century: Daniel Defoe and Isaacs Watts, the hymn writer, both resided there. This is because, being outside the five-mile limit from the centre of London, religious dissenters were allowed to live there. Defoe and Watts were notable representatives of that Nonconformist tradition. Such illiberal legislation had, I need hardly say, become a thing of the past in Poe's time, but the connection may be a significant one.

But, as I have said, Poe belongs to the American South. Some, for example, have seen a typical Southern landscape in the setting of "The Fall of the House of Usher", or have tried to trace the roots of the horror which pervades Poe's work in the guilt of a slave-owning society. I am unable to comment on this, for the South is not a part of America I have visited, nor have I sufficient knowledge of American literature to chart Poe's relationship to later writers in the Southern tradition, though I certainly think that this could be done. What is clear to me is that the nightmare of Poe's life and the nightmare which constitutes his imaginative work began in that room over the milliner's shop in Richmond, Virginia, where, almost certainly as a very small child, he witnessed his mother's body being nailed up in its coffin. It was at that juncture that he was adopted by a rich childless woman with an unfaithful husband, to be caught up in the resentments and animosities of those foster-parents. It is tempting to play the psychoanalytical game as a means of interpretation of Poe's work. This has been done very thoroughly by the Princess Marie Bonaparte. But there is not a lot of point in it — it is all too easy. Presuming, with Sigmund Freud, that the child has no apprehension of the fact of death, everything falls into place. Again and again the theme of premature burial recurs in Poe's work. Sometimes it is the narrator himself who is the victim. More often, it is the heroine of the story who has been buried alive, and who desperately fights her way out like the Lady Madeline of Usher to the world of the living. In other cases the hero's beloved succumbs to death but, by an effort of will, returns, like Ligeia, in the person of her successor, or like Morella, in her own daughter. We know that Elizabeth Poe, Poe's mother, was consumptive, was slight in build, with dark hair and remarkably striking large and luminous eyes. Poe's heroines have the same dark hair, and those same eyes, but these heroines are described as exceptionally tall. Of course, a mother will appear so actually in the eyes of a little child. This same Freudian theme even enters into the black humour of "The Spectacles", where the hero, too vain to wear spectacles to remedy his poor eyesight, is in danger of falling in love with his own grandmother. Poe was to find a surrogate mother in his aunt, Annie Clem, and to marry his own cousin, a fourteen-year-old child, poor little Virginia Clem. Virginia was consumptive, and there is a pathetic story of how, in their poverty, the only way she could gain warmth was to clasp the family cat to her bosom as she lay in bed, but this image becomes macabre when Poe transfers it to his story, "The Black Cat". A murderer has walled up his victim but has inadvertently buried the living cat along with her. It is its cries which lead ultimately to the discovery of his crime.

It is by a superhuman effort of will that Ligeia, in another story, overcomes Death and defeats the conqueror, Worm. Poe's universe is basically a materialistic one. His cosmology, as expounded in *Eureka*, is that of Laplace who, when Napoleon asked him about God, replied that he had no need for that hypothesis. Religion plays no part in any of Poe's stories nor, on a lower level, is there a single ghost, but he does seem to believe that the world is partly controllable, indeed partly created, by the human will. In "The Facts in the Case of M. Valdemar" a mesmerist is actually able to arrest the process of death and of putrefaction itself. While in one of his prose poems, a strange dialogue in which spirits converse together after destruction of our world, a blasted and hideous planet has come into being through the operation of an unhappy man's terrible curse.

The world of Poe's imagination has two polarities. On the one hand it is rooted in the life of the subconscious, in dream and nightmare and childhood fantasies. On the other, it is a world of pure will and pure intellect. In between these two polarities should exist what we regard as the ordinary world of everyday life and human relationships, but in Poe all this is frighteningly absent. It was through the power of his abstract intellect that Poe was able to invent the detective story and to solve the real life mystery of the murder of Mary Rogers under the fictional guise of "The Mystery of Marie Roget". In the pride of his intellect he believed that he could construct a universal philosophical system which would render obsolete the thought of both Bacon and Aristotle. But *Eureka*, his projected masterpiece, turns out only to be an example of those false riches which narcotics and alcohol offer to their devotees, or like the fairy gold which in folktales turns out to be only dead leaves and rubbish when the light of day falls upon it.

Poe's delight in his own intellectual skill led him, whose masters had been such romantics as Coleridge, Shelley and De Quincey, to learn from quite another tradition. He discovered the *Peri Bathos, or The Art of Sinking in Poetry*, by Alexander Pope. This masterpiece of Augustan intellectual irony became for Poe an armoury which furnished him with weapons against the mediocre poets who came his way as a reviewer. It was that same intellect which led him to the bleak vision of the future which appears in "Mellonta Tauta". The narrator of this story is crossing the Atlantic in a balloon. It is the 1940s and technology has got that far! One of the passengers has fallen overboard but no attempt, of course, was made to save him, as modern science has conclusively proved that no such thing as an individual exists.

Abstraction and subliminal dream are then the two constituents of Poe's world, each threatening the destruction of the other. It is significant that in that brilliant story, "The Murders in the Rue Morgue", the murderer turns out to be, not a human being at all, but an orang-utan. The ape is the symbol of the primitive within the unconscious man, which may at any time break out to destroy. Another story, "Hop-Frog", is on the widely used romantic theme of the clown's revenge (compare *Rigoletto*, for example, or *I Pagliacci*). In this story the dwarf Hop-Frog (the child is a dwarf in relation to the adult world) takes a terrible revenge against the prince and his courtiers (who have mocked him and threatened his child sweetheart) by tricking them into dressing up as apes. In passing, I would point out that the natural history of Poe's time greatly exaggerated the ferocity of the great apes, especially the gentle and rather sluggish orang-utan. But the three species of anthropoid apes, the orang, the chimpanzee and the gorilla, tended to get confused. Even before Darwin, their paradoxical resemblance to humanity was capturing the imagination. Here is a quiz question for you. Name three stories, written in English in the first half of the nineteenth century, in which an orang-utan plays a leading part. The first one I have already given you. The second is Thomas Love Peacock's satirical novel, *Melincourt*. This story ridicules what were known as rotten boroughs and pocket boroughs — Parliamentary constituencies which were entirely under the control of the local landlord since they contained either no voters at all or voters who were entirely dependent on his patronage. In Peacock's novel, an educated ape, Sir Oran Haut-ton, is put up as a Parliamentary candidate. The third orang, whose name is Sylvan, occurs in one of Sir Walter Scott's least read novels, *Count Robert of Paris*. It deals with the Crusaders in Constantinople, and Sylvan, who has been brought from the island of Taprobane, saves the heroine from being raped by killing her assailant, an evil and pagan-minded Byzantine philosopher.

But to return to our muttons. Let us have a look at "The Fall of the House of Usher". The house itself, the actual mansion, is fatally flawed by a crack that reaches from the top to the bottom of its structure. It is built over the waters of a dark tarn, which engulf it at the moment that the buried sister, the Lady Madeline of Usher, struggles back into life and consciousness. This struggle of the Lady Madeline and the violent noises which accompany it, are fused in Roderick Usher's mind with the sound of conflict against a dragon. This dragon is a figure in the ancient romance he is reading. Poe's attempt here at some kind of gothic style is not convincing, but the implied identification of the Lady Madeline with the dragon or serpent of rejected sexuality is significant.

The house, with its flaw, is identified with its occupant, Roderick Usher, the last representative of the house (in the sense of family) of Usher. He likewise is fatally flawed by incipient madness. Within this story is set the poem of "The Haunted Palace", supposedly composed by Roderick Usher himself. This poem is in fact in a tradition where the human body is allegorised as a house. In Book II of Spenser's Faerie Queene, the house of Alma is such an allegory. I think Poe may also have known the early seventeenth-century poet Phineas Fletcher's poem "The Purple Island", where the human body is allegorised as an island in which the different organs are cities joined by canals which are the veins and arteries. Significantly, in Roderick Usher's poem, it is the head alone which is allegorised as a palace. By implication the body and all that that implies is ignored.

An image related to "The Fall of the House of Usher" appears in what to my mind is one of the most successful of Poe's lyrics, "The City in the Sea", where another construct of human art and artifice, this time the city, is threatened by the final rising of the sea and of hell itself. Poe's imagery, in fact, is very noteworthy. Its symbolism points towards the symbolism of Melville, while its realism perhaps owes something to Defoe — who, as I have pointed out, had been a resident of Stoke Newington long before Poe spent some of his schooldays there. Poe's early visit to England, and of course the return voyage, may have been the only occasions on which he crossed the ocean (though Alexandre Dumas claimed to have met him in Paris in 1832). Nevertheless, his sea imagery in such stories as "A Descent into the Maelstrom", "MS. Found in a Bottle" and, above all, *The Narrative of Arthur Gordon Pym*, has a sense of actuality which is lacking in the ghoul-haunted landscape of many of his poems and prose poems. It is only at the very end of *Arthur Gordon Pym*, when strange white figures appear, symbols evidently like the White Whale, of death, that the seascape is transformed from a realistic into a symbolic one.

James Russell Lowell wrote of ". . . Poe, with his raven, like Barnaby Rudge, / Three-fifths of him genius, and two-fifths sheer fudge". "The Raven" is a paradoxical poem. It goes along with Poe's essay, "The Philosophy of Composition". In that document Poe claims to have constructed the poem step by step in order to achieve the maximum effect of beauty — according to him the only true aim of poetry and to be separated from moral or scientific truth. The most beautiful emotion, Poe claims, is that of sorrow, the most intense sorrow, grief for the death of a beautiful woman. The word "nevermore" is taken for its musical quality as much as for its meaning and has to serve as a refrain. Therefore something has to repeat it again and again, and what but a talking bird, a raven. In totally severing the link between truth and beauty, Poe goes beyond his romantic-masters, beyond Shelley, Coleridge, and even beyond Keats, though their thought seems to have been evolving precisely in this direction. But a far more radical break is made by the assumption that a poem is something to be constructed, coldly, and calculated, as one solves a mathematical problem, instead of being a product of inspiration or afflatus. To Wordsworth the poet was "a man speaking to men in the language of men", for Shelley the "unacknowledged legislator of mankind", but the archetype of the poet for Poe is a purely spiritual being: "the angel Israfel" "whose heart-strings are a lute." The idea that a poem is a deliberate verbal construct was to bear fruit in the twentieth century, notably in Paul Valéry, and even in Yeats's "fascination of what's difficult". Similarly, the idea that there is no such thing as a long poem was to be developed by the aesthetic philosopher Benedetto Croce and by the Anglo-American Imagist school. But the poem itself denies the very theory on which it purports to have been constructed. In the first place, we may question whether it is the masterpiece which its early readers, and probably Poe himself, took it to be. The remorselessly trochaic metre — a metre very effective in some other languages — is, at least to my ear, generally mechanical and dead when used in English. Part of the trouble is that as each line must start with a stressed syllable, it is impossible to begin a line in the most usual way of constructing an English sentence, i.e. with a noun preceded by the definite or indefinite article or by a verb preceded by a pronoun. In so far as "The Raven" does work as a poem, it works not by virtue of Poe's theory, but as yet another statement of the theme which haunts all Poe's work. The raven is a messenger from the world of the dead, from the lost Lenore — yet another of Poe's buried women whose presence continues to haunt their lovers in this waiting world. It has been suggested to me, in fact, that it is precisely because of the horror of this situation — the situation stemming from the childhood trauma of his mother's death and entombment — that Poe is obliged to deceive himself and his readers into taking the poem as a deliberate intellectual construct.

In Poe, as in the Symbolists, and (in English poetry) in Swinburne, who along with Dante Gabriel Rossetti owed much to Poe, poetry aspires to the condition of music. The words are of course chosen for their musical incantory power as much as for their meaning, and so are the names of Poe's heroines, in which the liquid consonants "l" and "r", and the nasals, "m" and "n", predominate. Such names are Lenore, Eulalie, Ligeia, Morella, the Lady Madeline, Annabel Lee. But these are recognisably names. What of the last in the series, "Ulalume"? That is not a name at all: it is a primitive infantile wail. The poem that is entitled "Ulalume" is in logical terms almost meaningless, although it is of course yet another statement of the continuing theme of the sepulchred beloved. Again, one may question whether it is a very good poem in objective terms, yet to read it frightens me. It is almost as if we heard the last cry of a soul desperately clutching at articulation before it falls into the abyss.

I said it is as if we heard the voice of a lost soul, but God forbid, that I should be thought to be standing in judgement on the man, Edgar Allan Poe. It is true that he was in some ways weak and self-indulgent (I am thinking of his alcohol and opium addiction). Such weakness and such indulgence was all too common in his, as it is in our own, society. In regard to opium one must remember that it was freely used in the early nineteenth century as a painkiller, almost as we use aspirin. It was not only Coleridge and De Quincey who were addicted to it, and to some extent wrecked their lives by this addiction. It was also used by other writers of a different kind, by George Crabbe, and by Wilkie Collins, both of whom managed to organize their lives rather well. Poe was able to survive as long as he did through sheer industry as a writer and a journalist. This is not the mark of a basically weak character; in the artist there is always a kind of inner strength and will to survive. Such a life as Poe's is in its own way a kind of martyrdom. I use the word martyrdom advisedly, bearing in mind the original meaning of the word martyr — a witness. But speaking of a very different writer, the modern Greek poet Constantine P. Cavafy, W.H. Auden spoke of his being "a witness to the truth", defining this as the prime duty of the poet. Poe in his own way was also a witness. Those who were closest to him seem to have found him gentle and affectionate, but the necrophile, the torturer, the untamed beast, lurked in his psyche as they lurk within each one of us. It was precisely because he had the strength to confront these monsters that his work has its universal appeal, that he was thus driven to explore the dark labyrinths within tells something about the society in which he lived. If a society rejects its poets and its prophets, they may be driven underground, not necessarily as political subversives, but as in Poe's case, psychological subversives. There is a tendency in some quarters today — I am thinking particularly of the European political left — to stress the duty of the artist to be politically committed. This can too easily be a way of bullying the artist. The very rejection of overt political values or social criticism is itself a kind of political statement, and if a poet rejects the world of normal human relationships and experience, to explore a dark underworld of fantasies, he should not be regarded as an escapist.

He is saying something about the health of his society which that society should take very much to heart.

The greatest of Poe's disciples was Charles Baudelaire. In however strange and even perverted a way, Baudelaire's sensibility was a Christian one. In a private notebook Baudelaire reminded himself to call, in his prayers, on his deceased sister and on Edgar Allan Poe as intercessors. Who is to say, in the economy of eternity, that such prayers for intercession are vain? If you believe, as I do, that the nexus which links all human personalities is not broken by death, then there is perhaps among the poets commemorated in this place none who needs our intercession more than Edgar Allan Poe.

[1988]

■ Tennyson

THERE IS a good deal to be said, I think, for presenting Tennyson to the reader of to-day through the medium of a short selection from his poems. About the destiny and reputation of his work there is a certain irony: he was the heir of the Romantic rebels who rose to be the Laureate of solid, Victorian England, the official singer of its belief in steady human progress, in the domestic virtues, and in a liberal religion which, often sorely perplexed, it strove to reconcile with the findings of Darwin. But most of what might be called, in the widest sense, Tennyson's "official" poetry (which must include the greater part of his sentimental narratives and would-be philosophic pieces, as well as his poems written for public occasions) is dead for us to-day. He was not a dynamic, creative thinker, but intellectually feminine by temperament. He gives voice to the leading ideas of the age, but we feel that he has taken them over uncritically, and at second hand. His unfailing art cannot conceal that the note of personal conviction is lacking. Moreover, his genuine poetic intuitions were often of such a nature as to conflict with his official persona. It was only by a long process of adaption that the voluptuous, melancholy Romantic of the 1830 volume of poems succeeded in grooming himself into the eminent Victorian laureate of 1850, who was finally to be raised to the peerage for his poetry. And happily for us, the spirit that inspired the former never wholly deserted him.

Precisely because the appeal of Tennyson's best poetry is so intensely individual, it is probable that no two of his admirers would make exactly the same selection from his work. Moreover, when the worst that can be alleged has been said of his emotional limitations and the frequent banality of his thought, it still remains true that his variousness and the general level of his craftsmanship are astonishing. There are beautiful passages of verse and unexpected departures into fresh poetic fields to be found throughout the whole range of his works — as in "Tithonus", "The Palace of Art", or "The Lotos Eaters" with its lovely Choric Song —

> Music that gentlier on the spirit lies,
> Than tir'd eyelids upon tir'd eyes . . .

One would wish to see cleared of all too frequent misprision, that complex, and even contradictory personality which was the real Tennyson. I have spoken of Tennyson as intellectually feminine; but there was also a vein of roughness, even of peasant coarseness, in his temperament—derived perhaps from his Lincolnshire yeoman forefathers. The Tennysons, he himself is reported to have said, were a blackblooded race, and in his boyhood his Calvinistic aunt could not look at him without being put in mind of the Scriptural text which commands the cursed to depart into everlasting fire. That roughness was overlaid by an intense, even excessive cultivation. Tennyson's father was a clergyman and a scholar, and his mother a woman of delicate refinement. From his first days he learned to know and imitate the Classics and the earlier English poets. He loved gardens, and above all cultivated English parkland, and delighted to luxuriate in sentimental tales of romantic love. Too much of his work is over-sweet, over-ornate, or even silly. But every now and then there breaks through his verse the more realistic note of the "Northern Farmer", and in the background is a melancholy and wild landscape, in which he remembers the Lincolnshire of his youth—the "glooming flats" of "Mariana", the haunted lakeside of the "Morte d'Arthur".

Born in 1809, at Somersby, he was not the only poet in his family, and his first printed verses appeared in a joint volume of schoolboy productions, the *Poems of Two Brothers* (1827), to which his brothers, Charles (who later took the name of Tennyson Turner) and Frederick, alike contributed. Charles (1808–79), who became a gentle and lovable but retiring country priest, confined himself almost entirely to writing sonnets. He is certainly only a minor poet, but within the narrow limits that he set himself he shows a sharpness and delicacy of observation, and a sense of the traditional pietas of rural life, which give one reason to pause and wonder whether he was, in some things at least, not more kindly endowed by the Muses than his more famous brother. Frederick (1807–98), though by no means inconsiderable, is a less readable poet, who found his characteristic expression in long narrative pieces on classical themes. He was a Swedenborgian, a spiritualist, and a friend of the Brownings—evidently a remarkable and original mind. Yet it was Alfred alone, with his ear for the music of words, his almost morbid hypersensitiveness, and above all his unquenchable desire for immortality, whether of fame or of the spirit, who was to win his way through to nation-wide and enduring celebrity. But this was only achieved after a struggle—a struggle which did not leave the poet unscathed. Tennyson was always acutely sensitive to hostile criticism. His poetical career could be uncharitably interpreted as a sequence of strategic tackings and doublings, until he had the wind of public opinion at last full behind his sails. In his later years his life and contacts were carefully stage-managed for him by a devoted and tactful wife, who, among other things, concealed from him all copies of hostile reviews. But in his first days as a poet he could not be so shielded. Both his sensitiveness and his craving for immortality sprang from a single root — his intense desire to be loved. That desire is expressed in an early sonnet which, though it is not among his best poems, is so illuminating from a psychological point of view that it may be quoted here in full:

> But were I loved, as I desire to be,
> What is there in the great sphere of the earth,
> And range of evil between death and birth,
> That I should fear, — if I were loved by thee?
> All the inner, all the outer world of pain
> Clear Love would pierce and cleave, if thou wert mine,
> As I have heard that, somewhere in the main,
> Fresh-water springs come up through bitter brine.
> 'Twere joy, not fear, clasped hand-in-hand with thee,
> To wait for death — mute — careless of all ills,
> Apart upon a mountain, tho' the surge
> Of some new deluge from a thousand hills
> Flung leagues of roaring foam into the gorge
> Below us, as far on as eye could see.

It is not surprising then that Tennyson first attained confidence in himself as a poet in his undergraduate days at Cambridge, when he found himself in an admiring circle of earnest yet brilliant young men, of which his beloved friend, Arthur Hallam, was a luminary. He discarded his boyish discipleship of Byron for that of Shelley and Keats; these were then still the "moderns", fashionable among the young, attacked by critics of the older generation as being formless and incomprehensible. Partly because of this, partly because he had already been over-praised by his own coterie, Tennyson's early volumes of poems, though the first of them (1830) contained some work, such as "Marianna", which he was scarcely to surpass, together with some pieces fatally open to attack, were remorselessly damned by some of the most influential reviewers. Tennyson was deeply wounded. The references to the "barbarous people /Blind to the magic /And deaf to the melody", in the half-autobiographical "Merlin and the Gleam", written almost at the end of his life, shows how long the memory of that rebuff remained with him. He relapsed into silence, publishing nothing from 1843 till 1850; years of obscurity and poverty (the cause of the long delay of his marriage), of melancholy, heavy port-drinking in London, and long nocturnal walks with the young Coventry Patmore. In 1833, also, had come the shock of Hallam's death, from which sprang *In Memoriam*. It was this poem, founded on what was undoubtedly the deepest emotional crisis of his life, which made his reputation. It appeared in 1850, and the same year he was made Poet Laureate. His subsequent career, till his death in 1892 was largely one of continuing success and prosperous security. He was never quite tamed, however. "Maud", for instance — that often lurid and hysterical melodrama — was thought extremely shocking on its first appearance in 1855. But *In Memoriam* expressed, or seemed to express, all the conflict of religious doubt and faith which characterised the age, and to conclude with a triumphal argument for the hope of immortality. Yet it is not this argument (in reality quite shallow, and depending on an already outworn philosophical attitude) by which the poem lives. If we isolate those passages which are most essentially poetical, there emerges, so to speak, a different and more intensely personal poem: a poem of poignant regret and remembered friendship set against the background of the English pastoral scene which Tennyson knew so well. Its climax is not philosophical, but an intuitive, though not clearly realised, moment of illumination, in which the poet's love for his lost friend, his feeling for Nature, and his own personal grief, are somehow blended in an emotion of unity.

To call Tennyson a mystic would be putting a strain upon language. But his poetry is marked, in flashes, by an abnormal, and, in reality, primitive feeling, in which the essential significance of the symbols he is using emerges. Some of the greatest poets, such as Shakespeare, or Tennyson's own master, Virgil, have possessed this faculty almost constantly. In Tennyson himself, perhaps, it is seen only in isolated lines or passages. We feel it, for instance, when, in the elaborately decorative "Palace of Art", we suddenly come on the stanza describing how

> ... mythic Uther's deeply-wounded son
> In some fair space of sloping greens
> Lay, dozing in the vale of Avalon,
> And watch'd by weeping queens.

This Arthur has the reality of the mythological archetype of the Wounded God, with which modern mythologists would connect him. The picture has a reality to which the Arthur of the *Idylls of the King* hardly attains, though it is present in the earliest written of the series, the "Morte d'Arthur" itself. Had Tennyson more consistently followed "the Gleam" he might have been a greater poet, even though it had lead him to the depths, there to discover more fully the obscene Kraken, which haunted the sub-world of the Romantic imagination. In so doing he could not have retained his place in the well-ordered world of mid nineteenth-century respectability. Those poets of the time who ventured farthest, such as De Nerval, Baudelaire or Rimbaud, were self-banished — from the sane light of common day, from the security of bourgeois society, from European civilisation and, finally, from poetry itself.

Tennyson is never in advance of his age. His mind was uncritical (he is almost the only English poet of equal standing who has left no prose writing to illuminate the principles of his art and craft), and he foreshadows no essentially integrated (in the truest sense, religious) attitude as did Hopkins, for example. But to the last he retains his primitive, almost savage, intuition of the mysteriousness of Man's birth and death:

> From the great deep to the great deep he goes.

It is this that underlies the over-refined Alexandrianism of his verse, and it is this, I think, that makes him more essentially a poet than his contemporary Browning. The latter, a townsman and an expatriate, is, for all his antiquarian and classical erudition, fundamentally rootless and cut off from tradition. He is the first and typical "false-modern". The attitudes of these two poets in the face of approaching death, expressed in their final poems, have often been cited as giving a key to their respective characters. Browning in the epilogue to *Asolando*, proposes to "greet the unseen with a cheer" — a thing no person with a really consistent attitude, either Christian, pagan or materialist, would think of doing. Tennyson's "Crossing the Bar", at first sight, seems to express nothing more than the vague hopes of Victorian liberal religion. But underlying it is the primitive, pagan conception of death as a voyage into the unknown waters from which life first emerged. The ancient Vikings, who may well have been among Tennyson's East Coast ancestors, held such a conception. More than a thousand years before Tennyson's time, the old English poet of Beowulf had told of Scyld scefing, the ancestor of the Danes — of his mysterious coming, and his sending forth to sea again in death: they only knew who received him at last who first sent him forth across the waters as a helpless child.

[1948]

II

Ezra Pound:
The Last Humanist

It MAY POSSIBLY be not quite irrelevant to our understanding of Ezra Pound, if we remind ourselves that he is represented — if only by a charming but very light-weight lyric — in the *Oxford Book of Victorian Verse*. Pound, born in 1885, was one of those whose formative years were spent in the period of calm and prosperity which preceded the 1914–18 war — a period in which, however, the portents of the coming storms could not be wholly undiscernible. But, as an American, he was, in some respects, several decades behind his time — as he himself, in *Mauberley*, has ironically suggested. Mr. Eliot has pointed out, in his introduction to Pound's *Selected Poems*, that there is a 'ninety-ish, Celtic twilight, or even pre-Raphaelite background to much of his early poetry. But it is possible also to regard him as the last exponent of a characteristic tendency in certain late or mid-Victorian writers. This tendency we discern in Arnold, Browning, Swinburne and Pater. All of these, in their different ways — the first and the last most specifically — are philosophers of culture. The culture which they uphold is a particular European tradition which can be traced back, through the Renaissance in France and Italy, to the Greeks. This tradition they oppose to the false values of contemporary philistinism, which they hope, by this means, to ameliorate. They love to think themselves back into their chosen periods of the past, and to treat of their own problems — emotional, intellectual, or spiritual — in such terms as, by analogy, they might have confronted real or imaginary characters in these periods. Thus, Arnold expresses his own very personal sense of tragedy in terms of the quasi-Homeric epic of *Sohrab and Rustum*. Browning, confronted by problems raised by the Higher Criticism of the New Testament, expresses himself through the mouth of an imaginary Greek poet of the first century A.D. He makes Fra Lippo Lippi or Andrea del Sarto discourse on the nature of the artist, and the relation of his personal life to his art. Pater presents the Victorian Aesthete's wistful approach to Christianity by writing the imaginary biography of a young man of the time of Marcus Aurelius, while Swinburne places the frustrated passion engendered by his own abnormal temperament into the mouth of Sappho.

All these writers, furthermore, are dominated by a special and marked enthusiasm for particular periods of the flowering of culture, and for particular figures — comparatively few in number. These form, as it were, a series of key-points, round which the whole of their work is deployed, and the standards by which their measurement of cultural values are made. This characteristic is very well-marked in Swinburne, the whole of whose work, extending as it does over a period of several decades, is dominated by a series of unwavering allegiances — to Sappho, Catullus, Villon, the border ballads, the Elizabethan dramatists, Landor and Hugo, in the tradition of literature, and to Mary Queen of Scots and Mazzini among historic figures. Much the same sort of thing, formulated more critically and intellectually, finds expression in Matthew Arnold's doctrine of "touchstones" — single lines of verse held to embody those virtues of style which he most approved, against which, in all too schoolmasterly a fashion, other poetry is measured.

Now, Ezra Pound also has his touchstones. They are certain writers — the "inventors" and the "masters" — who originated or brought to perfection certain technical devices, forms, or qualities of style, and who likewise furnish the standards by which poetry as a whole, particularly contemporary poetry, is to be judged. By reference, paraphrase, imitation, recommendation, or direct translation, these writers dominate alike the critical and the poetic work of Pound. They are in reality comparatively few in number, and the reader who has followed Pound's advice, and has taken the trouble to furnish himself with some knowledge and understanding of them, will soon find that they provide the key to Pound's own work. In the light of such knowledge, the *Cantos*, for instance, will not — as hostile critics seem to imagine — appear as a chaos, demanding from their readers a mass of eccentric and irrelevant erudition, but as a region easily charted by reference to its few major roads. To these "masters" and "inventors" Pound's own critical writings furnish, in many ways, the best means of approach. In particular, in *The ABC of Reading* and in the essay "How to Read" (included in *Polite Essays*) he has furnished his readers with a brief list of those writers a knowledge of whom he deems necessary to the discerning and intellectually mature student of literature, together with the reasons for their inclusion. It is by these writers that Pound's critical and imaginative universe is dominated, though not, it is perhaps necessary to add, bounded.

A consideration of them, their collective characteristics, and their historical relations both to one another and to the cultures which they represent, may give us a clue to Pound's own approach to art and to life, both in its strength and its limitations.

If we consider those writers whose names are most frequently on Pound's lips we find that they typically belong to what Professor Toynbee terms the "growth-stage" of the civilisations which produced them (or which they produced). Thus, Homer and Sappho represent the growth-stage of the Hellenic civilisation, the authors of the songs of the Shih King that of the ancient Chinese civilisation. These poets are preeminently concrete in style, giving us direct narrative or direct lyric. Their language serves to express objects, actions and emotions as immediately as possible, without metaphysical or rhetorical elaboration. Their world is that of man's mundane existence, but seen, as it were, in the clear light of early morning — transfigured only by a kind of primal innocence. The 'Tang poets, such as Li Po (Rihaku to the Japanese) belong to the growth-stage of a second Chinese culture (Toynbee's "Far Eastern" as distinguished from his "Sinic" civilisation). This second civilisation had grown up on the ruins of the old one, its ethos being a Confucian-Buddhist-Taoist synthesis, with "other-worldly" elements. The Mediaeval civilisation of Western Europe, was, historically, in an analagous relationship to the ancient Graeco-Roman civilisation — Christianity taking the place of Buddhism as the non-indigenous "other-worldly" religion which interpenetrated the old classical culture. Its growth-stage is represented in Pound's scheme by the line of Romance lyric poets which begins with the Provencal troubadours, and runs through the early Italians to Dante and Cavalcanti — (of this line Chaucer and Villon are later off-shoots). The Troubadours, and (I suspect) the Chinese 'Tang poets, are much more introspective than Homer and Sappho, or the poets of the Shih King; and Dante and the Italians of the *dolce stile nuovo* are, of course, deeply concerned with metaphysics. But they write while their civilisation is relatively un-subject to those stresses which lead men to ask unanswerable questions, and to be torn apart by indissoluble conflicts of spirit.

Those writers who most elicit Pound's admiration, and who represent later, more disintegrated phases of civilisation ("Civilisation" in Spengler's definition, as opposed to "Culture") form a much less coherent assemblage. Some of them, such as Catullus and the Alexandrian Bion, one might perhaps regard as having preserved, in their times, because of special reasons, a purity of style belonging to an earlier age. Catullus modelled himself closely on Sappho, and Bion, like the other pastoralists, was not un-influenced by the traditional Doric folk-poetry of Sicily. Propertius and Ovid, on the other hand, might be regarded as looking forward, from their historical position in the early Roman Empire, to the Romance poetry of the Middle Ages. Pound lays great stress on Propertius's line: "Ingenium nobis ipsa puella facit", which contains, in germ, the troubadour ethos of Courtly Love; and Ovid was, to the Middle Ages, the great "doctor" of love, as well as a romantic story-teller. It is the Mediaeval Ovid which finds expression in Golding's translation, another of Pound's touchstones.

In general, when dealing with these writers of a disintegrated culture, Pound's preference is for those who face up to the complexities of their situation with the intellectual weapon of irony, rather than by withdrawing themselves behind a screen of rhetoric, and by making their language hieratically remote from common speech. This quality of verbal irony — a form of "logopeia" — Pound detects in Propertius; it is found also in the seventeenth-century Metaphysicals, and in Laforgue and Corbière, and others of the French Symbolists. These — Metaphysicals and Symbolists — largely through their influence on Pound's pupil, T.S. Eliot, have become the progenitors of much modern English poetry. For in the twentieth century, the intellectual countering of a disintegration has become one of the main tasks forced upon the poet.

Lastly, we must consider three nineteenth-century English poets whom Pound has praised, and from whom many elements in his own style obviously derive. These are Swinburne, Browning, and Landor. Pound's praise, at any rate of the first two of these, has had its reservations. It could hardly be otherwise, for their faults are obvious, and of a kind particularly irritating to the twentieth-century reader. Their superiority to their contemporaries is not so obvious; in the opinion of the present writer, Browning may with justice be set beside, but not above, Tennyson; Swinburne by Rossetti; and Landor by Wordsworth. It is therefore instructive to enquire for what particular virtues Pound has picked them out of the general nineteenth-century Romantic rag-bag.

At their best, all three of them exhibit a certain cleanness of line, and a sharpness of physical impact — visual in the case of Landor and Browning, aural in that of Swinburne. They are, all three, extroverted writers, and are oriented towards the southern, Mediterranean culture which Pound himself admires. All three were no mean classical scholars. But they showed, in addition, an active political sympathy with the cause of Italian unity and freedom as it then presented itself. Fundamentally, I think, they belonged to a liberal tradition which was older than the nineteenth century. This was not so much Romantic Liberalism, with its belief in progress (represented by Tennyson — in his more liberal moods), but a classical, humanistic, aristocratic Republicanism. This aristocratic Republicanism was the creed of the Girondins in the French Revolution, and of the poet André Chénier, who met his death on the guillotine.

In the eighteenth century, it saw the world, not in terms of modern political necessity, but of Plutarch's idealised Greek and Roman heroes. It could not foresee the mob-violence of the Terror, still less the rise of Napoleon. Much of its idealism went into the framing of the American Constitution. This idealism was to be falsified by the development of Northern Big Business after the Civil War. This aristocratic Liberalism, limited by its too purely humanistic conception of Man, always makes insufficient allowance for the daemonic, destructive forces which human history may release. Of this tradition Pound is, perhaps, the last and most tragic representative.

Pound, an American, and therefore native to the periphery of Western Civilisation, has striven to affiliate himself to the "Mediterranean sanity". And beyond this, in his world-picture, is the profounder, though less passionate, Chinese sanity. Both these cultural traditions are founded, in their different ways, on a doctrine of the Mean, and are concerned, mainly, with the outward appearances of things. But the philosopher of culture, in the twentieth century — it is Pound himself, among others, who has taught us this — must be a philosopher of world culture. In spite of the diversity of Pound's interests, one cannot help noting his lack of response, in any of his published writings, to either the Indian or the Hebraic traditions. (The Indian tradition includes, of course, the Buddhist element in Far Eastern civilisation, just as the Christian element in Western and Eastern European civilisation is, at bottom a product of Hebraism. Islam may be regarded, for our purposes, either as an extreme, anti-Hellenic Christian heresy, or as a militant, de-nationalised Judaism.) Pound has spoken of "the Indian disease, asceticism, and the Hebrew disease, fanaticism". But if these are diseases, they are the diseases of civilisations for whom Man is not the measure of all things, because they possess the consciousness of realities which transcend the human. The Indian tradition, profoundly unhistorical, emphasises the immanence of the Absolute in all things. In the Hebraic tradition, the idea of Divine transcendence is related to an eschatological view of history.

In the second place, one notes Pound's lack of interest in the Drama, and, in particular, in Tragedy. Pound's early volume of essays *The Spirit of Romance* (1910), in which we may see many of his leading ideas in a still formative stage, includes, besides essays on the Troubadours, Dante, Villon, etc., a treatment of Lope de Vega's plays. Here we have a drama, mainly comic, with a maximum of rapid action, and a minimum of psychological interest. The same volume also includes an essay on Camoens — the most Homeric of the Renaissance writers of literary Epic. In *The ABC of Reading* he justifies the omission of the Attic dramatists from the list of books recommended to his ideal student on the grounds that "the words are only a part of the medium and the gaps between them, or deficiencies in their meaning, can be made up by 'action' " [though, at the very end of his life, Pound did in fact translate the *Trachiniae* of Sophocles]. But this argument, though convincing, can hardly be the whole of the truth. Elsewhere, Shakespeare's Histories are recommended, but on the grounds that they constitute "the true English epos". This is clearly an attempt to see Shakespeare in terms of Homer, from whom the Attic dramatists are also said to "decline". Now, the tragic consciousness, whether it finds expression in Drama or not, is the product of certain tensions which arise at a later, more complex, stage of civilisation, than that which finds its natural expression in heroic Epic. Man is called upon to face the destructive forces he finds within his own nature, and to ask what is his ultimate place in the Universe. Tragedy includes the problem of freedom, which may be freedom to self-destruction.

Aeschylus, Sophocles, and Euripides are each, after his own fashion, concerned with the problem of justifying God's ways to Man. And there is a line which leads from Sophocles to Virgil, and thence to Milton — where the tragedy of Good and Evil is played out on its ultimate, cosmic stage. Virgil is a tragic, as well as an epic poet; Aeneas, it has been wisely said, is not so much a feeble imitation of Achilles and Odysseus, as a forerunner of Hamlet. He is torn between his Roman destiny and Dido's passion; initiated by the Sybil, he has seen both Tartarus and Elysium.

Hence it is that the rhetoric of Virgil and Milton is not merely a formal evasion of the exigencies of plain narrative and common speech. Its inversions and sonorities are full of overtones, suggesting a complexity of human experience, and a sense of depth, which could not be otherwise realised.

It is this sense of depth, I think, which is ultimately wanting, both in Pound's critical writings and his poetry. It is to be found in his friend and pupil, T.S. Eliot, the range of whose mind and technical accomplishment are, perhaps, much narrower. The figures of Virgil and Aeschylus form part of the background of Mr. Eliot's imaginative world, and he has embraced, moreover, the tragic and meta-humanistic experience of Christianity. It is not my purpose here to suggest a comparison, either of the work or the personalities of these two men. Those of us who have come after them must be profoundly grateful to both for what they have taught us. Pound, on the one hand, has recalled us to a sanity and a humanism which are central to civilisation. Because of Eliot's words, on the other hand, we may be better skilled to face those tragic realities before which that sanity and humanism, and civilisation itself, may be found wanting.

[1950]

Structure and Source in Eliot's Major Poetry

FOR THE PURPOSES of this study, I would define as Eliot's major poetry the sequence of longer poems which begins with *The Waste Land* and concludes with *Four Quartets*. These, I suggest, have a common structure which is largely idiosyncratic. They are all more or less cyclical, and are developed in a way which clearly owes much to musical form (as is, of course, explicitly the case with *Four Quartets*). My purpose is to show how this method of composition evolved, to suggest some precedents in earlier poetry, and at the same time to point to one or two possible sources of the imagery of the poetry, some of which may not hitherto have been recognised. Furthermore, I suggest that this major poetry has itself an overall unity of structure, so that as a corpus it might legitimately be considered as one long major poem, which develops according to a plan which clearly owes much to Dante's *Divine Comedy*. I do not, of course, suggest that this plan was deliberately envisaged by Eliot, but that it developed spontaneously out of his poetic thinking and method of composition.

That Eliot is a major poet I think there need be no doubt. And I suggest, a major poet in terms of our Western tradition is basically a poet capable of creating major structures. It is rather notorious that in an early essay Eliot described himself as "a minor poet". This, I think, was not just false modesty. His original intention, I suggest, had simply been to do in English something like what Laforgue had done in French — to write poetry which was to a large extent a marginal comment on reality, ironic and allusive. But from *The Waste Land* onward he was seized by a daemon which had quite different plans for him, and which destined him willy-nilly, for major status.

I have said nothing about Eliot's plays. These form a major sequence which runs parallel with and is intimately connected with his major non-dramatic poetry. But the structural determinant in the case of the plays is different. It is indicated in the early "Essay on Dramatic Poetry" in which he speaks of the advantage which both the Greeks and the classical French dramatists had in being able to restate again and again generally-known mythical themes, and he also points to the ritual of the Mass as providing an ideal model for poetic drama. It is clear that from *The Family Reunion* to *The Elder Statesman* the first of these principles operates. But the plays progressively disentangle themselves from the myth, so that while *The Family Reunion* might be regarded as a restatement, partly in Christian, partly in post-Freudian terms of the *Oresteia*, the comparatively slight drama of *The Elder Statesman* is only remotely related to the *Oedipus at Colonus*. In the case of *Murder in the Cathedral*, it is the model of the Mass which principally determines the structure, with the sermon in the middle and the murder of Becket corresponding to the consecration, and the address of the four knights to the audience ironically corresponding to the communion of the people. The final chorus could be considered as a *Gloria*, which, of course, is said or sung after the Communion in the 1662 Book of Common Prayer Eucharist.

It is customary to consider "The Love Song of Alfred J. Prufrock", published in 1915, as the starting-point of Eliot's mature poetry. I would see it rather as belonging to the earlier category of Laforgueian poetry, though it has features which point forward, particularly to *The Waste Land*. One of these is a possible use of Arthurian source material, which has not, so far as I am aware, been noticed. The line

> Though I have seen my head (grown slightly bald)
> brought in upon a platter,

may not simply be an allusion to the execution of John the Baptist. Eliot had attended classes on the Arthurian legend at Harvard, and it is not impossible that he had read the Welsh *Peredur* (readily available in Lady Charlotte Guest's translation of the *Mabinogion* in Everyman's Library). This tale is a version of the Percival legend, in which the hero, like Prufrock, fails in his quest because he has failed to ask an important question. But in *Peredur*, for the Grail theme has been substituted a perhaps more primitive revenge motif. Peredur, like Percival, witnesses a mysterious procession in which both a bleeding spear and a blood-filled vessel are carried, but in the latter is a severed head — that, as he later finds out, is of a slain kinsman of his own. This revenge motif links Peredur with Prince Hamlet, to whom, of course, Prufrock also alludes.

The metre of *Prufrock* is peculiar. It is not simply free verse, but in its lines of irregular length, many, but not all of which rhyme, suggests a free version of the Dantesque Canzone. This, together with its epigraph, points to Eliot's growing preoccupation with Dante, which, as I have already suggested, was to bear fruit in the overall structure of the later major poems.

What is peculiar about the structure of *The Waste Land*, and one of the things which doubtless most baffled its first readers, is the absence of any narrative links. This was accentuated by Ezra Pound's excision of many passages from the original version. On the whole, critics have regarded these excisions of Pound's as judicious, and certainly the omitted passages are poetically inferior. But the effect was to make *The Waste Land*, when it finally appeared in 1922, perhaps too much like an imagist poem. For despite his debt to Pound, Eliot was never really an Imagist, nor did he ever appear in any of the Imagist anthologies. The critical theories of Benedetto Croce, who defined poetry as pure expression, and who held that Dante's *Divine Comedy* was merely a collection of short poems with irrelevant narrative links, were also operative. For my part, however, I regret particularly the elimination of the passage describing Phlebas's voyage from the Mediterranean to Britain. This powerful passage was in need of revision, doubtless, but its total exclusion from the plan of the poem makes the following short poem, which is in fact Phlebas's epitaph, obscure. Phlebas's voyage is, in the Mediterranean world of his time, as venturesome and as much a voyage into the unknown as the early voyages to America, without which the Eliot family could not have emigrated to the New World. It is a voyage to an unknown and savage land, like the Romans' voyage to Britain suggested by Conrad in *Heart of Darkness*, a story to be quoted later on in the epigraph to *The Hollow Men*. Jessie Weston, whose *Ritual to Romance* furnished part of the scheme for *The Waste Land*, suggested that the parallels between the Celtic legends of the Holy Grail and the Mediterranean rituals centred on the cult of the Dying God, might be due to the latter having been brought to Britain by Phoenician and other Mediterranean merchants. This is in fact an unnecessary hypothesis. There is no real evidence that the Phoenicians ever made landfall in Britain, and the parallels which Jessie Weston detected can best be explained in terms of a common heritage from the culture of the Bronze Age or earlier. Nevertheless, this does make the voyage of Phlebas of crucial importance in understanding the poem.

The Waste Land is preceded by an epigraph from the *Satyricon* of Petronius. The passage in question is taken from that part of the latter work commonly known as "The Banquet of Trimalchio". This describes a banquet of immense opulence and vulgarity given by Trimalchio, a rich freedman. Most of his guests belong to the same *nouveau riche* class and retain the superstitious beliefs of their slave origin. It is one of these who describes the Sibyl hanging in her basket and wishing to die. The *Satyricon*, of which we possess only fragments of a work of considerable length, is in effect something like a picaresque novel, set in the Greek-speaking cities of southern Italy at the time of Nero, and giving a scarifying picture of society obsessed with sex and terrified by the fear of impotence. That Eliot sees analogies between this society and that of post-war Europe is clear. But formally the *Satyricon* belongs to the Latin genre of the Varronian satire. Features of the Varronian satire were the alternation of prose and verse passages, and the use of literary quotation and allusion, quotations from Greek writers in the original language being frequently incorporated. It has been suggested that the *Satyricon*, like Joyce's *Ulysses*, parallels the plot of Homer's *Odyssey*. The wanderings and misfortunes *of* Odysseus in the latter work are due to his having incurred the wrath of Poseidon (by blinding his son Polyphemus). Encolpius, the first person narrator of the *Satyricon*, seems similarly to be afflicted by the curse of impotence through having incurred the wrath of Priapus.

If, then, *The Waste Land is* to be put into any category, it is clearly to be classed as Varronian satire. Edmund Wilson came near the mark, but just missed it, when he suggested that *The Waste Land* could be considered as Juvenalian satire. *The Waste Land* does not alternate prose and verse, as does Varronian satire, but it does alternate free blank verse and regular rhymed verse in much the same way, and its use of literary allusion, quotation and parody are clearly in the spirit of Petronius. The absence of narrative links can best be explained by supposing that the accidentally fragmented nature of Petronius's work furnished a model.

There are, however, two works of nineteenth-century English poetry which likewise dispense with narrative links. They are also related to *The Waste Land* in theme. The first of these, as Anne Ridler has pointed out, is James Thomson's *The City of Dreadful Night*. This remarkable poem, the product of a man who suffered from severe depressive illness and alcoholism, is a vision of a city which is at one and the same time a contemporary industrial city, with its gaslit street lamps, and an image of a spiritual state of despair and dereliction (Thomson, a friend of Charles Bradlaugh, was a committed unbeliever). The epigraph to Thomson's poem is from Dante's *Inferno* describing the City of Dis. This is the city in which the heretics are punished, in their burning tombs. Thomson's poem consists of a number of sections, the overall description of the city being given in a series of eight-line rhymed stanzas which alternate with episodes in other metres in which various of its inhabitants are described, or their conversations overheard. All of them are victims of the poet's own melancholy despair, and the final passage of the poem describes the great brooding figure of Melancholia, based on Dürer's engraving.

Though the poem is unequal, its overall effect is extremely powerful. Two lines —

> The extreme nudity of flesh is shameless:
>
> The unsexed skeleton mocks shroud and pall

come nearer to Baudelaire and to Eliot than anything else in Victorian poetry. That Eliot had read this poem I know is certain. Struck by the resemblance of *The City of Dreadful Night* to *The Waste Land*, I once asked him if he had read Thomson's poem. His reply was characteristically Eliotic and ambiguous. He said, "It was my favourite poem when I was sixteen." I had no idea whether this implied that he regarded the poem as an immature taste, or that it had deeply influenced him.

The second nineteenth-century precedent for *The Waste Land* is, I believe, Tennyson's *Maud*. This poem, which Tennyson called a "Lyrical monodrama", is not one of his most successful, but one on which he set great store. This is understandable, for it represents a courageous attempt to come to terms with the realities of contemporary industrial England and also to break with conventional form. It was written shortly after Tennyson's marriage (which had been delayed owing to Tennyson's having lost most of his private fortune in injudicious speculation). As is sometimes the case when a bachelor marries comparatively late, the marriage, though happy, seems to have entailed a certain nervous shock to Tennyson. For a time he had eye trouble and was advised by his doctors not to read. Edward Fitzgerald, who was visiting him at this time, attempted to divert him by playing him Mozart (not then an altogether fashionable composer) on the piano, and reading from the Persian poems of Hafiz. Tennyson had studied classical Persian with the same teacher as Fitzgerald, Cowell. *Maud* — especially its best known lyric "Come into the garden, Maud" — is full of echoes of Hafiz's imagery. More importantly, the Persian manner of structuring a poem by means of a series of intuitive image-links, rather than logically and lineally, may have influenced the form of Tennyson's poem. *Maud* consists of a series of dramatic lyrics spoken in the first person by the unnamed hero, which are in a wide variety of rhymed metres. The plot, as it emerges, is one of nervous breakdown. And in his madness, the hero sees his own anguish as mirrored in the general condition of England, with its inequalities of wealth and the misery of the post-industrial slums. The final solution comes when England enters the Crimean War, thus finding a purpose for itself. The poem ends when the hero finds himself on board a troopship to set sail for Russia:

Let it go or stay, so I wake to the higher aims
Of a land that has lost for a little her lust of gold,
And love of a peace that was full of wrongs and shames,
Horrible, hateful, monstrous, not to be told;
. . . .

For the peace, that I deem'd no peace, is over and done,
And now by the side of the Black and the Baltic deep,
And deathful-grinning mouths of the fortress, flames
The blood-red blossom of war with a heart of fire.

This conclusion is, to our twentieth-century way of thinking, fairly ap-palling. But the rose-fire image is striking. It is the climax of a series of antithetical images of rose and lily that runs through the poem, signifying passion and purity respectively, and it might be considered as foreshad-owing "the rose and the fire are one" of "Little Gidding". Tennyson's rose of war is in its own way purgatorial. *Maud* anticipates *The Waste Land* in more than one respect. I have already indicated its relative freedom of form and its dispensing with narrative links. But it also resembles Eliot's poem in the way that a theme of personal crisis (in this case the hero's frustrated love for Maud) is linked with a wider social crisis.

I have already noted that the structure of Eliot's major poems is musi-cal. This is part of the heritage of Symbolism. Verlaine and Mallarmé in different ways had striven to recapture for poetry what had been lost to music, and were particularly impressed with the music of Wagner. There can never be a complete analogy between the procedures of poetry and those of music. The latter art can recapitulate whole passages without their seeming tedious, because their key-signature has been altered. It can also represent simultaneity by the harmonic and contrapuntal interweav-ing of differing voices. Poetry, on the other hand, is confined to a single voice, and there is nothing analogous in the speaking voice to a change of key. It can only suggest, not imitate, actual musical effects. One such suggested effect is brought about by Eliot by the repetition of key phrases and quotations, rather in the manner of the Wagnerian *leitmotif*. And Eliot, I have been informed, never laid claim to any profound knowledge of music, and too much stress must not be laid on his use of musical form, either in *The Waste Land* or in *Four Quartets*. Wagnerian echoes — from *Tristan*, from *The Ring*, and by way of a quotation from Verlaine, from *Parsifal*, are notable throughout *The Waste Land*, but they refer as much to the texts of these operas as to their musical nature. Wagner's *Ring* cycle can be interpreted as an allegory of the development and fate of capitalist society, in a way closely analogous to Marxist thinking. Such an inter-pretation had been given by Bernard Shaw in his *The Perfect Wagnerite*, and might well have interested Eliot, then a bank employee. The gold is stolen from the Rhinemaidens by Alberich and the dwarfs (whom the notoriously anti-Semitic Wagner saw as the Jews). The gods (the old ruling class) appropriate the gold in order to pay the giants (the new industrial class) for their construction of Valhalla. The giant Fafnir kills his brother Fasolt and becomes a gold-hoarding dragon (monopoly capitalism). The gold is finally released by Siegfried (the new young revolutionary generation of the 1840s) who reawakens the Sleeping Beauty, Brunnhilde (Germania). In accordance with Wagner's Schopenhauerian pessimism, the whole cycle breaks down in *Götterdämmerung*, and the gold returns to its original owners, the Rhinemaidens. Shaw saw the drama's climax as really completed with Siegfried's awakening of Brunnhilde, and *Götterdämmerung* as merely the unnecessary survival of Wagner's earlier scheme to compose a tragedy on the theme of Siegfried's death. In Eliot's *The Waste Land* the rape of the gold from the Rhinemaidens is connected with the general theme of rape and seduction that runs through the poem. In particular, I think, he saw an analogy between this rape and an episode which appears in a medieval French prose romance, *The High History of the Holy Grail*. In this work, we are told how the wasteland was brought about through a certain knight attempting to rape and to steal her golden cup from a maiden who appeared at a well to offer water to thirsty travellers. *The High History of the Holy Grail* was translated into English by the Victorian poet and antiquary Sebastian Evans, and like Lady Guest's *Mabinogion*, was readily available in Everyman's Library. In his introduction to the work, Evans put forward the theory that it was written in England and had a political purpose. In fact, that the wasteland represented England under the interdict imposed by Pope Innocent III in the reign of King John. This theory is not, I think, historically tenable. But it may well have suggested to Eliot a way in which the Arthurian material could be used to comment on a contemporary breakdown in English society. The Arthurian myth was certainly important to Eliot. In a conversation I had with him towards the end of the Second World War, we discussed the way in which the Germanic mythology treated by Wagner had been misappropriated and distorted for their own purposes by the Nazis, and he gave it as his opinion that it was fortunate that "our own mythology" (by which he clearly meant Arthurian material) had not been misused in this way.

If we regard the sequence of Eliot's major poems as following a Dantesque pattern, then *The Waste Land* will correspond to *The Inferno*. The Christian solution appears in it, it seems to me, more as an unrealised possibility than a complete statement. But if *The Waste Land* is an inferno, it corresponds mainly to that section of Dante's poem before Dante and Virgil enter the inferno proper, where the uncommitted are punished, following a phantom banner and continually tormented by gnats and flies. Eliot seems to suggest that twentieth-century man is in the main incapable of enough existential commitment to evil to merit full damnation. *The Hollow Men* and "Gerontion" are two poems closely linked to *The Waste Land* and may be considered as appendages to it. In the former poem, Eliot's vision of mankind as simply a collection of old Guys in a cactus desert reaches its most negative point. "Geron-tion", on the other hand, looks forward to the "Ariel" poems and to *Ash Wednesday* — Eliot's purgatorial poetry, linked to his conversion.

The title of "Gerontion" is simply the diminutive of the Greek *geron*, an old man. But surely the connection with the name of the protagonist of Newman's dramatic poem, *The Dream of Gerontius*, is not accidental. The link between the two poems becomes plain, I think, if we frame such a phrase as "a dying man's vision of death and judgement" which would apply equally to both. The Christian imagery in *The Waste Land* is Paschal. There are references to the betrayal and trial of Christ, and to the resurrection appearance on the walk to Emmaus. "Gerontion", on the other hand should, in my opinion, be considered mainly as a Christmas poem. This is clear, of course, from the echoes contained in it of a Christmas sermon by Lancelot Andrewes, with his meditation on the "verbum infans" — "the word within a word, unable to speak a word". The rather puzzling phrase at the beginning of the poem, "The goat coughs at night in the field overhead", should, I think, be interpreted astrologically. It is surely a reference to the sign of Capricorn. The sun enters Capricorn at the winter solstice, so that Christmas Day falls within this sign. When we consider that "The Journey of the Magi" belongs to the feast of the Epiphany, and that Simeon's prophecy was made at the presentation of Christ in the Temple and "A Song for Simeon" is therefore associated with the feast of the Purification (February 2nd), we see that we have a series of poems associated with the ecclesiastical calendar, whose cycle ends with *Ash Wednesday*, a poem for the beginning of Lent. In all these poems the characteristically Eliotic theme that birth and death are the same is prominent. Phlebas's death by water in *The Waste Land*, prefigures — but I think only prefigures in the natural cycle — the rebirth through baptism. The theme becomes explicit in "The Journey of the Magi":

> I had seen birth and death,
> But had thought they were different; this Birth was
> Hard and bitter agony for us, like Death, our death.

This is finally to be transformed into the "in my beginning is my end" in "East Coker".

In *Ash Wednesday* itself the desert imagery of *The Waste Land* is still present but it has been transformed. Images of fecundity are also present and the dark lurid colours of London fog give place to clear blues, greens and white. The "Lady of the Rocks, / the lady of situations" becomes the veiled lady who honours the Virgin in contemplation. The main source of this imagery is of course the closing cantos of Dante's *Purgatorio*, where Dante enters the Earthly Paradise to encounter first Matilda gathering flowers and then Beatrice herself. But Eliot is after all a symbolist, not, like Dante, an allegorist. In Dante we feel that however complex the fourfold allegory may be, it is always capable of intellectual explication, however much it may bear with it the resonance of archetypal imagery. With Eliot this is not so. The Lady suggests the Church, the Virgin or a redeemed nature-spirit, but all these meanings flow into each other. The two white leopards are terrifying and destructive powers of grace, related to the "Christ the tiger" phrase of "Gerontion" and also to the image of the Furies as bright angels in *The Family Reunion*, but not capable of precise explanation. Besides the references to Cavalcanti, to St John of the Cross and to the liturgy, there are other possible sources for the imagery of *Ash Wednesday*. The bones lying under the juniper tree suggest Gretchen's song from her prison in the last scene of Goethe's *Faust*, Part I:

> My mother, my mother!
> The wanton woman — My mother hath slain me
> My father, inhuman, for supper hath ta'en me —
> My little sister hath, one by one,
> Laid together each small white bone,
> 'Mong almond blossoms to sleep in the cool; . . .

> (Anster's translation)

Gretchen's song is taken from a folktale, of which one variant given by Grimm is called the Juniper Tree, the bones of the murdered child being buried under a juniper bush (there are also two English versions entitled *The Rose Tree* and *Orange and Lemon* — see Jacob's *English Fairy Tales)*. Goethe does not in fact mention the juniper tree and the almond blossoms appear to be Anster's own importation. The roots of this story seem to lie in primitive child sacrifice, and give a further resonance to Eliot's poem. George Macdonald's allegorical romance *Lilith* has some images which remarkably suggest *Ash Wednesday*. The hero of this story enters an alternative world which is dominated by the evil, but ultimately redeemable, Lilith. Because there is a prophecy that she will be overthrown by her own daughter, she has stopped the flowing of the springs, thus creating a "wasteland situation". She also sends a white leopard to destroy any newly-born children. The hero encounters a mysterious veiled lady who is likewise accompanied by a white leopard. This lady turns out in fact to be de Quincey's "Our Lady of Sorrows". Whether Eliot had in fact read Macdonald's story I do not know, but it seems not altogether improbable. Another image which occurs in Macdonald's children's story, *The Princess and Curdie*, is of a fire made up of roses. This fire is purgatorial and initiatory in character. Curdie, the hero, is made by the princess's great-grand-mother (a kind of mother-goddess figure) to plunge his hands into this fire. The experience is agonising, but from now on his hands are sensitised, so that when he grasps the hand of any evil person he feels not a human hand but the paw of whatever beast typifies that person's evil qualities. This may possibly have suggested the fire "whose flames are roses and whose smoke is briars" of "Little Gidding". Another possible influence on the imagery of *Ash Wednesday* is H.G. Wells's story "The Door in the Wall". In this the protagonist as a boy finds himself in a secret garden where there is a goddesslike figure accompanied by panthers and other wild beasts. On two occasions in his adult life he sees the door which led into that garden but worldly considerations prevent his entering it. He finally re-enters the secret garden only in death — but the ending of the story is ambiguous. If this story is an influence, it relates *Ash Wednesday* to the "secret garden" image which becomes important in "Burnt Norton", and which is expounded in *The Confidential Clerk*. Eliot may very possibly have read as a boy Frances Hodgson Burnett's story *The Secret Garden* (Mrs. Hodgson Burnett settled in America and her work was well known there at the end of the last century). The secret garden of this story had been left locked because its owner's wife met her death after falling from a tree in it and prematurely giving birth to a sickly child. The discovery of the garden by the little girl who is the principal character of the story, and its recreation, symbolise her own redemption from being a spoilt, unpleasant child into a normal, healthy one, and also the husband's own reconciliation to his past. It seems to me that these themes bear some relation to Eliot's own biography — the failure of his marriage and the breakdown of his first wife.

The *Four Quartets* have had a vast mass of commentary written upon them, to which I have little to add. They represent the culmination of Eliot's cyclical and musical method, but attempts to correlate them closely with Bartok's Quartets (which Eliot heard during the war at a National Gallery concert) or with Beethoven's last quartets, do not seem to me to constitute a very fruitful approach. It is worth noting, however, that all four of these poems are poems of place, and we should perhaps relate them to the seventeenth- and eighteenth-century tradition of the English place-poem. This tradition has little precedent in classical antiquity, though the germ of it may be sought in the "Moselle" of the late Latin poet Ausonius. The beginning of the tradition in English starts with Ben Jonson's *Penshurst*, a poem in praise of a great country house. This provided the model for Andrew Marvell's *Upon Appleton House* — a poem which certainly influenced Eliot in "Burnt Norton", providing in particular the image of the kingfisher's wing. Burnt Norton itself is a deserted country house in Gloucestershire to which Eliot made a visit with a lady companion, as I have been informed. Helen Gardner assures us that he was not aware of the story that this house had been burnt down by its eighteenth-century owner in a drunken frenzy. We must therefore discount the close coincidence between this story and the disaster which overtook the ruined house in W.B. Yeats's verse drama *Purgatory*. Nevertheless, Eliot much admired this play and it certainly provides much of the imagery, not only for "East Coker", but also for "Little Gidding", where in the scheme of the four elements which dominates these poems, fire is now in the ascendant. This fire is the purgatorial fire which first appears in the fire-sermon section of *The Waste Land* and which runs through all Eliot's poetry. So, likewise, does the complementary image of water. The lack of this element is the basis of *The Waste Land*, and, in the form of the image of a sea voyage, is for Eliot always associated with transition from an old life to a new one. This is most notably the case in "Marina" where the voyagings of Shakespeare's Pericles come together with Eliot's own yachting experiences off the coast of Maine as a boy. "Marina" is the poem most intimately connected with Eliot's conversion. Pericles' rediscovery of his lost daughter is the rediscovery in conversion of a lost self, which bears with it also the terrible burden of guilt which is incumbent on Hercules' recovery of his sanity in Seneca's play *Hercules Furens* (which provides the epigraph for the poem) only to find he has destroyed his own children.

In *Four Quartets* the water imagery dominates "The Dry Salvages". The germ of this poem might be sought in another work which has a key position in the development of the English place-poem. This is Sir John Denham's "Cooper's Hill". Eliot mentions Denham as a poet worthy of reconsideration in an early critical essay. In "Cooper's Hill" the place-poem moves away from the country house to a view of landscape. Cooper's Hill itself is in the neighbourhood of Windsor, and Denham's meditations involve a sight of the Thames

> Hasting to pay his tribute to the sea
> Like mortal life to meet eternity.

Denham's "Cooper's Hill" established the place-poem as a dominant Augustan genre. Notable examples are John Dyer's "Grongar Hill" and Pope's "Windsor Forest". The last great poem written in the eighteenth century is also an example of this type. I refer to Wordsworth's "Tintern Abbey", which first appeared in *Lyrical Ballads* of 1798. Here the eighteenth-century moralisings upon landscape are transformed into a profound meditation upon time, place. Although Eliot, one assumes, respected Wordsworth, he does not seem to have been deeply influenced by him. Nevertheless, the four poems of *Four Quartets* develop the poem of place exactly from the point to which Wordsworth had brought it.

Four Quartets continue to develop the Dantesque structure of Eliot's major poetry to where a paradisal vision might seem a possibility. But it is a possibility only, culminating in the "rose and the fire are one" of "Little Gidding". It is as if Eliot implied that man is not yet ready for paradise but must remain within a purgatorial ambience. In this respect, just as each of the several poems has a cyclical progression, "Little Gidding" might be said to close the whole great cycle which begins with *The Waste Land*, itself a poem of implied rather than realised possibilities, both of damnation and redemption.

[1985]

Daughters of Memory:
The Anathemata of David Jones

THE ANATHEMATA, like its predecessor, *In Parenthesis*, exists, like the *Cantos*, and like *Finnegans Wake*, in that region where the conventional (and convenient) distinction between verse and prose ceases to be meaningful; and like them, it is certainly epic in its scope. Whether it will prove to have the enduring importance of the work of Joyce and Pound is another matter. But it is certainly one of the most significant (and exciting) books to be published within the year. For here, at least and at last (in a poetic landscape dominated by the ghosts-between-two making their Italian visits) is a volume of major pretensions, which offers something to the enrichment of the language, and through this, to the enlargement of our sense of our common heritage.

But this claim, I think, requires a certain qualification. Mr. Jones is not (in Pound's phrase) among the "inventors". As soon as one opens *The Anathemata*, one is conscious of the debt, amounting to direct imitation, to Pound's own *Cantos*. The verse form used, the employment of key words in the original foreign tongues (Latin, Greek, Welsh), even the typographical devices, are the same. The principal difference is that, where his tension slackens, Mr. Jones is content to modulate into the rhythms of prose — and this prose is the incantatory prose of *Finnegans Wake* (Joyce so to speak, with a Welsh accent). And, on a closer inspection, we detect the ubiquitous presence of the Joycean pun. (Not very happily, I think — for the Welsh share the eloquence of the Irish, but not their wit.) Joyce and Pound, in fact, evolved something that would serve as an epic style for the modern poet — imprisoned, as he necessarily is, in the subjective world of his own dreams and personal memories. They evolved it by facing, remorselessly, the lack of significance to which this subjectivity reduces all human experience in history. Neither Pound nor Joyce has any supernatural faith. Hence, their universe is, in each case, one of pure flux. For Joyce, history is cyclical in time — as it was for the Greeks and the Indians. It is possible, that without the idea of revelation, and, finally, of incarnation, history must always be seen as cyclical — the Eternal Recurrence of Nietzsche, and what Jacob Boëhme called "wicked endlessness". For Pound, indeed, some measure of positive significance is given to human action, by the pattern imposed by sane, as opposed to insane, economics. But his poetic world is essentially one in which each particular image is autonomous, as in Joyce, in the end, each particular word becomes autonomous. This autonomy of the word, or the image (ideogram) is analogous to the autonomy of the twelve tones in the music of Schoenberg and his school, and arises, one cannot help suspecting, from the same cultural impasse.

But is it not possible that we have passed the crisis? Schoenberg's followers, and the Master himself in his later works, have, we are told, begun to find a way out of the vacuum produced by their own abandonment of the concept of key. Without their departing from the rules of the game as laid down in the formulation of the twelve-tone system, the old concords, and even the old conception of melody, have begun to reintroduce themselves. And so it may prove to be also in the sphere of post-Joycean, and post-Poundian literature.

For Mr. Jones has taken over intact the Epic style which Joyce and Pound forged out of their (and our) despair. His poetry, simply *qua* poetry, lacks the intense visual or aural, impact of theirs. But there is in it a positive, integrating factor, which gives it a further significance — a significance, which may transcend purely literary criteria. So that the pure literary critic must, perhaps, suspend judgment.

This positive, integrating factor is (as also in *Four Quartets*) the writer's personal faith. But this personal faith is one that Mr. Jones (like Mr. Eliot) is able to identify as the Catholic faith of the Church, and hence as having a validity which goes beyond a mere subjective vision, and which is, by its nature, bound up with the pattern of history. This pattern is no longer cyclical, or a fugue of autonomous images. Rather, it is an ordered progression of all the images, in and out of Time, from Creation, through Redemption, to Re-creation.

I would not, however, compare *The Anathemata* with *Four Quartets*, which are essentially lyrical meditations, but rather — in spite of the great differences of form and style — with the epic lyrics of Charles Williams. (The fact that both writers are partly concerned with the same mythical material — the "matter of Britain" — furnishes an incidental, though not I think, a coincidental, resemblance.) The Taliessin poems of Charles Williams are also works upon which pure literary criticism should hesitate to pronounce judgment. Mr. Jones himself, in an article published a few years ago in *The Tablet*, has given us far and away the most perceptive and the most balanced estimate of Charles Williams' poetry. He put his finger on what is, undoubtedly, the main weakness of Williams' work considered purely as poetry: his failure to present the visually concrete and particular image. And, curiously enough, a not dissimilar defect marks *The Anathemata*. This lack of visual concreteness is at first surprising in Mr. Jones, who is perhaps better known as a painter of visionary power, than as a writer. But we find it also in Blake's Prophetic Books. I would add, in passing, that the extremely beautiful wood engravings which Mr. Jones has incorporated in this volume, are almost as integral to his text, as are Blake's engravings to his. Compared with the *Cantos* with which it so much invites comparison, *The Anathemata* is lacking in *density*. But read continuously — and, especially read aloud — its incantatory power, and the imaginative logic of its construction, will become apparent.

Mr. Jones has provided a running commentary of footnotes. The reader should be well advised (as the author himself suggests) to ignore them, at any rate at a first reading of the work. There is a touch of provincial pedantry about them, and Mr. Jones ought to know that footnotes always make a poem more, and not less, obscure. (The notes to *The Waste Land* were, I think, the perspicacious possum's only false move; stupid people have been inking their eyebrows over them ever since, instead of enjoying the poetry.) A poet should leave exegesis to exegetes. The only special equipment needed for an understanding of *The Anathemata* is some acquaintance with the Welsh traditions of the *Mabinogion*, (say, in Lady Guests's translation, with its very full notes), and with the language of the Roman liturgy. For this is Mr. Jones' own testament. He is, he tells us in his Preface "a Londoner, of Welsh and English parentage, of Protestant upbringing, of [Roman] Catholic subscription". These phrases represent very closely, the points of departure tor Mr. Jones' poetry. They mark, as it were, his particular paradigm, his personal variation, on the theme of our common Western heritage, which is the real subject of the poem. We can only enter the poetry by recognizing this, and relating it to our own paradigm. (I am myself, for example, a Londoner, but of country upbringing; of English parentage (but with some heritage of Welsh blood) and tradition; and of (Anglican) Catholic subscription. That is to say, rather closer to Mr. Jones than some of my readers, but still having to make important adjustments.)

In Parenthesis could be regarded (in spite of the author's caveat) as a more or less straight "war-book". Its language was mainly the language of prose as we know it, though liberated by the impact of Joyce's *Ulysses*. But really, like *Ulysses*, it was Epic — Mr. Jones' personal *Iliad*, in which his 1914–18 war-time experience was set in the perspectives of Welsh heroic saga, just as Bloom's prosaic day in Dublin was illuminated by gleams from mythological overworlds. *The Anathemata* is his *Odyssey*, a voyaging home through the seas of memory, at once a *nostos* and a *nekuia*. The ancients made the Muses the Daughters of Memory. When Blake indignantly repudiated this idea, as a false invention of the rationalizing intellect, he did not know that Mnemosyne signified more than the empirical memory of things perceived and recorded by the senses. Mnemosyne (as Keats knew) is a mighty goddess, standing for the transmitted communal wisdom and experience of the tribe. She is sister to Themis, who (far beyond abstract Justice) signifies the community's intuitive sense of what is is fitting and customary. Memory, in this sense, finds its equivalent, in Christian terms, as the concept of Tradition within the Catholic Church. And the strands of personal memory in *The Anathemata* ("the thing dedicated") draws the poet back into this great universal tradition.

The opening of *The Anathemata* inevitably suggests that of Pound's *Cantos*. But the image that emerges is not that of Ulysses descending to a pagan Hell, to call up the thin bloodless ghosts, but that of the Christian pontiff-priest offering the sacrifice for the living and the dead, and in so doing recalling the passion and Resurrection of Christ, and with it all history, for all history is *in* Christ (a theme also treated by Charles Williams in "Taliessin at Lancelot's Mass" in his *Taliessin through Logres*.)

It is the word *anamnesis* which is the real key to this poem, as Mr. Jones, in one of those notes I've just been complaining about, points out. He quotes from the great Anglican scholar, Dom Gregory Dix's *The Shape of the Liturgy*: "It (anamnesis) is not quite easy to represent accurately in English, words like 'remembrance' or 'memorial' having for us a connotation of something *absent* which is only mentally recollected. But in the scriptures of both the Old and New Testament *anamnesis* and the cognate verb have a sense of 'recalling' or 're-presenting' before God an event in the past so that it becomes *here and now operative by its effects*".

This poetry, in fact, is throughout *liturgically* organized. And it is this, I would suggest, that provides the positive, integrating factor, which makes *The Anathemata* something more than a mere exercise in the manner of Joyce and Pound. In modern poetry only *Murder in The Cathedral* (though in a quite different way), certain poems of Charles Williams, and, perhaps, David Gascoyne's sequence of poems on the Crucifixion, provide anything like a parallel.

It is thus, in the first part of the work, "Rite and Fore-time", that the whole of the past is evoked; down from the Celtic and pre-Celtic culture of Europe, in whose cult-symbolism can already be discerned those images — the Mother, the Sacred Tree, the Sacrificed God — which are to achieve their full significance in a Christian context. Mr. Jones also makes use of the myth of the Trojan origin of the Britons (familiar to English poets from Layamon to Spenser, Shakespeare, Milton and Blake) which links the destiny of London (Troynovant) to that of Rome. Thence he passes to later, historical migrations to Britain — Phoenician and Anglo-Saxon. Mr. Jones' evocations of the sea are hauntingly beautiful, as in this litany to the Patroness of Mariners, recalling as it does both passages in Ezra Pound's *Cantos*, and the sea-litany of "The Dry Salvages":

> Maiden help y'r own
> Maiden help y'r own
> > > Maiden aid us.
> Themis, pray,
> Phoebe, Telphousa
> > > pray.
> Agelastos Petra
> > > cleft for us!
> Paphia remember us that are indentured to your mother.
> And us marines, remember us
> > > as belong to y'r panzer'd lover.
> Sea-wives of Laconia
> > > bid your Cytheréa
> be mindful of her nativity.
> Ladies of Tyre and the Phoenician littoral pray. The Lady to
> have a native pity on this ship's company — consider: how
> many inboard, along of us, belong to *her*!
> In all the sun-lands of our cradle-sea
> you many that are tutelar
> > > regard our anathemata.
> Pay our vows Iberian ladies
> > > to the Lady of Iberia
> for making by her coasts toward this place
> we *did call* her by her name:
> > > > remind her.

The Lady presides also over London, and the many City churches dedicated to the Blessed Virgin, which gather to themselves pre-Reformation and pre-Christian associations. And the street-cry of the lavender-seller reminds the poet that this plant is said to have been first introduced by the Romans. In the sixth section of the work, *Keel, Ram, Stauros*, the image of the Cross is called up. It is identified as the wood of the ships carrying the immigrants on their sea journey to Britain, and is also the sacred tree, *ashera*, from the Phoenician East.

The last two sections of the work are closely linked to the liturgy. "Mabinog's liturgy" is a meditation on the office for Christmas Day. The whole section is a sort of holy pun on the word *Mabinogion*. This, in Welsh, means a tale to be taught to a youthful apprentice bard, but also means a story of the infancy of Christ — hence, it may be applied to the gospel of the birth of Christ proper to Christmas. *Maponos* (The Youth, or Son) was an ancient Celtic god (who appears, in Welsh heroic tradition as Mabon, son of Modron — the Son of the Mother) whom the Romans identified with Apollo. And the tales called "The Four Branches of the Mabinogion" are largely concerned with the miraculous births of mythical heroes — Pryderi and Llew — which shadow that of Christ.

The last section, "Sherthursday and Venus Day", deals with the events of the Passion, seen as an eternal event, the eternal offering of Himself by the eternal Priest, for the living and the dead:

> He does what is done in many places
> what he does other
>   he does after the mode
> of what has always been done.
> What did he do other
>   recumbent at the garnished supper?
> What did he do yet other
>   riding the Axile Tree?

These, the concluding words of the whole work, not only sum it up, but also recall the image of the sacrificing priest with which it began. For the movement of the images in this poem is also cyclical. But the circle is not the wheel of Maya, the "wicked endlessness" of *Finnegans Wake* or Yeats' "Phases of the Moon". We think rather of that "great ring of pure unending light" under the form of which, another Welsh poet, Henry Vaughan, glimpsed Eternity.

[1953]

■ Hart Crane

IF ONE WISHED to dismiss Hart Crane's poetry, it would be easy to sum him up as a splendid failure. But to make that the last word, would be to miss the whole point about American literature, and American poetry in particular, which cannot be judged by the absolute standards of the European tradition, as if it were no more than a colonial offshoot of English literature. There are roughly three types of American writer, and the least significant are those — such as Emerson, James Russell Lowell or Longfellow — who attempt to create, in New England or elsewhere, a literary environment which shall be, as near as possible, a replica of that of Europe. These, I say, are the least significant — though their work can be judged by European standards without any radical re-adjustment of mind being demanded of the critic. The second type includes those, who, dissatisfied with their native background, make the return-pilgrimage to Europe — to London, or Paris. Such are Henry James and T.S. Eliot. The foundations of their work are profoundly American, but they have severed themselves from their roots, and assimilated the older and more complex culture of Europe. Often, indeed, they bring to it a sensitivity, and a wider sense of values, such as are scarcely to be found among its own legendary guardians. The third type includes men like Whitman, Melville and Poe. They remain as outlaws within an American society to which they are radically maladjusted. Neurotics, living a life of frustration or disaster, they are, by absolute standards, no more successful as artists than in their lives — though they may achieve canonisation after death at the hands of pundits. They adumbrate myth, rather than literature. Their work is top-heavy, formless, megalomaniac. Poetry fitfully struggles to be born in it, too often smothered by rhetoric, or a failure of style. Yet these are the real key-figures of American literature, to whose work we return again and again, and for whom, at length, we come to feel a personal sympathy, and, finally, reverence. Their work alone can give us something which is not already contained in the matured culture of Europe, and in its totality it has a greatness of conception which is of more significance than any purely formal virtues.

To this third class Hart Crane also belonged, and indeed, in one poem, he paid personal homage to Melville, and likewise incorporated the figures of Whitman and Poe into his private mythology. Growing up in an age of poetic intellectualism, restraint, and "neo-classicism", he is, or strove to be, a reckless, prodigal and romantic writer, attempting to recapture the abandon of Marlowe and the other Elizabethans. He has little in common with Pound and Eliot, of whom he was a younger contemporary, and still less — for all his deliberate cultivation of imagery drawn from urban and mechanised civilisation — with the group of young English poets, who, under the leadership of Auden, were coming to the fore at about the time of his death. But his personal attitude and his feeling for words shows, I think, a distinct affinity with that developed a little later by a slightly younger group of poets, including Dylan Thomas, David Gascoyne, and George Barker. It seems to me that his influence on English poetry is therefore likely to increase, especially if his work, which is at present not readily accessible in this country, becomes more widely known. It is noteworthy that in the work of Dunstan Thompson, a young American poet who was over here during the war years, the influence of Hart Crane is seen blending, quite naturally, with that of Barker and Thomas.

The story of Hart Crane's life is in most ways a terrifying story — the record, no less than the life of Poe, of the progressive disintegration of a personality up against the whole weight of American philistinism and materialism. From the first, the conditions of his environment were almost symbolic of the *impasse* of American civilisation. He was the son of a cultivated mother of old New England stock, and a father who was a rich candy-magnate. The marriage was unsatisfactory, and they were subsequently divorced. From a boy, Hart Crane felt himself to be the target of both his parents' emotional possessiveness, and to this situation, perhaps, we may trace the development of his homosexuality. His father attempted to train him in the family business, starting him from the bottom, and deliberately tried to prevent him from writing poetry. He broke away, but found continual difficulty in obtaining regular employment, or was forced into such uncongenial environments as the cultural desert of Pittsburg. He sought refuge in an addiction to alcohol — and to sailors — and, at the end of his life, came to identify himself with all the *poètes maudits* — with Baudelaire, with Rimbaud, and with Christopher Marlowe. The critics' appreciation of his long poem, *The Bridge*, finally gained for him a travelling fellowship which took him to Mexico. But by this time he had sunk into a slough of physical excess, and spiritual impotence and despair. Knowing that he had done none of the work, which the conditions of the fellowship demanded, and that the chances of its being renewed were slight, he drowned himself in the Bay of Mexico, throwing himself overboard from the stern of the ship on which he was returning to the U.S.A. In broad daylight, in a calm sea, he sank without a struggle and without trace.

Yet, although it destroyed him, Hart Crane, in his poetry, made the attempt to accept modern American and industrial civilisation, in all its implications. His poem, "For the Marriage of Faustus and Helen", celebrates the union of the modern "Faustian" spirit with the idea of traditional beauty:

> Anchises' navel, dripping from the sea, —
> The hands Erasmus dipped in gleaming tides,
> Gather the voltage of blown blood and vine;
> Delve upward for the new and scattered wine,
> O brother-thief of time, that we recall.
> Laugh out the meagre penance of their days
> Who dare not share with us the breath released,
> The substance drilled and spent beyond repair
> For golden, or the shadow of gold hair.
>
> Distinctly praise the years, whose volatile
> Blamed bleeding hands extend and thresh the height
> The imagination spans beyond despair,
> Outpacing bargain, vocable and prayer.

In his most ambitious poem, *The Bridge*, he goes further, and attempts to create a whole mythology for the new American civilisation. Whitman, Poe and Emily Dickenson are invoked, no less than Isidora Duncan, the story of Pocohontas, the legend of Rip Van Winkle, Columbus in mid-Atlantic, and Plato's Atlantis. The leading symbol is the Bridge itself—Brooklyn Bridge. It is an image not only of man's triumph in construction, but of his ability, in doing so, to create beauty. It is that which unites men within the city, and which unites the city with the country beyond. Finally, as a symbol of union, it is apostrophised, almost, as God. The poem structurally owes much both to *Ulysses* and *The Waste Land*. Like them, it gives the wanderings of the hero about the city where he lives, during the space of a single day, together with his mental journeyings in the world of myth and the past, which impart to the whole the context of epic. But while Joyce in Dublin and Eliot in London found only despair and the end of civilisation, Hart Crane, consciously at least, tried to express a positive attitude of acceptance in his vision of the city.

But the continual forced rhetoric of his poem makes us suspect that he is attempting the impossible; that the marriage of Faustus and Helen cannot, in fact, be consummated. And Hart Crane's life and poetry do not exemplify what he strove to express, the splendid promise of American civilisation, but rather its tragedy. Whitman before him, had given form to a vision of democratic brotherhood springing in part from the high hopes which the foundation of the young American republic had inspired, in part from a subjective intuition rooted in his own homosexuality. The victory of the North in the Civil War brought, not the ideal society for which he hoped, but the growth of industrial capitalism, and increase of materialism and inequality among men. Whitman (as Stephen Spender has pointed out) was forced to become, in *Sea Drift* and his poem on the death of Lincoln, a great poet, no longer of the acceptance of life in all its forms, but of death. Hart Crane is the conscious successor of Whitman, but a Whitman faced with the far greater complexities of modern scientific and mechanistic civilisation. The poet, in *The Bridge*, after his journey round the city, returns, in the evening, by the subway under the river. Here he encounters, in the grotesque figures of the tired workers crowded together in the unnatural light and foetid atmospheres of the Tube, a symbol of the obverse side of the civilisation which he has been trying to celebrate, the hidden aspect of the city. And here the last of his mythological figures, the ghost of Poe, haunts him:

> And why do I often meet your visage here,
> Your eyes like agate lanterns — on and on
> Below the toothpaste and the dandruff adds?
>
> — And did their riding eyes right through your side,
> And did their eyes like unwashed platters ride?
> And, Death, aloft, — gigantically down
> Probing through you — towards me, O evermore!
> And when they dragged your retching flesh,
> Your trembling hands that night through Baltimore —
> That last night on the ballot rounds, did you
> Shaking, did you deny the ticket, Poe?

Poe, the impotent, whose mathematical intellect drove all the faculties of his nature to inhabit a womb-world of nightmare, who tried to reduce poetry to a mechanical science, and who, hating American democracy, met his death in the disorders attendant on a local election, is fittingly the presiding genius of the journey through the Gates of Wrath.

Hart Crane's obsession with the symbol of Unity tells its own story. Like every homosexual, he is attempting an absolute union which can never be achieved. He is striving to derive from the dead and mechanical an emotion and power which belongs only to a vision of society organically conceived. Yet his attempt is a heroic one, and illustrates a problem lying near to the heart of our modern predicament, and which is particularly the concern of the poet. But as an artist, he is most successful when he ceases to seek the impossible, and is most personal, as in the sequence of love poems entitled *Voyages*. In these the emotions of tenderness, ecstacy and despair all meet in the one image of the sea:

> Mark how her turning shoulders wind the hours,
> And hasten while her penniless rich palms
> Pass superscription of bent foam and wave, —
> Hasten, while they are true, — sleep, death, desire,
> Close round one instant in one floating flower.
>
> Bind us in time, O Seasons clear, and awe.
> O minstrel galleons of Carib fire,
> Bequeath us to no earthly shore until
> Is answered in the vortex of our grave
> The seal's wide spindrift gaze toward paradise.

As for Swinburne, the sea for Hart Crane is the Great Mother, who is also Death and Eternity. And it was she who claimed him at last.

[1947]

■ Charles Williams

CHARLES WILLIAMS died in 1945, yet, even after the lapse of some ten years, it is very difficult to arrive at a balanced estimate of his place in modern English literature. Criticism has, indeed, largely neglected him; and in particular it has neglected that part of his work, the later poems, by which he would certainly have wished primarily to be judged. There appear, however, to be signs that interest in his work is steadily growing, especially among the younger generation, though it is probably for his prose fiction that he is best known. His novels are "metaphysical thrillers", in which the supernatural always plays a prominent part. They belong, broadly, to the same literary genre as the stories of Sheridan Le Fanu (in *Through a Glass Darkly*), Arthur Machen, Algernon Blackwood, and M.R. James. This is a tradition of English writing (an offshoot, really, of the earlier tradition of the "Gothic" romance, of which the detective story is another offshoot) which, whatever its entertainment value, criticism does not feel called upon to take very seriously. Witchcraft, converse between the living and the spirits of the dead, a magic stone that can transport you at will in time and space, the images of the Tarot pack, a modern quest for the Holy Grail — these, surely, are things which may entertain our fancy, even produce a pleasurable shudder of a winter's evening — but have nothing to do with our rational, day to day experience, and hence cannot form the material of serious literature.

Yet the reader, encountering the properties I have mentioned above in the pages of a novel by Charles Williams, quickly becomes conscious of a factor which distinguishes his work from that of other writers of this kind. The supernatural is being taken seriously, and is being brought disconcertingly close to our own experience. Magic is seen, not as something which may provide a fanciful escape from a dull reality, but, at least, as the image of something which is part of the world as we know it. It is, in these stories, the abuse of a real spiritual power for selfish ends. Hence, it holds the possibility of real damnation, just as does the abuse of other forms of spiritual power — love, for instance, or poetry.

Charles Williams believes in the supernatural. But his mind is at the same time highly rational, even (in a sense) sceptical. However bizarre the events that occur in his novels may be, they are always, essentially, logical, and subject to the same laws which apply to our everyday experience. And the people to whom they occur are everyday people — middle-class people for the most part, who work in shops and offices, or as professional men or clergymen, and who live in London, its suburbs, and the home-counties. Charles Williams himself lived and worked among such people (as an employee of the Oxford University Press's London Office, and lecturer in the City Literary Institute) and he believed in their fundamental decencies. It is among such people that he has mostly found his readers rather than among the "intellectuals" (whom he tended to distrust). His novels belong, it may be, to "middlebrow" literature. They were written partly, it would appear, for entertainment, partly to bring in money. But in turning, only half-seriously, to the novel form, Charles Williams employed ideas which he held with profound seriousness. These ideas are most fully developed in his other prose-writings — literary critical, historical, and religious in character, and above all, in his poetry and plays. The corpus of his published work is large, and some acquaintance with its varied aspects is necessary if we are to gain a correct estimate of his stature. But primarily, he was a poet. All his work is to be understood in terms of his conception of the poet's experience, and its relationship to spiritual truth.

As a poet, he stood, in some sense, apart from the age in which he lived, in much the same way as William Blake did from his. This was due (as also in Blake's case) to his overriding spiritual preoccupations:

> The young poets studied precision;
> Taliessin remembered the soul.

Fundamentally, he was a traditionalist, wishing to continue the great tradition of Dante, Milton and Wordsworth, but also of the Metaphysicals. This, together with his distrust of the highbrows, for long made him suspicious of what was being done by modern poets, and he was late in finding a style really adequate to his thought. His early volumes, such as *Poems of Conformity* (1917) and *Divorce* (1920), show great virtuosity of style, yet it is always imitative. There are pastiches of Herrick, Rochester, and other seventeenth-century poets, some poems with a somewhat pre-Raphaelite colouring, and others again which show the strong influence of the early Yeats, Abercrombie, Chesterton, and perhaps Kipling. This technical virtuosity is matched by an equal intellectual power. Many of his leading ideas and themes are already developed in these early volumes — but the result is hardly ever quite satisfactory as poetry. We feel that the poet is limiting himself (as did Bridges, whom Williams admired, and the Georgians) by attachment to false, and static conceptions of poetic tradition. The living tradition of English poetry was, at the period these poems were written, directing itself into very different channels. Under the guidance of Ezra Pound, Eliot, and the later Yeats, the younger poets were learning to accommodate their rhythms to colloquial speech, and to discard the overworked associations of romantic diction.

Yet, even had he been prepared to adopt it, this colloquializing tendency, this re-affirmation of the "low" style, would not have served Charles Williams's purpose. He aimed at a poetry of epic scope, using the traditional British theme of the Arthurian legend. The "Taliessin" poems are, in fact, a series of epic odes (rather like the classic Greek odes of Pindar or Bacchylides) using this mythological material, as a symbol of spiritual experience, in somewhat the same way as the mythology of Blake's Prophetic Books is employed. Some of its episodes he treated earlier in the style of Chesterton — quite an inadequate one to his purpose. But with the publication of *Taliessin through Logres* (1938) Williams emerged, in middle life, as a mature poet. The style of these poems is wholly original, and fully as "modern" in its own way, as that of T.S. Eliot. But whereas the latter, actuated partly by a negative mysticism, stripped his language of all ornaments to an ascetic bareness, Williams, with his "affirmative" approach to the same beliefs as Eliot held, required a language rich with imagery, ceremonial and hieratic. It is remote, indeed, from common speech, but it is equally remote from the enervated romantic diction of the Georgians. It does, however, perhaps owe something to Hopkins, whose poems Williams had edited, but it is not "Hopkinsese".

Nothing could be more unlike the "social realist" poetry then in fashion. The poetic canons of the thirties are classically (and admirably) illustrated in Michael Roberts's *Faber Book of Modern Verse*; and in the original edition of this anthology, Charles Williams finds no place. But before the decade was out, a certain reaction against these canons began to become apparent; and one poem of Williams, "The Crowning of Arthur", was included in the edition revised by Anne Ridler.

Though quite independently of any knowledge of Williams's work, younger poets like George Barker and Dylan Thomas began to write in a style which did not eschew a certain romantic rhetoric. There was also a growing feeling, accentuated later by the experience of the war (which drove people back to their inner resources), that a merely "social-realist" interpretation of experience was inadequate for poetry.

Younger poets became interested in mythological and religious symbolism, as a means of expressing areas of experience inaccessible to the intellect alone. Among some of these, Williams began to find readers. His influence is discernible in the work of Sidney Keyes and Vernon Watkins, and, in another way, in that of Anne Ridler and Norman Nicholson. These last were not attracted to Williams's style, but sharing his religious faith, were impressed by the way in which he gave significance to the apparently trivial, and to everyday relationships.

Among poets of Williams's own generation, T.S. Eliot has expressed his interest in Williams's work, and the influence of the latter's ideas in the *Four Quartets* and *The Cocktail Party* is at least to be suspected. (The *doppelgänger* theme, drawn from a passage which both poets quote from Shelley's *Prometheus Unbound*, occupies a key position in both *The Cocktail Party* and Williams's novel *Descent into Hell* (1937).) W.H. Auden, who by the end of the war had reached a position of Christian orthodoxy, has been certainly influenced by his reading of Charles Williams. *The Descent of the Dove* is quoted in the notes to *New Year Letter*. The image of a landscape corresponding to the human body, in *The Age of Anxiety*, derives from the scheme of *Taliessin Through Logres*, while "Memorial for the City", in *Nones*, is in direct imitation of Williams's mature style.

I mention this influence of Williams on other writers, in order to suggest that he need no longer be regarded as a figure eccentric to the age, but as a thinker and poet of stature, to be reckoned with seriously. It is to the "Taliessin" poems that I wish primarily to direct the reader's attention. But these, as I have already said, present considerable difficulty. They are to be interpreted with reference to Williams's leading ideas, and these are most readily deducible from consideration of his prose writings.

II

I have mentioned above Charles Williams's relationship to T.S. Eliot. It may be helpful if we regard them, in some sense, as complementary figures. Both are poets of a religious experience which verges on the mystical. Both were able to formulate that experience in terms of orthodox Christian faith, as this is interpreted by the Catholic tradition within the Church of England. But the roads whereby they reached this position were very different. Eliot's starting point was the Puritan tradition of New England; though we must not forget his interest in the idealist philosophy of Bradley, and his early studies in Sanskrit, and in Indian religious thought. Williams, on the other hand, passed through a more unusual, and perhaps a more dubious route. In his early years he was a member of the group of "Rosicrucians" in London, known as the Order of the Golden Dawn, whose leader was MacGregor Mathers. This association of students of ceremonial magic, cabalism, alchemy and other occult subjects is of some importance for the literary history of the early years of this century. It is well known that, at a time before Williams's association with the Golden Dawn, Yeats was one of its prominent members. At a later time, members included Arthur Machen, and Algernon Blackwood, while the sinister figure of the "black magician" Alistair Crowley crossed its path, and attempted, unsuccessfully to direct it to his own objects. Another member was A. E. Waite, the author of numerous voluminous and learned writings on occult subjects, including studies of the Caballa, and of the Holy Grail legend. These books, though written in a highly involved and obscure style, show considerable imaginative insight, and also a respect for historical scholarship decidedly uncommon in writers of this kind. They may certainly be read as source-books of many of Charles Williams's ideas. Waite was, in fact, in spite of the "gnostic" tendency of his thought, a practising Catholic; but it did not need his influence to point Williams, from the vague and sometimes trivial fantasies of occultism, towards the living tradition of Christian orthodoxy — for he had been brought up as a Churchman from boyhood. Arthur Machen, another of his "Golden Dawn" associates, was likewise an Catholic. The source of some of the themes in Charles Williams's novels can be discerned in Machen's stories (notably *The Great Return*). But the heavy, slightly sickly tone of some of Machen's prose (as if redolent of stale incense), and the rather prurient reference to "nameless evils", etc. is something quite foreign to Charles Williams.

Another important influence, was Williams's contact with the Christian mysticism of Evelyn Underhill, whose letters he edited (1943). It is notable that Miss Underhill's novel, *A Pillar of Dust*, is, in almost every respect, the model for Charles Williams's own writings of this kind. He also became friendly with the Roman Catholic poet, Alice Meynell, who assisted him in finding a publisher for his first book of poems, *The Silver Stair* (1912).

His early interest in occultism explains much of the bizarreness (intriguing to some, repellent to others) of the machinery of Charles Williams's novels, and, more importantly, the difficult symbolism of his later poems. In particular, the idea that the various parts of the human body can be related to spiritual states (which is basic to the understanding of the "Taliessin" poems) doubtless owes much to the Cabala. But as a poet, he employed these symbols, just as did Yeats, merely as they provided him with images for what he had to say. Everything in his work must be related to his basic orthodoxy, and in particular to his belief in the Incarnation. This doctrine implies a belief in the relevance, indeed in the dignity of the material creation, and in the possibility of its ultimate redemption. In the light of such beliefs no poet could lose his head, to the detriment of his art, among cloudy pseudo-mystical symbols.

There is also another element in Charles Williams's character, which must not be left out of account. This is a certain scepticism — what he called "the quality of disbelief". For him, doubt is something very close to faith — perhaps one might say, something to be included in faith — and he always emphasizes man's right, even duty, to question. In *The Descent of the Dove* (1939), which is a history of the operation of the Holy Spirit in Christendom, he gives important and honourable place to Montaigne and to Voltaire. Of Montaigne he writes:

> Our Lord the Spirit, having permitted contrition to exist, permitted sheer intelligence to exist; he inspired — one may say so — Montaigne ... He recalled men to the recollection that they began with a hypothesis; that faith — the kind of faith he beheld active around him, which had (it was estimated) killed 800,000 human beings and wrecked nine towns and two hundred and fifty villages — that faith had first been a hypothesis and had been generally translated into the realms of certitude by anger and obstinacy and egotism. Even of profound spiritual experience the sentence that he put up in his library was true: "Men are tormented by their opinions of things, not by the things themselves." Thomas à Kempis had said it in another idiom: "The Holy Ghost has delivered us from a multitude of opinions".

And of Voltaire:

> Voltaire seems actually to have thought on a low level; he did suppose that the fact that there were a thousand reputed Saviours of the world proved that there was no Saviour of the world, and that the different circumstances and natures of many mothers of many gods disproved the Virginity of the Mother of God. We know that neither affirmation nor denial are as simple as that. But in matters of public morals Voltaire shocked and justly shook the Church. The mechanical operation of cruelty which proceeded under the automatic rigour of the still officially Christian governments was halted, for a few brief moments, by the incredible energy of the old man of Ferney ... Voltaire attacked in force and with a passion of sincerity: "I will not laugh while such things are done." He wrote across the brain of all future Christendom: *"Ecrasez l'infame."* Christendom will be unwise if ever she forgets that cry, for she will have lost touch with contrition once more. She had forgotten — or at least her rulers had forgotten — Man; the candles burned to the Incarnate, but the co-inherence of all men was being lost.

Again, in *He Came Down from Heaven* (1938), he characteristically lays emphasis on Mary's question immediately she received the message of the Annunciation: "How shall these things be?" For him, this is a resumption, though on a new plane of experience, of Job's impassioned questioning of God in the Old Testament. "Man was intended to argue with God, Humility has never consisted in not asking questions." In private conversation he seems sometimes to have gone further. Thus, he is reported by Professor C.S. Lewis to have said that, though he was ready to accept as revealed doctrine the proposition that existence is good, he added that it would never have occurred to him, unaided, to suspect it. On another occasion, it is said, he suggested that perhaps the individual, after death, might accept immortality as a "final act of obedience".

Thus, though in the main, Charles Williams may be regarded as belonging to the tradition of Christian transcendentalism in English poetry — the great tradition of Spenser, Vaughan, the later Wordsworth and Coleridge, and Coventry Patmore — there is also a sense in which he may be regarded as a Christian existentialist, almost as a Christian sceptic. He was one of the first, in this country, to realize the importance of Kierkegaard, and is reported to have been largely responsible for the Oxford University Press's issuing its series of translations of this thinker. "To live in the unconditional", wrote Kierkegaard (Williams quotes this passage with approval), "inhaling only the unconditional, is impossible to man; he perishes like the fish forced to live in the air. But, on the other hand, without relating himself to the unconditional man cannot, in the deepest sense, be said to 'live'."

III

In the writings attributed to "Dionysius the Areopagite", which form a fountain-head of the tradition of Christian mysticism, there are defined two ways by which the human soul may come to God. These are the Negative and the Affirmative ways. Viewed from the point of view of the former, God is defined in negative terms. He is to be reached by detaching the soul from love of all things that are not God — the things of the created world. This is the way of the Rejection of Images. But the Christian God is immanent as well as transcendent. Hence, everything in the created world is also an imperfect image of Him. The Way of Affirmation consists in the recognition of this, and in the acceptance, in love, of all things, not for their own sake, but as images of the Divine. Charles Williams was fond of expressing this through the maxim of an ancient writer: "This also is Thou: neither is this Thou." This way, lived to the full, is not necessarily less hard than the Way of Rejection, for it will, sooner or later, involve the affirmation of the images of suffering and loss, along with the others.

In the historic Christian tradition (at least in the West) the emphasis has tended to be on the Negative way, rather than on its complement, the Way of Affirmation. This may possibly be due to the influence of monastic ideals, in the Middle Ages, and after. For the Negative is clearly a way that can most conveniently be taken by the cloistered contemplative. Perhaps its greatest exponent is St. John of the Cross, and in our own day, T.S. Eliot has expressed something of it in his later poetry, particularly *Four Quartets*.

> I said to my soul, be still, and wait without hope
> For hope would be hope for the wrong thing; wait without love
> For love would be love of the wrong thing; there is yet faith
> But the faith and the love and the hope are all in the waiting.

But for Charles Williams the Way of Affirmation was pre-eminently the way of the poet, and of the lover — a way which all poets and lovers at least partially followed, whether they knew it or not. Even the verses of St. John of the Cross were a gesture of recognition made by the one way to the other. For the two ways are not mutually exclusive. In *The Figure of Beatrice* (1943) Williams says: "The tangle of affirmation and rejection which is in each of us has to be drawn into some kind of pattern, and has so been drawn by all men who have ever lived."

Among poets, he believed that Dante had most fully expressed one aspect of the Affirmative way, bringing it into relation with the ordered intellectual system of medieval Gothic theology. This following of the same way, along with the perversions of it into which the soul might be tempted, forms the central theme of Williams's own work. The significance of this point of view, for the Christian thought of our time, must not be neglected. The traditional emphasis in Christian thought on the Negative way, to the exclusion of the Affirmative, may be traced to the historical influence of the monastic ideal. Monasticism arose as a result of the condition accompanying the breakdown of the Roman Empire. Men withdrew from the world for the sake of the world, in order to salvage, in safe refuges, something of the values which were everywhere being destroyed. We must be profoundly grateful that it was so. Today, European civilisation is faced with a situation analogous to, yet also different from, that which heralded the approach of the Dark Ages. Perhaps once again it will be the task of the Christian Church to preserve for posterity our threatened values. But many believe that this can be done, not by a return to the monastic ideal, but by some organization of an essentially "lay" kind, of Christians living and working in the world, yet under the law of Grace. In his poem "The Founding of the Company" (in *The Region of the Summer Stars*) Charles Williams tells of the creation of such a group, committed to the Affirmative way:

> Grounded in the Acts of the Throne and the pacts of the themes,
> it lived only by conceded recollection,
> having no decision, no vote or admission,
> but for the single vote that any soul
> took of its own election of the Way;
> the whole shaped no frame nor titular claim to place.
> As the king's name held the high lords
> in the kingdom's glory, so the Protection this,
> but this was of the commons and the whole manner of love,
> When love was fate to minds adult in love.
> What says the creed of the Trinity? *quincunque vult*;
> therefore its cult was the Trinity and the Flesh-taking
> and its rule as the making of man in the doctrine of largesse,
> and its vow as the telling, the singular and mutual confession
> of the indwelling of the mansion and session of each in each.

The beginning of the soul's election of the Way lies in what Charles Williams termed the Romantic experience — a moment of Vision, in which some image of the created universe is seen as embodying the transcendent Good. But Charles Williams's use of the term "Romanticism" must be distinguished from the use of the word by some other modern writers. It does not, for him, mean an affirmation of emotional values to the exclusion of formal and intellectual ones, and not, certainly (as for T. E. Hulme) a denial of the essential limitations of human nature. At best, Charles Williams would have regarded these as inaccurate or imperfect statements of Romanticism — and "Hell", he once wrote, "is inaccurate". The false romantic makes the mistake of regarding the romantic experience as meant for him, instead of him for it. The greatest false romantic was Milton's Satan.

IV

In a lecture which I heard him deliver at Oxford in 1943, Charles Williams distinguished five principal modes of the Romantic experience, or great images, which occur in poetry. They are:

(a) The Religious experience itself. Having posited this, Williams proposed to say nothing further about it. Obviously, in a sense, it is in a category apart, and includes the others.

(b) The Image of woman. Dante's *Divine Comedy* is the fullest expression of this mode, and its potential development.

(c) The Image of Nature. Of this Wordsworth in *The Prelude* (the actual subject of the lecture he was giving) was the great exponent.

(d) The Image of the City. Had Williams not been addressing an audience composed of English Literature students, I have no doubt that he would have cited Virgil, in the *Aeneid*, as the great exponent. As it was, he points to "what were, until recently, known as our younger poets" [by which he meant the Auden school] as expressing, in their Vision of the Unjust City, a negative aspect of this experience. (An even better, and positive, example from modern poetry would have been provided by Hart Crane's *The Bridge*, but Charles Williams had not read this poem.)

(e) The experience of great art. Of this, Keats's "Ode on a Grecian Urn" was a partial expression.

The last of these modes, like the first, seems to stand in a special category. It is, it might be said, included by the others, just as the others are included in the first. And it also seems to me doubtful whether it could ever lead to a more than partial expression, without being subsumed in one of the others. Something further, however, must be said of these others, and of Charles Williams's interpretation of them.

In the first place, it will be seen that they are, psychologically, closely linked, especially as, in European poetry, Nature and the City are commonly personified as female figures. Dante's love for Beatrice was inextricably involved with his love for the city of Florence, and his ideal of the Empire. Wordsworth's attitude to nature is fundamentally that of a lover; he speaks of the great poem he planned, of which *The Prelude* was to be the first part, as "spousal verse". It is therefore impossible to treat of any one of these three great images in isolation.

Of Charles Williams's attitude to Nature, there is little which need be said. He greatly admired Wordsworth, and his essay on him in *Reason and Beauty in the Poetic Mind* (1933) is profound as well as sympathetic. Nevertheless, in his own poetry, Nature as such has hardly any part to play. His poetry lacks particularity of observation. Natural objects, in Charles Williams's poems, are always symbolic, stylized, even heraldic. Landscapes are always emblematic of states of mind. Thus the description of the wild scenery of Orkney in "Lamoracke and the Queen Morgause of Orkney" — very powerful in its way — serves only to externalize the undisciplined passion of Morgause and her lover:

> Caves and hollows in the crags were filled with the scream
> of seamews nesting and fleeting; the extreme theme
> of Logres rose in harsh cries and hungry storms,
> and there, hewn in a cleft, were hideous huge forms.

Perhaps his most important natural symbol is that of the Forest, which occurs in the "Taliessin" poems as Broceliande. This forest may be interpreted in various ways — as the pre-conscious mind, as the perplexities of thought and decision through which we pass in this life. It is a place at once innocent and dangerous. But in Williams, it is primarily a literary symbol. Dante's "*selva oscura*", the forest of Shakespeare (in *As You Like It* and *A Midsummer Night's Dream*) and of Milton's *Comus*, Spenser's "wandering wood", in which the Red Cross Knight encounters Error, and the forest of Keats's "Ode to a Nightingale", are all parts of it:

> The forest itself has different names in different tongues — Westermain, Arden, Birnam, Broceliande; and in places there are separate trees named, such as that on the outskirts against which a young Northern poet saw a spectral Wanderer leaning, or, in the unexplored centre of which only rumours reach even poetry, Igdrasil of one myth, or the Tree of Knowledge and Life of another. So that indeed the whole earth seems to become this one enormous forest, and our longest and most stable civilisations are only clearings in the midst of it.

If Charles Williams has little to say of Nature, his theory of Romantic Love is the very mainspring of his work. His beliefs on this subject are most completely set forth in *The Figure of Beatrice* (1943). But for their full understanding, one must have a wider acquaintance with his work, and particularly of his early poems, many of which are actual love-poems addressed to his wife.

The act of "falling in love", as Charles Williams saw it, was a religious experience. To say this, is not simply to dignify a human emotion bringing it into relation with a category expressive of the highest values. Williams's interpretation of love as a religious experience was both precise and literal. For the lover, at the moment of his first falling in love, the beloved was actually an image of the divine perfection. Dante saw Beatrice as such — as "the youngest of the angels", a being of complete perfection. This does not abolish the "real" Beatrice, the girl in Florence, who doubtless had many serious faults. But at his first meeting with her, described in the *Vita Nuova*, Dante sees Beatrice in the image of her perfection—as God sees her; that is, as she would have been, had there been no fall of Man, and as she may potentially be, when this image is restored to Heaven.

Charles Williams insists very strongly on the objectivity of this experience. Our modern psychological way of thinking, though it must perforce admit that such experiences do happen, would always tend to interpret by means of terms such as "projection" and "sublimation". Williams will have nothing to do with this. Religious emotion is not sublimated, unconscious sex. Rather, every lover is, in some degree, whether consciously or not, a religious mystic. Furthermore, the experience is one of encounter. "The most difficult thing in the world", he once said, "is to realize that other people exist." To treat the beloved as a mere instrument, as something upon which romantic emotion may be projected, is one of the most terrible dangers of the Way. This is illustrated in the novel, *Descent Into Hell* (1937). One of the characters of this story, the historian Lawrence Wentworth, whose final "descent into hell" is the conclusion of the book, frustrated in his desire for a girl who does not love him, chooses instead an actual succubus in her image which, unlike her, is completely subservient to his will. He shuts himself up in his house, losing all interest in the real world, being completely absorbed by this auto-erotic activity. Finally, he refuses to recognize the real girl when, in a moment of terror, she comes to him for help. It is because it is an experience of encounter with another, essentially independent personality, that the initial ecstatic "Beatrician moment" is only the beginning of the Way. The pattern has to be worked out in its fullness, and for each human being this pattern will be different. But the challenge of experience will entail a further and more complex series of affirmations. For Dante this challenge lay in the marriage to another, and the subsequent death, of Beatrice. But the more usual pattern, at least today, would lead to marriage, and its responsibilities and problems.

There is, of course, much in common between this view of love, and that set forth by Plato in the *Symposium*. But the aim of the Platonic lover is to pass from the contemplation of phenomenal beauty in the person of the beloved to a purely intellectual and abstract ideal. Charles Williams's thought, however, is Christian, and not Platonist. The aim of the Way is not the exaltation of Eros to a transcendent plane, but its transformation into Agape—Christian love within the framework of Christian Marriage. Williams is bound by his belief in the Incarnation, which implies an affirmation of the importance of the particular, and of material experience. It may well be, as M. Denis de Rougemont has suggested, that the characteristic western view of Romantic love originated, among the Provencal troubadours, in heretical (Dualist) circles. But Dante brought what had hitherto been a purely secular ideal into harmony with the whole framework of medieval Catholic theology. This harmonization of Dante's Williams aimed to perpetuate, and to reinterpret for the world of today.

He did, in fact, write a book on the "outlines of Romantic Theology", in which his ideas on the subject were set forth. It remained unpublished — partly, it seems, because authorities were doubtful about the propriety of its publication from a theological point of view. It will be remembered that Patmore's *Sponsa Dei*, a work of a similar nature, was for like reasons suppressed on the advice of Gerard Manley Hopkins. It is probable that we need not have any regrets about this, for such matters are better expounded in the language of poetry, than in that of discursive prose. Among Williams's poems, a group of early sonnets and other poems, in *Poems of Conformity* (1917), are important for giving further insight into his ideas (as does the chapter on "The Theology of Romantic Love" in *He Came Down from Heaven* (1938).) In these poems, a very close analogy is worked out between the experience of the individual lover and the events of the Incarnation, up to the Ascension. The latter represents the inevitable departure of Eros, after marriage. This departure is necessary in order that Agape, the Holy Spirit, may come.

V

If a recognition of his belief in the Incarnation is necessary for the understanding of Charles Williams's views on the nature of human love, the important place he gives to the image of the City is best referred to his belief in the doctrine of the Trinity. The God of Christians is not an Absolute of metaphysical abstraction, but a dynamic relationship of three Persons, united in one substance. This relationship is one of mutual love. It is also a hierarchical relationship, though each is co-equal and co-eternal. Since Man is made in the divine image, this pattern of co-inherence is realized more or less perfectly wherever on earth human beings exist in social relationship. Every manifestation of a just political order on earth is therefore in some degree an image of the divine order of Heaven, and the quest for a just society therefore becomes likewise a mode of the Affirmative Way. Virgil's ideal vision of Augustan Rome presents a version of this experience. It is, of course, perfectly true that Augustus's Rome was only in one respect the beneficent state, bringing peace and justice to the nations, which Virgil celebrated, and that its other aspect was exploitation and corruption. The realization of this contradiction would exactly correspond to a lover's discovery of discrepancy between his lady's base behaviour and his romantic vision of her. The latter experience is examined by Charles Williams in his criticism of Shakespeare's *Troilus and Cressida* (in *Reason and Beauty in the English Poetic Mind* (1933)) and in his poem, "The Coming of Palomides".

> Division stretched between
> the queen's identity and the queen.
> Relation vanished though beauty stayed . . .

The same experience, in relation to the City, is partly the theme of "Taliessin on the Death of Virgil", the basis of which is the tradition that Virgil, on his death-bed, asked that his *Aeneid* might be destroyed (an idea that is the theme of Hermann Broch's novel, *The Death of Virgil*).

> Virgil fell from the edge of the world
> hurled by the thrust of Augustus' back; the shape
> he loved grew huge and black, loomed and pushed.
> The air rushed up; he fell
> into despair, into air's other.
> The hexameter's fulness now could find no ground;
> his mind, dizzily replete with the meaningless sweet sound,
> could found no Rome there on the joys of noise.
> He fell through his moment's infinity
> (no man escapes), all the shapes of his labour
> his infinite images dropping pell-mell; above
> loomed the gruesome great buttocks of Augustus his love,
> his neighbour, infinitely large, infinitely small.

Virgil's final despair is interpreted as springing from his disillusion with the Empire, the perception of its negative aspect, symbolized by the "gruesome great buttocks" of Augustus. Being a pagan, Virgil lacks the faith to see beyond the imperfect image to the reality behind it. The image of the City, for Williams, can comprehend all human social groupings, whether large or small. He worked for most of his life in the London offices of the Oxford University Press. In the privately printed *Amen House Masques* (1927), charming *jeux d'esprit* written for performance at the Press's staff parties, he sees the office itself in this light, and the late Sir Humphrey Milford (then head of the Press) appears as Augustus Caesar. Charles Williams was a Londoner and he had a great love for the city of London. In his last novel, *All Hallows Eve* (1945), there is a vision of London, which is seen as timeless, its whole historical past co-existing with its present in it:

She saw a glowing and glimmering City, of which the life was visible as a roseal wonder within. The streets of it were first the streets of to-day, full of the business of to-day — shops, transport, men and women ... Then, gently opening, she saw among those streets other streets ... other Londons into which her own London opened or with which it was intermingled. No thought of confusion crossed her mind, it was all very greatly ordered, and when down a long street she saw, beyond the affairs of to-day, the movement of sedan-chairs and ancient dresses, and beyond them again, right in the distance and yet very close to her, the sun shining on armour, and sometimes a high battlemented gate, it was no phantasmagoria of a dream but precise actuality. She was (though she did not find the phrase) looking along time. Once or twice she thought she saw other streets, unrecognizable, with odd buildings and men and women in strange clothes, but these were rare glimpses and less clear, as if the future of that City only occasionally showed. Beyond all these streets, or sometimes for a moment seen in their midst, was forest and the gleam of marshland, and here and there a river, and once across such a river a rude bridge, and once again a village of huts and men in skins. As she came down towards what was to her day the centre of the City, there was indeed a moment when all houses and streets vanished, and the forests rose all around her, and she was going down a rough causeway among the trees, for this was the place of London before London had begun to be, or perhaps after its long and noble history had ceased to be, and the trees grew over it, and a few late tribes still trod what remained of the old roads ...

It was not for her yet to know the greater mystery ... In this City lay all — London and New York, Athens and Chicago, Paris and Rome and Jerusalem; it was that to which they lead in the lives of their citizens.

VI

It will be seen that Charles Williams's thought is based not on abstract premises but on the experience of human relationships — man's relationship to a personal God and to his fellow creatures, whether as individuals or in society. All such personal relationships involve sacrifice — a free giving to others of part of the personality — and exchange. The idea of exchange finds its supreme embodiment in Christ's giving of Himself as a sacrifice for Man's sin. But it is the type of all other relationships, including that of economics. This is brought out in the poem "Bors to Elayne: on the King's Coins", which succeeds in embodying in strictly poetical terms the suggestion of an economic theory based on just values. The idea of exchange is also at the root of Williams's characteristic doctrine of Substitution — a doctrine which he seems to have intended quite literally and practically. I have not space to discuss this, his most daring, perhaps his most controversial doctrine, here in detail. It is best set forth in his novel, *Descent Into Hell* (1937), where it forms a major theme; and also in the chapter on "The Practice of Substituted Love" in *He Came Down From Heaven*. Pauline Anstruther, the heroine of *Descent Into Hell*, is troubled by a recurring terror — she is haunted by a *doppelgänger*, or image of herself. She tells her fear to the poet Peter Stanhope (who is a *persona* of Williams himself). He tells her that he will "carry" her fear for her, just as one might carry a parcel:

> 'When you go from here, when you're alone, when you think you'll be afraid, let me put myself in your place, and be afraid instead of you.' He sat up and leaned towards her. 'It's so easy,' he went on, 'easy for both of us. It needs only the art. For what can be simpler than for you to think to yourself that since I am there to be troubled instead of you, therefore you needn't be troubled? And what can be easier than for me to carry a little while a burden that isn't mine?' . . .

> 'And if I could,' she said. 'If I could do — whatever it is you mean, would I? Would I push my burden on to anybody else?'

> 'Not if you insist on making a universe for yourself,' he answered. 'If you want to disobey and refuse the laws that are common to us all, if you want to live in pride and division and anger, you can. But if you will be part of the rest of us, live and laugh and be ashamed with us, then you must be content to be helped. You must give your burden up to someone else, and you must carry someone else's burden. I haven't made the universe and it isn't my fault. But I'm sure that this is a law of the universe, and not to give up your parcel is as much to rebel as not to carry another's. You'll find it quite easy if you let yourself do it.'

It is, he explains, the logical application of the injunction to "bear one another's burdens". By so doing, he is able to release her from her fear, but she in her turn must be ready to take upon herself another's suffering when the time comes. This happens when Pauline is granted a vision of one of her own ancestors, a Protestant martyr in the Marian persecution, in the agony of spirit which overcame him when he faced the stake. She takes this suffering upon herself, and he is enabled to go forward with faith to martyrdom, crying, "I have seen the salvation of my God". At the same moment, she once more beholds the *doppelgänger*. But it now appears as her own self transfigured, and she is able, at last, to confront it without terror. "He dead and she living were made one in peace. Her way was haunted no more."

VII

A great deal of space has been given above to the exposition of Charles Williams's leading themes, because some knowledge of them is necessary for an understanding of his work as an imaginative writer. In the remainder of this essay it is proposed to touch upon his work as a novelist, a dramatist and, finally, as a poet, remembering that he was also critic, biographer, and lay theologian. In so doing, I hope to remain within the customary boundaries of literary criticism — calling attention to his imaginative and technical achievement, rather than treating these works merely as vehicles of ideas, however important these ideas may be.

His novels, as has already been suggested, are, though perhaps the most widely read of his works, probably the least important. The kinds of theme that preoccupied him are hardly confinable within the terms of the "serious" naturalistic novel — or at least, it would take the genius of Dostoievsky to make them so. His novels are entertainments, within that tradition of the supernatural romance already indicated. In this respect, he might be compared to Mr. Graham Greene, the best of whose novels, such as *Brighton Rock* and *The Power and the Glory*, are really conventional "thrillers" adapted as vehicles of theological ideas. But Mr. Greene has a technical accomplishment as a fiction writer (he is whole-heartedly such, being embarrassed by no poetic genius) that Williams could not command; though, it may be suggested, Mr. Greene's religious thought exhibits a relative poverty besides the richness and subtlety of Williams's. The form which Williams chose was an artificial one. His dialogue, for instance, lacks realism. It is highly stylized, and sometimes falls into a certain preciosity which irritates many readers. There is also, perhaps, especially in his earlier novels, a certain tawdriness in the presentation of evil. *War in Heaven* (1930), the first to be published, makes use of the traditional paraphernalia of the witches' Sabbath and the Black Mass. But as he developed, he learnt to treat such matters with an increasing subtlety, and to present evil in a less sensational, and hence, far more terrifying manner.

The underlying theme of all his novels is the quest for some symbol of spiritual power. The good characters learn to humble themselves before it, submitting themselves to it, while others seek to pervert it to personal and selfish ends. This theme is presented most simply in *War in Heaven* which hence, though not the best, is in many ways the easiest to understand of Charles Williams's works. The quest is the traditional one for the Holy Grail; but the setting is contemporary England. The Grail is a chalice in a country church, outwardly indistinguishable from any other chalice. The seekers include, on the one hand, an ordinary English archdeacon, a young poet, and the Duke of the North Ridings, a romantic Roman Catholic aristocrat; and on the other, a group of occultists, and Sir Giles Tumulty who represents the modern "Faustian" intellect. Sir Giles is a traveller, scientist and anthropologist. Without any beliefs himself, he regards all religions as on a par with the primitive superstitions he has encountered on his travels. His one emotion is a consuming and wholly a-moral curiosity. This character is further developed in *Many Dimensions* (1931), the theme of which is Law—human, natural, and divine. Human law is embodied in the character of Lord Arglay, the Lord Chief Justice of England, who is now the opponent of the fundamentally lawless Sir Giles. Natural and divine law are represented by the Stone (once set in the crown of King Solomon) which is here the object of the quest. This Stone will work miracles. By its aid, the categories of Time and Space can be transcended. It can be divided, and each piece retains all the properties of the whole. Yet though the subject of this novel is the miraculous, it is remarkable for the intellectual logic with which it is worked out. Sir Giles and his associates, having gained possession of the stone, carry out a series of scientific experiments with it. We are here almost in the world of H.G. Wells's early scientific romances. The stone is placed in the hands of a man condemned to be hanged, who is told to wish that he may not die. He does not, but having been hanged, remains alive and conscious, but horribly, his neck broken, and without the use of his bodily faculties. Another "subject" is told, by means of the stone, to project himself into the past. This he does, but having done so, simply continues to live his past life up to the time when he made the wish, repeats it, and is once more projected back to the same point in the past, where the process continually recommences. He is imprisoned, as it were, in a closed tunnel of time, with no hope of escape. There is a working out of metaphysical possibilities here, such as the author of *The Time Machine* did not envisage.

In *Shadows of Ecstasy* (1933) (written before *War in Heaven*, though published later) spiritual power is represented by the primitive magic of Africa, which the principal character, a white man, has mastered, and seeks to unleash for the destruction and domination of Europe. This is a prophetic book—for it anticipated, in a sense, the canalization of primitive, unconscious forces for evil ends which was to be achieved by Adolf Hitler.

In *The Greater Trumps* (1932) the leading symbolism is the images of the Tarot pack. These are the archetypal images, which various events and characters in the book are seen as embodying. It is characteristic of Charles Williams's capacity to see the eternal in the commonplace, that the Emperor card (signifying eternal law) is here represented by the figure of a policeman holding up the traffic. *The Place of the Lion* (1931), the most brilliant, perhaps, of the novels, also deals with the theme of archetypal images. The heroine, Damaris Tighe, is a young lecturer in philosophy. She has made a study of the history of the archetypes in neo-platonic and medieval thought. But her approach is purely academic and intellectual. She has never envisaged her subjects as being living forces of the imagination. In the book, a group of adepts succeed in drawing down these archetypal images into the phenomenal world. As they appear they assimilate their ectypes to themselves, so that the destruction of the phenomenal world is threatened. They also appear to individuals as evil or good, according as they have been imagined. Thus it is that the Eagle (representing intellect) appears to Damaris, because of her failure in imagination, as something hideous and obscene — a pterodactyl, in fact. The process is finally reversed by the hero, Anthony Durrant, repeating the act of Adam in "naming the beasts" — that is, defining them by the particular qualities, and hence restoring the world as we know it.

Williams's last two novels, *Descent into Hell* (1937) (of which I have already outlined some of the main themes) and *All Hallows' Eve* (1945), are somewhat in a category apart. They are dark and difficult books, in which the sense of evil has become more oppressive, and the characters pass across the frontiers which separate the living and the dead. To break down these frontiers, as a final expression of his inordinate lust for power, is the object of Simon the Clerk in *All Hallows' Eve*. Clerk Simon is based on the figure of Simon Magus, the traditional founder of the Gnostic heresies, and is also an Anti-Christ figure. He has imposed himself on his followers, who blasphemously accord him the title of "Our Father" as a spiritual leader. He is certainly the most powerfully drawn, and the most wholly evil, of all the characters in Williams's novels. But the two principal characters of the book have already crossed the frontier Simon is trying to break through. They are Lester Furnivall and Evelyn Mercer, two young girls, killed in an air-raid on London during the war. The story is thus seen not from the point of view of the living, but of the dead. The two girls exist in some kind of intermediate state, just beyond death. But they progress to sanctity or damnation in accordance with the laws of their own characters, formed during life.

VIII

It will be seen that Williams's novels, in proportion as they become more serious, tend to push their subject-matter beyond the limits where the novelistic conventions can contain it. In the field of poetic drama, he was freer to be an innovator and experimenter in technique. His earlier plays, like his early lyric poems, have something of an air of pastiche about them. But the best of his later plays are wholly original, and will (it may prove) furnish many hints to younger writers who are seeking to grapple with the still unsolved problem of re-creating a living poetic drama.

The starting point of Williams's mature work in the drama is the same as Mr. Eliot's: a church festival drama, to be staged within a ritualistic framework. *Thomas Cranmer of Canterbury* (1936) immediately invites comparison with *Murder in the Cathedral*. Both were written for the Canterbury festival, and have a similar subject — the martyrdom of the protagonist. *Cranmer*, however, is more original in technique, allowing for a much wider presentation of the historical forces involved, and is further removed from naturalism. The greater complexity of the play is made necessary by the character of the hero. Cranmer's historical personality was more complicated than that of Becket. Becket's struggle with Henry II could be represented as a straightforward clash between spiritual and temporal power, and his martyrdom signalizes his final victory over the king. Cranmer, on the other hand, sought, up to the very last, to temporize with the secular power. The climax of his tragedy is his final acceptance of the suffering, which his character, naturally humane and gentle shrank from. This acceptance is symbolized, in the play, by the figure of the Skeleton, who partly acts as chorus. The Skeleton at first seems to represent evil, but is finally seen as the dark, reverse face of God. The Skeleton thus addresses Cranmer before his martyrdom:

> I am Christ's back; I without face or breath,
> life in death, death in life,
> each a strife with, each a socket for, each,
> in the twisted tear of good will, backward-running speech,
> the derision that issues from doctrines of grace
> through the division man makes between him and his place.
> Christ laughs his foes to scorn, his angels he charges
> with folly; ah, happy who feel how the scorn enlarges!
> I am the thing that lives in the midst of the bones,
> that (seems it) thrives upon moans, the thing with no face
> that spins through the brain on the edge of a spectral voice.
> Rejoice, Son of Man, rejoice . . .

In his novels, Charles Williams was sometimes tempted to represent evil in a melodramatic fashion. In his plays, in the figure of the Skeleton, the Accuser in *Judgement at Chelmsford* (1939), and the Third King in *Seed of Adam* (1948), it is much more subtly treated. The Accuser suggests the Satan of the Book of Job; he is God's minister, not his opponent. This series of characters may be said to culminate in the Flame in *The House of the Octopus* (1945), who represents the Holy Spirit watching over and guiding the Church.

All these plays of Williams are religious dramas, written for groups of church actors. But they are far removed from the sentimental conventions of the run of "religious drama" (which he is once said to have humorously described as "women with pitchers at wells"). Williams held that the religious dramatist must discover "those images of human experience in which the desired religious design can be so achieved poetically that what is 'palpable' to us is the poetic and not the religious purpose". *Seed of Adam* is a nativity play; yet it is the most original in technique of all his plays. In it, the ordinary categories of time and space are abolished, and the Nativity is depicted as an eternal, symbolic event. Adam is also Augustus Caesar. His numbering of his subjects is the desperate attempt of fallen man to overcome his limitation through exact knowledge. The first two Kings, the Tzar of Caucasia and the Sultan of Baghdad, represent human material and imaginative power respectively. The Third King (the one traditionally represented in iconography as an Ethiop) is the core of the apple which Adam ate. With him he brings his "little mother Myrrh", Hell, the worm in the core of the apple. She is a negress, who threatens to devour all. Only Mary can accept, and offers herself in love. Her birth pangs are represented by Hell's attacking Mary with her scimitar. But Mary breaks into the Magnificat till even Hell herself is compelled to join in the words "and Holy is His name!"

Judgment at Chelmsford (1939) is another example of Williams's power to transform what might be dead and conventional into something organic and exciting. It is a pageant play, written to celebrate the centenary of the foundation of the diocese of Chelmsford. It is so designed that small groups of actors from separate parishes may each present scenes of local history within an over-all framework. Nothing might be expected to be more banal or formless. As it is, the formal unity of the play is magnificent. The allegorical figure of Chelmsford comes to take her place beside the great sees of Christendom, but is met at the gates of Heaven by the Accuser. The series of historical scenes is then unfolded, moving backwards in time but in a logical progression probably suggested by

Dante's *Commedia*. First is shown the limbo of modern life, then the inferno of Matthew Hopkins, the early seventeenth-century "witch finder", and the Essex witches. We move to a purgatorio, whose climax is the martyrdom of the Abbess Osyth by the Danes, and hence to a paradiso represented by the legendary marriage of St. Helena of Colchester to Constantius Chlorus, father of Constantine the Great, which symbolizes the ideal union of Church and City. The play ends with St. Helena's pilgrimage to Jerusalem, and her finding of the True Cross.

IX

I come now to Charles Williams's sequence of poems on the Arthurian legend, *Taliessin through Logres* (1938) and *The Region of the Summer Stars* (1944). It is on these, I believe, that any claim for him to rank as a major writer must finally rest. This is not the place to attempt a detailed examination of these complex and often obscure poems. The reader is referred to Professor C.S. Lewis's valuable commentary, included, with Williams's unfinished prose study of the Arthurian legend, in *Arthurian Torso* (1948). I may perhaps be able to indicate their place in the tradition of English poetry, and touch upon some of their leading themes.

The "Matter of Britain" has, of course, ever since the Renaissance, continually suggested itself to English poets as the ideal subject for epic treatment. It is known that Milton, Dryden and Wordsworth all at one period of their careers contemplated an Arthuriad. But the only major poet, finally, to tackle the subject was Tennyson. Yet the *Idylls of the King*, though better than most modern critics will allow, are not the epic poem which Tennyson probably planned. For all their charm, they are remote and unreal; the characters are sentimentalized — especially when we think of the almost Homeric directness of Malory — and the morality is commonplace. A modern poet, attempting the same subject-matter, must first of all free himself from the Neo-Gothic and Pre-Raphaelite associations which inevitably spring to mind when the names of Arthur, Lancelot, Galahad, and the rest are mentioned. This Charles Williams has done; he has gone behind the sham medievalism of Tennyson, and even the genuine medievalism of Malory (who still remains, however, his chief source, though he had also read widely in the earlier sources of the Arthurian Legend, including the Welsh *Mabinogion*) and created a world which is completely his own. It is partly a world of timeless poetic symbolism like that of Blake's prophetic books, partly the world of the sixth century A.D., the world of the Byzantine empire, in which the historical Arthur is believed to have lived. In the preface to *The*

Region of the Summer Stars (1944), Williams writes: "Logres is Britain regarded as a province of the Empire with its centre at Byzantium. The time historically is after the conversion of the Empire to Christianity but during the expectation of the return of Our Lord (The Parousia)." It is this last which is, in fact, the central theme of the poems. It is signalized by the coming of the Grail. But owing to the breakdown of unity — the treachery of Mordred, the civil war between Lancelot and Arthur (owing to the former's adultery with Guinevere) — the historical process is reversed. "Logres is overthrown and afterwards becomes the historical Britain, in which the myth of its origin remains."

The symbolism of the poems is further explicated by the end-paper design to *Taliessin through Logres*. Here the Empire is represented as a human figure. The head is in Logres (Britain) for it is in Britain that the myth is to be enacted, and the historical process become conscious and articulate. The breasts are in Gaul (where Christendom is nourished by the milk of learning and culture). The hands, at Rome, symbolize the manual acts of the Pope, which are the acts of the Church (blessing, laying on of hands, etc.). Byzantium, the seat of the Emperor (who, Williams tells us, is to be regarded as Operative Providence), is the navel — traditionally the seat of the soul. Jerusalem is the genital organs — the place both of Crucifixion and Redemption. At the furthest remove from Logres (but nearest to Byzantium) is Caucasia, the buttocks — this represents the natural, but still essentially good, human functions. Beyond the Empire, to the east and south, is the antipodean empire of P'o l'u, where order gives way to anarchy. P'o l'u is not, Williams warns us, formal Hell, yet it perhaps represents as much of Hell as the finite human mind can conceive. To the west is Broceliande, which is both a forest and a sea, and beyond this Sarras the Land of the Trinity, to which the Grail finally departs. Broceliande, of which I have already had something to say, roughly represents the Unconscious (in Jung's sense). Its ruler is Nimue, the Lady of the Lake — who is the great goddess of Nature. On its confines is Carbonek, the castle where the Grail and the sacred Spear are kept. This is the castle of King Pelles, the father of Helayue, who becomes by Lancelot, the mother of Galahad. The establishment of Logres is due both to the Empire (the command of the Emperor) and to the powers of Broceliande — Merlin and Brisen (the twin offspring of Nimue), who are Time and Place, prophetically considered. Readers of Blake may find it helpful to equate the poetic geography of Charles Williams with Blake's "States". There is an almost exact correspondence between Sarras and Eden, Broceliande and Beulah, Albion and Logres, and P'o l'u and Ulro.

Within Logres itself, the working out of the myth is seen through the eyes of Taliessin, the king's poet. He represents the poetic imagination and is a *persona* of the author. He is "druid-born" but has become Christian. An early poem—(not included in the two series I am considering) tells us of his visit to Byzantium to request the Emperor to establish the kingdom of Logres. He is in love with Dindralne, the sister of Percivale, but they are separated, for she enters Religion. She represents the Negative way, as he the Affirmative. In contrast to Taliessin is the Saracen knight Palomides, who is connected with mathematics as Taliessin with poetry, and is the rejected lover of Iseult. He is in pursuit of the questing beast, one of Williams's subtle images of Evil. The beast appears at the moment when Palomides becomes conscious of the discrepancy between his ideal image of Iseult and her human imperfection.

> I heard the squeak of the questing beast,
> where it scratched itself in the blank between
> The queen's substance and the queen.

The beast leads Palomides into a sterile region, which has been compared to Eliot's waste land:

> When I came out of the cave the sky had turned,
> I have climbed since down a dead mountain,
> over fossils of space in the petrifaction of time,
> by the track at the slant-eyes' edge in this city of astrologers.

Here he learns to accept his own failure, and goes to be baptized:

> it was true I should look a fool before everyone;
> why not look a fool before everyone?

In the three poems relating to Palomides Williams explores a sceptical, intellectual consciousness which contrasts sharply with his "Romanticism", but is of importance in estimating his work as a whole. These themes (and others) are peripheral to the main one—the quest of the Grail. Galahad, who achieves it, and reaches Sarras, and the three other knights who are granted a sight of it, Percivale, Lancelot and Bors, like Blake's Four Zoas, partly represent the human faculties—spiritual, intellectual, emotional and physical. More importantly they are four ways of love—divine, virginal, romantic yet sinful, and ordinary married love. Bors is connected with economics and the providing of food. In *The Calling of Arthur*, where Arthur, at Merlin's (prophetic Time's) calling, overthrows the effete tyranny of King Cradlemas, and establishes the kingdom, we are told:

> Bors is up; his wife Elayne behind him
>   mends the farms, gets food from Gaul; the south
>   is up with hammer and sickle and holds Thames mouth . . .

When we remember that the poem was written in the thirties, the hammer and sickle reference must not be missed.

Taliessin through Logres forms a series of lyrics, written in different stanza forms, making a very original use of internal rhyme and alliteration. These poems belong to the tradition of the Ode rather than the Epic. The poems in *The Region of the Summer Stars* are described as "generally . . . incidental to the main theme". They are in the nature of straightforward narrative or monologue, and hence, once the symbolism of the earlier sequence has been grasped, are easier to understand. Charles Williams never really solved the problem of presenting a direct narrative in contemporary poetic terms (but I do not think *any* modern poet has solved this problem), but some of his dramatic monologues, notably *The Meditation of Mordred*, are remarkably effective.

> The nit-witted wittols of worldly wisdom tear
> their throats at the abolition of the Byzantine tribute,
> now the coined dragons stay in their pockets at home.
> Kin to kin presently, children; I too am a dragon.
> My father dwelled on the thought of the Grail for his luck,
> but I can manage without such fairy mechanism.
> If it does prove to be, which is no likely thought,
> I will send my own dozen of knights to pull it in.
> My cooks would be glad of such a cauldron of Ceridwen
> To stand by their fires — magic . . .

It is no accident that Charles Williams, like Yeats, but independently, seized upon the image of Byzantium to express the City. It was the union of sensuous colour with geometrical and abstract form in the subsumption of art and life into ritual, in the historical art of Byzantium, which attracted both poets. Williams's poetry may perhaps best be understood in terms of that art. It is non-naturalistic, mathematical and ritualistic. He never attempts particularities of descriptions of nature, or of human character. Yet human emotion is profoundly explored in his work. When we first open the Taliessin poems, it is like entering a Byzantine cathedral. We are dazzled by the profusion of colour and ornament, and at the same time, it may be, chilled by the apparent inhumanity of the figures which confront us. But as we become accustomed, we begin to see the magnitude of the structure, and the deeper humanity which is conveyed by the formalism of portraitures. And above all, everything is subordinated to one great design. It is the final purpose of all art — to praise:

The organic body sang together,
the acts of identity adored the Lord
the song sprang and rang in Byzantium . . .

Bless him in Caucasia, bless him in Lateran
bless him in the blazons of London-in-Logres,
bless him, praise him, magnify him for ever;

if there be worlds of language beyond Logres,
bless him, praise him, magnify him for ever;
if there be any wit in the rolling mass of waters,
if any regimen in marshes beyond P'o l'u,
if any measurement among the headless places,
bless him, praise him, magnify him for ever.

To me, at any rate, such articulation is that of a major poet.

[1955]

Cecil Day Lewis:
A Real Poet After All

L.A. PARSONS, introducing a selection of Day Lewis's poems, said of him, "quite early in his life he came to think of himself as first and foremost a poet, and thereafter he never allowed the exigencies of earning a living, whether as a schoolmaster, a publisher or a writer of detective stories to deflect him from his total commitment to poetry. But it also meant that he seized eagerly on every opportunity to write a poem ... " I suspect, indeed, that Day Lewis followed the advice, often given to poets, to write something every day to keep their hand in. It is very foolish advice, for as Keats said, "If poetry comes not as naturally as leaves on a tree, it had better not come at all", and we know that Keats was no lazy or slapdash writer. Far too many of Day Lewis's poems, especially those from the volumes published after 1940, seem to go to immense pains to say nothing very compelling or original. "Pegasus" is an example. It tells the story of Bellerophon's capture of the winged horse as we have all known it since boyhood, and the latter animal is made to speak the poetic moral:

> I am brute
> And angel. He alone, who taps the source
> Of both, can ride me. Bellerophon, I am yours.

Well, anybody who understands anything about poetry, knows that that is true. But how little, alas, does Day Lewis's actual work exemplify it.

In the 1930s, Day Lewis's name was inevitably linked with those of Auden, MacNeice and Spender. He espoused the left-wing principles of that group in a more committed way than his contemporaries, and seems to have been the only one of them who was for any length of time an active member of the Communist Party. I am still inclined to think that the poems he wrote during that period are his best. "The Nabarra" is an energetic narrative poem dealing in a quasi-epic manner with a naval episode in the Spanish Civil War. It is good, at least in the kind of way that Tennyson's "The Revenge" is good, and is a useful poem for introducing schoolboys to poetry. "The Conflict" is surely one of the classic poems of the thirties:

> Move then with new desires,
> For where we used to build and love
> Is no man's land, and only ghosts can live
> Between two fires.

One reads this poem today with a certain irony. Some of us, indeed, believe and trust that what it is saying is in fact not true, and that the only hope for survival of the values of our civilisation lies in avoiding precisely that political polarisation which the poem postulates. But if it were true, Day Lewis's subsequent progress to the establishment heights of the Laureateship offers a rather sour comment on it.

Day Lewis's juvenilia show that he early possessed a delicate lyrical gift, slightly old-fashioned even by the Georgian standards of the time. If it had not been for the influence of Auden, one feels that he might never have crossed the frontiers of the modern movement at all. His other most fruitful models were all late Victorian — Hopkins, Hardy and Meredith — though, of course, they are exceptional among Victorians for their intellectual awareness. Day Lewis was inclined to follow his models too closely, so that many of his poems are suggestive of pastiche or even parody. The early influence of Hopkins was often particularly disastrous, leading to such things as the notorious poem beginning:

> Why, seeing a communist, do we all feel small?

It is well-known that Day Lewis was also the detective story writer Nicholas Blake. One of Nicholas Blake's stories, *Head of a Traveller*, is about an eminent poet who has written himself out because things had been made too comfortable for him. He has a rogue brother who returns from abroad to destroy him, and he murders him. This tale would seem to have a symbolic autobiographical content of which the author must partly have been aware. Reading through the selection from the later volumes of Day Lewis's work one seems to be in the presence of a man betrayed by his own qualities of amiability — a combination of Anglo-Irish charm and English middle-class niceness. Day Lewis with his light tenor voice was an almost too mellifluous reader of his own and others' verse. He used the position of eminence that he had attained most conscientiously, sitting on I know not how many tedious committees for the promotion of the interests of poets and poetry. He accepted the Laureateship, which he held for all too short a space, as a further opportunity unselfishly to serve his chosen art — though his actual Laureate poems were a disaster. One could not help liking and admiring him; but where, one may ask, was the poet all the time?

For there was after all a real poet there. Of all his models, Hardy was, I think, the one closest to his heart. He shared Hardy's feeling for the timeless beauty of the English countryside and his courageous agnosticism — though Hardy's disbelief had a more tragic edge to it. Day Lewis on the other hand was incapable of that root of bitterness which sometimes poisons Hardy's verse. He accepted the transience of life and the transience of love with clarity and compassion. Of all his poems *An Italian Visit* is one that strikes me as in the main particularly unfortunate both in plan and execution. It reads like a tourist brochure in verse, for the most part. But at its heart is "Elegy Before Death", a poem of lucid and poignant beauty in which the same sense of transience is realised. "At Lemmons", written not long before the author's death, concludes on a note of quiet courage:

> Above my table three magnolia flowers
> Utter their silent requiems.
> Through the windows I see your elms
> In labour with the racking storm
> Giving it shape in April's shifty airs.
>
> . . .
>
> Round me all is amenity, a bloom of
> Magnolia uttering its requiems,
> A climate of acceptance. Very well
> I accept my weakness with my friends'
> Good natures sweetening every day my sick room.

This kind of purity appears less often in Day Lewis's work than it ought to, in what is, quite frankly, too large a corpus of work.

[1977]

■ Auden

Many of his admirers have objected that Auden revised too extensively and thereby spoiled some of his best-known early poems. The question of Auden's revisions and rejections is not solely I think a textual one. It is symptomatic of the author's own self-doubt, and his difficulties in finding a true poetic identity. He began as something of an *enfant terrible* and ended as a figure of the Anglo-American establishment. The consensus view, I suppose, is that he was one of the most significant English-speaking poets of the century, second only in importance to Eliot, and indeed, in the opinion of some, his equal or superior. I believe that this view very much overrates Auden, and that in a few years time he will be much less widely read and admired than he has been in the last forty years or so. For his own generation Auden seemed to personify all the youthful enthusiasms of the thirties — their revolutionary politics and psychological confusions:

> Now the leaves are falling fast,
> Nurse's flowers will not last;
> Nurses to the grave are gone,
> But the prams go rolling on.

This is, I suppose, typical early Auden, not least in its preoccupation with nursery imagery. In that, at least, he was consistent. The posthumous "A Lullaby" is to me quite embarrassing:

> Now you have licence to lie,
> naked, curled like a shrimplet,
> jacent in bed, and enjoy
> its cosy micro-climate:
> *Sing, Big Baby, sing lullay.*

For my part I was born a little too late, or too provincial in my education to have fallen under the spell of the early Auden. When I got to Oxford in 1939 he was definitely out of fashion with my friends and contemporaries. We were all for neo-symbolism or even the apocalyptic surreal of Dylan Thomas. I didn't even bother to read Auden very much at that time. I discovered him just after the war, and for me his best period will always be the forties and early fifties, with such poems as "Song for St. Cecilia's Day", "Atlantis" and "The Shield of Achilles". This we must now call middle-period Auden. It is the period of his early residence in America and of his recommitment to Anglican Christianity. He himself traces his own development in the following lines:

> When pre-pubescent I felt
> that moorlands and woodlands were sacred:
> people seemed rather profane.
>
> Thus, when I started to verse,
> I presently sat at the feet of
> *Hardy* and *Thomas* and *Frost*.
>
> Failing in love altered that,
> now Someone, at least, was important:
> *Yeats* was a help, so was *Graves*.
>
> Then, without warning, the whole
> Economy suddenly crumbled:
> there, to instruct me, was *Brecht*.
>
> Finally, hair-raising things
> that Hitler and Stalin were doing
> forced me to think about God.
>
> Why was I sure they were wrong?
> Wild *Kierkegaard*, *Williams* and *Lewis*
> guided me back to belief.

He goes on to identify Goethe and Horace as his final mentors. As for Goethe, that "purveyor of unusable wisdom" as Eliot, in a moment of irritation termed him — his shadow falls chillingly across the third and last period of Auden's verse. It seems to me that in his later years Auden virtually ceased to be a poet at all and became a writer of maxims and aphorisms — a few of them profound, many of them merely clever. I would much rather read his prose writings of this period, such as *The Dyer's Hand*, than most of his later verse. Like the passage quoted above, a great deal of this is couched in pseudo-classical metres. It would be charitable to call these Horatian. They derive obviously from the practice of Goethe and his German contemporaries. This procedure has always been quite disastrous when transplanted to English, and the Anti-Jacobin parody of Southey's Sapphics ought to have put a stop to it once and for all.

Auden was one of those writers of verse who was content to communicate in popular form not so much his own personal insights as the ideas and currents of thought, floating, as it were, in the atmosphere of his time. Such writers include Pope, Byron, Tennyson and Kipling. All of them fall short — yes even Pope, I'm afraid — of the very highest rank. From each of them, with the exception of Tennyson, the very name of poet has at one time or another been withheld. After all, the word "poet" does mean "maker". The highest and truest poets are creative and solitary visionaries who stand above and beyond the currents of their time. I believe that something of this quality did adhere to Eliot: to Auden it emphatically did not. Eliot spoke of poems as "raids on the inarticulate", and adapted with approval Mallarmé's phrase about purifying the dialect of the tribe. One could not possibly think of Auden's verse in connection with either of these concepts. His poems are not open-ended. They do not reveal new dimensions of meaning each time we read them, as truly great poetry does. As for his dialect — his diction is too often a mélange of schoolboy and undergraduate slang, vogue words, popular scientism and, especially in his last period, odd and archaic words quarried, one suspects, from dictionaries and paraded with something very like affectation. Although in his early period Auden was certainly affected by the fashionable Freudianism of his day, it is significant that he seems to have preferred allegory to symbolism, and rejected the ambiguous language of the unconscious:

> For dreams, I quite irrationally reproach You.
> All I know is that I don't choose them: if I could,
> They would conform to some prosodic discipline,
> mean just what they say. Whatever point nocturnal
> manias make, as a poet I disapprove.

But in a sense he also disapproved of poetry itself:

> Although you be, as I am, one of those
> Who feel a Christian ought to write in Prose,
> For Poetry is Magic born in sin . . .

Although Auden in his later years regarded himself as Anglo-Catholic, this view of poetry seems to derive from a very Protestant interpretation of the relation of nature to grace. In so far as it was not part of Auden's basic puritan heritage, he must have taken it from Kierkegaard and Niebuhr, and certainly not from Williams and Lewis. By the way, these do mean Charles Williams and C.S. Lewis, not William Carlos Williams and Percy Wyndham Lewis, just in case some reader has got it wrong — an all too typical instance of Auden's off-hand namedropping.

Have I been suggesting that this particular emperor, if not exactly starkers, is distinctly less adequately covered than anyone has hitherto presumed to point out? Well, I think it was about time someone did something of the kind. Yet, after all, when this has been said, enough that is memorable and beautiful remains and will continue to remain. There are the grave, finely turned baroque poems of the middle period which I have already referred to. But above all from among the undergraduate posturings of the early Auden there emerge the poignant moments of a pure and singularly personal lyricism. "Lay your sleeping head, my love" is surely one of the great love lyrics of the English language. It has a haunting quality, such as may spontaneously recur to the mind of anyone who has read it even in his own moments of intense passion. To have achieved only this would have ensured Auden some kind of immortality. So peace be to his sleeping head too.

[1976]

■ William Bell

WILLIAM BELL was born on July 1st, 1924, at Belfast, and came of Ulster Presbyterian stock. His boyhood, however, was spent in Derbyshire, where he attended a preparatory school and I think that the hill scenery of that county had a decisive effect on his poetic development. The son of a doctor, he went later to Epsom College, and proceded, in 1942, to Merton College, Oxford, where he was shortly awarded a Postmastership in Physics. He took his B.A. in 1944, and left Oxford to become a cadet in the R.N.V.R., serving in the Fleet Air Arm. This did not lead to his being sent abroad. Demobilised, as a sub-Lieutenant, two years later, he returned to Merton, where he now decided to read English. He had been writing poetry ever since his schooldays, and in 1946 he published a small collection of twelve *Elegies*. This, however, attracted little attention, except among his friends. He was happy at Oxford, for that city and its traditions meant much to him, and his vacations were largely given over to his favourite pursuit of mountaineering, which was finally to cost him his life. The sense of danger and of solitude which he experienced among the mountains is expressed again and again in his poetry. A skilful and courageous climber, in 1946 he had been awarded the Carnegie medal for bravery, when he saved the life of a boy trapped on a cliff-face near Arbroath. In the summer of 1944 he had fallen a considerable height from a mountain in Wales. He was detained for about ten days in Bangor Hospital with head injuries. This episode seems strongly to have affected his imagination, and from this time onwards the image of falling from a height occurs in his poetry with an ominous frequency. In August, 1948, he was holidaying, with three Oxford companions, in the Swiss Alps. On Sunday, the twenty-fifth, they set out to climb the Matterhorn. Together with Ian McKean, a member of the present party, Bell had climbed the Matterhorn on the same day of the previous year, when they were accompanied by a guide. On this occasion, however, they decided, in order to save money, to dispense with guides. After a partial ascent, one of the party, feeling ill, turned back. The other three continued their climb, saying that they would return that afternoon. They were experienced climbers, but, before they reached the summit, they also, as the evidence of their footprints in the snow later showed, decided to turn back. While descending they encountered some unknown obstacle, and, roped together, fell some three hundred feet to their deaths. On the following day a search party was organized. The bodies were discovered, in the deep snow of a ravine, by Swiss guides. Curiously enough, the remains of an unknown man, who had apparently met his death in 1936, were found in a crevasse a few yards away. The bodies of William Bell and his companions were buried in the cemetery of the commune at Zermat, where a stone, with the inscription, NON ENIM ACCESTIS AD TRACTABILEM MONTEM, has been erected to their memory.

My own friendship with William Bell began at Oxford in the winter of 1942. I had just graduated, and had a little reputation for verse-writing. The introduction was effected by a common friend, at a dance. We immediately settled ourselves in a corner, close to a barrel of beer, and began to discuss poetry. I already knew that he wrote poetry; he, too, knew of my name, and began by expressing a dislike of the type of verse which I and some of my Oxford friends were at this time trying to write. He asked me (this was always his opening gambit), "Did I believe in the Muse?" It was an axiom with him that the Muse, who personified the psychologists' Unconscious, was the source of all real inspiration, and that every true poet must have an objective belief in her. I answered yes, and asked him (probably rather pompously) who he considered pre-eminent among contemporary poets. Our fruitful differences of opinion began to declare themselves. W.B. Yeats and Ezra Pound were the particular objects of his regard. I also remember his making a strong defence of the poetry of George Barker. Years later, he told me that he had not really been well acquainted with Mr. Barker's work; his championship had been based on a cursory reading of a single poem. This surprised me, as I thought I had detected certain affinities between his own work and that of Mr. Barker, which at that time I was beginning to know better, and to admire.

It was only with difficulty that I persuaded him to show me his own poems. His aggressively confident manner, which antagonized many who did not know him better, concealed a real modesty and sensitiveness. He distrusted the "Romantic" formlessness which was beginning to be fashionable among undergraduate poets at Oxford, and still more the left-wing intellectualism of the nineteen-thirties. His own style had been formed by a careful study of Yeats and Pound. Later he was to pass, through them, to other models — Provençal, early Italian, and early English lyric, as well as, to some extent, Mallarmé and Heredia. By this means he gradually attained to an extraordinary eloquence and mastery over form. This is apparent even in his immature work, where, naturally, personal feeling plays a secondary rôle. He worked incessantly at his poems, and, finding little encouragement to publish them through the usual channels, altered and re-modelled them continually. This has made my task of selection somewhat difficult. The manuscripts which came into my hands after his death include material for a number of projected collections. The title, *"Mountains beneath the Horizon"*, which I have adopted for the present volume, seems to have been intended for a book of sonnets, of which he composed more than a hundred. His poetical experiments also include a sequence of "Elegies" (in Italian Canzone forms) dedicated to various friends, a very long semi-satirical narrative in heroic couplets, and a large number of shorter lyrics, classified as Albas, Ballades, Hymns, Eclogues, Ranting Ballads, and so on.

Bell's spontaneous and sometimes reckless eloquence was apt to betray him into an over-elaborate verbal ingenuity. His imagination was aural rather than visual; hence his feeling tends to express itself in generalized, emblematic, and apparently conventional imagery. All this may easily tempt the casual reader into the "stock response" of dismissing, as mere literary exercises, poems which are essentially alive and personal. Except for some of his later sonnets, his love-poetry is set in a Dantesque or Petrarchan mode. This is remote from what we expect in a modern poet. The personal experience, for Bell, forms the starting-point for a metaphysical exploration — but one which the early Italian or Provencal poets whom he studied would have understood.

Characteristic of Bell's work is a continuous and at times repetitive use of mythological imagery. This, at first sight, appears to be merely decorative, and not imaginatively organic. The images are drawn from the quasi-Pythagorean world of Ovid's *Metamorphoses*. Certain figures — Narcissus at the pool, the birth of Venus, for instance — had a particular attraction for him. But we may take them to symbolize the interaction between human and external nature, and the imaginative transmutation of one into the other. Prometheus bound to the Caucasus, Andromeda chained to her rock, are connected, for him, with the image of the Crucifixion. Dante's ascent of the Mount of Purgatory, and Petrach's climbing Mount Ventoux (which signalized the beginning of the post-Renaissance attitude to Nature, as something to be appreciated for its own inherent æsthetic qualities), are linked with his own mountaineering experiences. Behind his poetry there is a religious sense of communion with a sacramental Nature — such as he found expressed in the best of Wordsworth's poetry, and in the pantheistic prose of W.H. Murray (the author of

Mountaineering in Scotland, etc.) whom he greatly admired, and with whom he corresponded.

But though Bell tended to see all mythical images as expressive of truth, he was not a Pantheist, but accepted, without question, the validity of the Christian revelation, in which all the lesser myths find their consummation. In conversation and in argument, indeed, he could be almost Johnsonian in his dogmatism.

We are dealing with the fragmentary and unequal work of a very young man. But his letters, and a paper, read to an Oxford society, on Poetic Inspiration, show that he had thought to some purpose about his art. On the one hand, his poetry expresses his love of the inaccessible and the ideal — suggested by his mountain-imagery; on the other, a continual striving after technical perfection, and his sense of form and of tradition. The traditions of the Navy, and of Oxford, with her ancient civility and scholarship, the hierarchic principle embodied in English Churchmanship — these things meant much to him. From them he gained a profound sense of the nature of certain aspects of human experience. From the Navy, in 1945, he wrote:

> You remember Charles Lamb's holiday, and how he made himself unhappy by looking for happiness? That is itself a little difficult to understand, and maybe laughable when it is understood. But can a man treat his whole life like that? You must have heard —— say "Life holds nothing after forty" (which is rather a slander, by the way, on his dear parents)? Is it possible to look ahead for twenty years of declining youth without being sad? ...
>
> Indeed, one can have some consolation from the past. There is something imperishable, once, if you reflect that you climbed a mountain, and were happy at the top of it. That you have had friends whom you loved generously (and how few they are!) or that you produced a perfect line of verse ... Yet that consolation is the most dangerous of pleasures: you will never love a friend, nor write a fine line, nor worship the creation, for consolation. And I think that the real consolation is to be found by looking to the future. Particularly I remember —— —— ... He is a man who was never married, who has no children to perpetuate his exceptional mind; and a man who has no faith in the Atonement, and that method of perpetuation. But despite that, he has a dignity and assurance that almost convince me that these qualities, and his generous love for people, and all created things, are enough in themselves. ... His criticism of my work I respect, but no more than your own. It is himself I admire so greatly. And he is not the only man of the kind, though he is the most outstanding. I enjoy, often, the company of the fathers of my friends, and old sailor-men, and labourers, for the same reason. If you asked them the reason for

their contentment, they probably couldn't answer, or they might produce a string of platitudes even more elementary (though maybe more brief) than that which I am writing to you to-night. But it is easy to neglect the truth that is to be found in a platitude, even when it is a comforting truth.

I have mentioned the consolation of the past. And the consolation of the future. You know, I cannot help the feeling that when we cease to believe in the fire of Hell, and in the enormity of its torment, we lose one of the greatest aids to our happiness. The thought of that might make a man who was dying of a filthy disease praise God for another minute to complete his reconciliation. I suppose that a true love of God can do the same. It can only be one of these that can make a man endure the life of a hermit without complaining. Anyway, there is still a certain amount of comfort to be had from looking at either the past, or at the future. But it is looking at the present, which, you would expect, should complete one's happiness, that poisons it. Any pleasure at which we catch ourselves is at once unsatisfactory. How can I express it? If you are in a state of perfect physical comfort, and yet realise it, you will feel the unbearable itch: in other pleasures it is more complete: sometimes the view of your own mind when you are drunk or kissing a girl can be revolting, and even if the pleasure is perfectly innocent. Self-consciousness always evokes the mental counterpart of the itch ...

It is perhaps not surprising that the man who could write these words at the age of twenty-one, should seek a release from himself in violent physical and mental action. His death, only three years later, cut tragically short a talent which held a singular promise of development.

[1950]

III

■ Tasso's *Gerusalemme Liberata* as Christian Epic

Ariosto and Tasso are the two great exponents of the Romance Epic in sixteenth-century Italian literature. But whereas Ariosto represents the high noon of the Renaissance, Tasso's poetry is often described as signalizing its decline — a sunset, if a glorious sunset. More accurately it represents the transformation of the humanistic impulse of the Renaissance into that peculiar blend of humanism and a revived Christian culture, which found its most characteristic expression in the Baroque, and which was intimately associated with the Counter-Reformation. Tasso's *Gerusalemme Liberata* was completed twelve years after the closure of the Council of Trent. Its style and diction remain singularly lucid and pure and have little or nothing about them which can be characterised as baroque. But the ideals which inspire the poem, and much of the psychological treatment of its principal characters (especially the heroines) are largely to be explained in terms of post-Tridentine Catholic theology, devotion, and political aspirations.

By all those criteria by which poetry may be objectively evaluated, Ariosto must be accounted a greater poet — indeed a poet of a higher order — than Tasso. The *Orlando Furioso* exhibits that serene objectivity, that complete liberation of the pure creative impulse, which, in English literature, we find only in Shakespeare, and, on a smaller scale, in Chaucer. Ariosto is, perhaps, the most purely Latin in spirit of all modern European poets. For the English reader, there will always be something alien about him. For all his acknowledged and manifest greatness, he presents, as Mr. C.S. Lewis has pointed out, in his *Allegory of Love*, this paradox — his poetry seems to be lacking in just those qualities which Anglo-Saxon readers often identify with poetry itself. These are the Romantic qualities: fundamentally they are the appeal to the subconscious and the primitive, the evocation of the archetypes, and of racial and childhood memories. For Ariosto, in spite of his romantic subject matter, and his carefree disregard of the Neo-classical canons of form, is a pure classicist. A very good case could be made out for regarding Tasso

---

[The translation quoted in the text is that of Edward Fairfax (1600).]

as the first real representative of that Romanticism which, whether we
admit it or not, has come to dominate our whole present-day conception
of poetry. The sources of his sensibility reach far back into the ancient,
even the primitive world. But at the same time he anticipates, more
than any of his contemporaries, much that is characteristic of European
literature in the four centuries which followed his death.

I have called Tasso a Romantic. But it is important to realise that
the *Gerusalemme* is, with Camoens' *Os Lusiados* and Milton's *Paradise
Lost*, (and as the *Orlando Furioso* is not), in the central stream of devel-
opment of the Homeric-Virgilian Epic tradition, and that Tasso himself
was completely aware of this fact. The history of this Epic tradition
is to a large extent the history of European civilisation itself, and its
continuity, at least down to the eighteenth century, was never broken.
Such mediaeval Latin poems as Joseph of Exeter's *De Excidio Trojae*
bridge the gap which apparently separates the end of the classical tradi-
tion in Claudian from the Renaissance humanistic revival signalized by
Petrarch's *Africa*. From Boccaccio's *Teseide* onwards, the Renaissance
poets began to experiment in vernacular epic, conforming to the Virgilian
pattern, but incorporating material derived from the Mediaeval romances
of chivalry. The task of the Renaissance Epic poet was to re-interpret
the ancient, pagan themes and images, in terms of his own Christian and
Humanistic culture. In this he was assisted by the allegorical method
which he had inherited from the Middle Ages. Not only was an allegor-
ical interpretation applied to the texts of Homer and Virgil themselves,
but the Middle Ages had developed two characteristic epic themes of its
own — the Pilgrimage of Man's Soul from this world to the next, and
the Battle of the Virtues and Vices. As Dr. Tillyard has pointed out in
The Miltonic Setting, both these themes underlie the neo-Classical su-
perstructure of *Paradise Lost*, and this is even more true of the work of
both Camoens and Tasso, where it is, indeed, explicit. The fusion of
Epic and Allegory had already taken place in Dante, whose *Commedia*
on the one hand descends from a long line of Pilgrimages of the Soul,
and on the other derives from Virgil's adaption of Odysseus' descent into
the Underworld, which itself has a pre-Homeric history stretching back
to the ancient Sumerian *Gilgamesh Epic*.

It is easy to dismiss the allegorical interpretations, with which Ariosto
and Tasso glossed their poems, as *ex post facto* and poetically irrelevant,
even while admitting the significance of the allegory in Dante, and tol-
erating it in Spenser. It does not seem to add to our appreciation of the
poem to be told that Jerusalem stands for the civil happiness of Man,
that Goffredo represents the Understanding, and Rinaldo and the rest of

the Christian heroes other faculties of the soul. And when Tasso tells us that Ismeno and Armida are servants of the Devil leading men astray by false opinions, he appears to be talking nonsense. For Armida is ultimately converted, and baptized, as a result of her love for Rinaldo. But these interpretations are mere pointers, which enabled Tasso to tap deeper, subconscious levels of significance. Jerusalem as an allegory of Man's civil happiness sounds like a dead letter. But the Heavenly City is a symbol far more ancient and universal, common to the author of the Apocalypse and St. Augustine, John Bunyan and William Blake, and it is also to be found outside this Judaeo-Christian tradition: some of the Buddhist *mandalas* illustrated in Jung's *The Secret of the Golden Flower* are supposed to represent the plan of a Heavenly City. Tasso, like Virgil and many other great poets, possessed, I think, an intuitive grasp of the significance of such symbols. Modelling the incidents and characters of his poem closely upon Homer, he repeatedly handles his material in such a way as to suggest this primitive symbolism, yet re-stated in terms of his own culture and religion.

The Epic, as the European Homeric-Virgilian tradition has understood it, is more than just a long narrative poem with an exalted theme. Mr. Pound has defined Epic as "a poem containing history", and this at least makes plain one important element in a conception which, in its own historic development, has become highly complex. But it is not only that the subject of an epic must be one that is regarded as historically true by the audience to which it is addressed. The historical event of which an epic poem is the record must be one in which myth and fact are seen to coincide. The historical events themselves conform to a basic mythic pattern or archetype, such as is reflected in religious ritual and symbolism. The event is one in which the whole community feels itself to have participated, and which is the type and source of its present and future destiny. The part played in the consciousness of the Jewish nation in historical times by the epic theme of deliverance from Egypt and entry into the Promised Land, is an excellent example of this sort of historical myth. Indeed, the parallel between the story of the Exodus and the conquest of Canaan, as told in the Old Testament, and Virgil's *Aeneid*, is striking, if the leading motifs of both stories are briefly summarised. In both a Leader, in response to divine command, conducts an often reluctant people to a promised Land, where a great destiny has been prophesied for them, and which, tradition affirms, was the original home of their ancestors. Settlement in the land is achieved, with divine help, in spite of stiff resistance from the present occupiers of the land.

Halfway through the journey, the Leader comes to a place of initiation (Sinai, Cumae) where his mission and that of his people, is re-affirmed.

It will probably be objected that the above definition of Epic is applicable to the "literary" Epic of Virgil, and his Renaissance imitators, rather than to the "authentic" Epic of Homer. The tale of Troy, it will be said, was merely an incident in the overrunning of Minoan civilisation by the Indo-Germanic invaders from the North. The Trojans themselves were equally new-comers, closely related to the Achaeans; their relatively unimportant citadel has been identified and excavated at Hisarlik. It is a mere chance that Homer (whoever he may have been) has perpetuated this story, rather than many other heroic lays and sagas, now lost.

On the archaeological and historical evidence for this, I am not, of course, competent to pass judgment. But it seems to me that if the arguments advanced by Mr. R. Carpenter in his book, *Folktale, Fiction and Saga in Homeric Epic* will stand the test of criticism, we must look elsewhere than Hisarlik for Homer's Troy. Mr. Carpenter suggests (as a mere guess, it is true) that the historical basis of the *Iliad* may be the unsuccessful raid (recorded in Egyptian inscriptions) of the combined forces of the "Peoples of the Sea", of whom the Aikhawasha (Achaeans) formed a part, upon the Nile Delta, and that upon this distorted memory has been superimposed an equally garbled tradition of the expulsion of the Etruscans from Asia Minor, some two centuries later. Homer assimilates the manners and customs of his Trojans and Greeks, just as Mediaeval European Romance writers (to say nothing of so historically conscious a poet as Tasso himself) to a large extent assimilate the manners of Christians and Moslems. But it is surely significant that Priam, in the *Iliad*, is credited with the un-Greek (and un-Indo-Germanic?) practice of polygamy. Moreover I am convinced that the main outlines of the Trojan story derive (in spite of the historical verisimilitude which Homer gives to them) at least as much from a ritual and mythic pattern, as from any historical event. This pattern is the beleaguering of the fortress of the Otherworld, in order to rescue the captured, but ever-virgin, Goddess of Spring and Vegetation — a motif which appears in Mediaeval romance, and in folk-tales from all over the world, and whose ritual is perhaps reflected in the numerous "Troy" games of modern Europe, and others, familiar to our childhood, such as Prisoner's Base, King of the Castle, and Tom Tiddler's Ground. Similarly, I do not think that we are to seek for the origin of the Wooden Horse in some siege engine or battering ram supposed to have been used by the primitive Archaeans (as has been seriously suggested). Rather, is he not a near relation of the Hobby

Horse of the old English May games, and the Mari Llwyd of the Welsh midwinter festival described by Mr. Vernon Watkins?

If then we may believe *Folklore and Saga*'s guess is right, the history of the Epic, from Virgil onwards, will be seen to be a logical development of the original Homeric theme. I have said that the history of this development is to a large extent the history of European civilisation itself. It is the war of Europe and Asia which forms the grand Mythological theme, seen as the conflict of Reason and Passion, of an ordered civility, and formless, instinctive, destructive forces. Herodotus showed an apprehension of the same theme, when he began his history by citing the mythological stories of Io, Europa, Jason and Medea, Paris and Helen, as providing the clue to the wars between Greece and Persia. Xerxes is said to have made offerings at the tomb of Hector before invading Greece, claiming that the object of his expedition was to avenge Troy. Alexander, in his invasion of Asia, was clearly actuated by the same myth. In the *Aeneid* this theme is the struggle of Rome and Carthage personified in the reasoned *pietas* of Aeneas, and the orgiastic passion of Dido. After the Christian Middle Ages, in Ariosto, Camoens and Tasso, the conflict becomes that between Christendom and Islam. In Milton, it received its final universalisation as the cosmic conflict of Good and Evil. The historical myth becomes the original event of all History, in which is involved, not the destiny merely of a nation, an empire or a civilisation, but that of mankind as a whole. In accordance with this development, the character of the epic antagonist undergoes a corresponding development. Hector is just a hero on the other side, for whom we feel as much, or more, sympathy as for Achilles. Virgil's Turnus, though he has a legitimate grievance, opposes his own will to that of the gods and the destiny of the City. Tasso's Solimano is not only proud, but ruthless, passionate and cruel as well. His very name suggests the contemporary Grand Turk — Suleiman the Magnificent — seen as the potential antagonist of a re-united Christendom. All these figures culminate in that of Milton's Satan, who opposes his own individual will and pride to the Divine Justice itself.

Tasso's poem represents the religious and political ideals of the Counter-Reformation, as Milton's does those of Puritanism. Tasso's primary purpose is to exalt his patron, Alfonso D'Este, of whom his hero, Rinaldo, is the fictitious ancestor. But in choosing as his subject the First Crusade, he points to the ideal which was to haunt the mind of Catholic Europe right through the seventeenth century — that of a re-united Catholic Christendom, which should subdue by force the powers both of the Turk and of Protestantism. The Muse whom Tasso invokes:

O Musa tu che di caduchi allori
Non circondi la fronte in Elicona,
Ma su cielo infrai beati Cori
Hai di stelle immortali aurea corona—

[*O heavenly Muse, that not with fading bays*
Deckest thy brow by the Heliconian spring,
But sittest crown'd with stars' immortal rays
In Heaven, where legions of bright angels sing.]

— is by implication, the Blessed Virgin, whom the art of this period in particular delighted to represent as the Queen of Angels, the Woman of Revelation crowned with seven stars, as in Velasquez' *Immaculate Conception* in the National Gallery. The Muse of Milton is Urania, Sister of Divine Wisdom, or the Holy Spirit himself. Milton addresses himself to no patron, but to the individual reader. His theme is the temptation, and moral choice, of Adam and Eve (and also, the free choice for good or evil, of Satan and the Messiah). But I think the Puritan ideal of the Reign of the Saints on Earth also underlies his poem. This hope he had seen tragically deferred in the England of his own day. Hence, perhaps, the pressing need to speak of Man's disobedience and to justify God's ways. Milton's, alone of the great epics, has, on the human level, an unsuccessful issue.

We may now, I hope, begin to grasp something of the manner in which, both on the conscious and subconscious levels, Tasso approached his material. The choice of the First Crusade as a subject was as inevitable for him as that of the Fall of Man finally became for Milton. Its factual truth was unchallengeable; Tasso could draw on chroniclers like William of Tyre for the historical framework of his poem. But, even today, with our awareness of the mixed motives, and the frequent rapacity and brutality of the Crusaders, we can see the first Crusade as one of those moments in history in which historical fact and religious myth seem almost to coincide. How much more so for a Romantic Counter-Reformation Catholic like Tasso! Furthermore, the story of the first Crusade offered a fruitful analogy with the Homeric archetype in the *Iliad*. In both we have a siege, and an expedition of the combined forces of European civilisation, under a single leader, against those of Asia—its object, the capture of a city, and the avenging of an insult. The Cyclic poets who succeeded Homer, also showed the representatives of a legendary Further East— Memnon and his Ethiopians, Penthesileia and her Amazons—coming to the assistance of Priam; and Aladino, King of Jerusalem, is similarly assisted in tho *Gerusalemme*. Tasso was thus enabled to imitate Homer closely, but substituting a Christian supernatural "machinery" of God, the angels and devils, for the Homeric Olympians, and always revaluating his characters and incidents in Christian terms. But to this he added another, and very important element — that derived from Mediaeval Romance. It is this element that provides the greater part of what is most original and memorable in the poem.

In incorporating these Romance elements in a Classical Epic framework, Tasso was following the example of Boiardo and Ariosto, who, before himself, had both enjoyed the patronage of the Ferrarese court. But there is an important difference between Tasso and these predecessors. Boiardo and Ariosto say, in effect, to their readers: "These stories of Charlemagne and his Paladins — Orlando and the rest — are a fardel of Gothic nonsense and old wives' tales. They entertained a barbarous age, but intelligent, classically-educated people like ourselves need something a bit more sophisticated. But it will be fun to dress up these extravagant stories (and spin more extravagant ones of our own) with all the solemnity of Homeric and Virgilian epic machinery, and all the grace and polish of style we can muster. So we will have Orlando run mad for a princess of Cathay (who shall be a little like Homer's Helen, as well); and we will have a hippogriff, and a voyage to the moon, and a magic ring, and saints and angels and devils, and the Andromeda-story (set in the Hebrides) and — anything else you care to fancy. But it shall all be beautifully and graciously done — by no means a burlesque or a travesty." Matthew Arnold, who could not even see it in Chaucer, would certainly have denied "high seriousness" to Ariosto. In fact, Ariosto has the very highest kind of poetic seriousness. For, whatever the extravagance of his design, his characters are always convincingly alive, and he never departs from the truth of human passion.

The seriousness of Tasso is of quite a different kind. As we have seen, he is specifically a religious writer, just as Milton is. (This is not to imply that Ariosto is irreligious, any more than Shakespeare.) Tasso is incapable of humour — fortunately, unlike Milton, he does not even attempt it. His treatment of his material is innocent of irony. The Romance themes are grafted on to the Classical stock. The result is something new, yet wholly organic. This grafting was, of course, too much for the neo-Classic critics of Tasso's own day. In response to a good deal of academic brow-beating, he re-wrote his epic as the *Gerusalemme Conquistata* — from which the romantic episodes have been excised — performing on his own work much the same operation as, in the eighteenth century, Richard Bentley perpetrated on *Paradise Lost*.

Homer's *Iliad* forms the principal model for the classical part of the *Gerusalemme Liberata*, though there are also, of course, echoes of the *Odyssey*, the *Aeneid*, and, in the story of Clorinda's birth, of the *Aethiopica* of Heliodorus. (Contemporary criticism allowed Tasso to regard this early Byzantine novel as a kind of prose epic, and therefore a legitimate subject for imitation.) Many of the incidents, and most of the heroes, are closely imitated from those of Homer's poem. Thus Rinaldo corresponds to Achilles, Goffredo to Agamemnon, Aladino to Priam, Raimondo to Nestor, Boemondo to Odysseus, Tancredi to Tydides and Gernando to Ajax. Single combats and sorties by individual warriors, occur similarly in both poems. But Tasso continually transforms the pagan heroic values of his ancient models, to give them a Christian character. His heroes never boast of their lineage or prowess. Instead of mutilating the bodies of their slain opponents, or leaving them to be devoured by birds and wild beasts, they give them honourable burial. Virgil begins his epic:

> Arma virumque cano . . .

"Arms and the man" implying the self-sufficient pagan hero who gains his victory by simple force. In Tasso, this phrase becomes:

> Canto l'armi pietose, e'l Capitano . . .

The arms are dedicated to a religious purpose. Goffredo, the leader, owes his position to the unanimous voice of the Christian army. Unlike Agamemnon, his authority is never disputed. Calchas, in the *Iliad* is a mere soothsayer. Peter the Hermit, in the *Gerusalemme* has the apostolic authority implied in the Christian conception of priesthood. When Rinaldo is brought back from the magic island where he has been seduced by Armida, Peter the Hermit admonishes him:

> "Quanto devi al gran Re che 'l mondo regge!
> Tratto egli t' ha dall'incantate soglie:
> E te smarrito agnel fra le sue gregge
> Or riconduce, e nel suo ovile accoglie;
> E per la voce del Buglion t'elegge
> Secondo executor de le sue voglie
> Ma non conviensi già, che ancor profano
> Nei suo gran ministieri armi la mano;
>
> Chè sei de la caligine del mondo
> Si della earne tu di modo asperso,
> Che'l Nilo, o 'l Gange, o l'Ocean profondo
> Non ti potrebbe far candido e terso.
> Sol la grazia del Ciel, quanto hai d'immondo

Puó render puro: al Ciel dunque converso
Riverente perdón richiedi e spiega.
Le tue tacite colpe, e piangi e prega."

[*"Much are you bound to God above. who brought*
You safe from false Armida's charmed hold;
And thee a straying sheep, whom once He bought,
Hath now again reduced to His fold,
And 'gainst His heathen foes, these men of nought,
Hath chosen thee in place next Godfrey bold;
Yet may'st thou not, polluted thus with sin,
In His high service war or fight begin.

"The world, the flesh, with their infection vile
Pollute thy thoughts impure, thy spirit stain:
Not Poe, not Ganges, not seven-mouthed Nile,
Not the wide seas can wash thee clean again;
Only to purge all faults, which thee defile
His blood hath power, Who for thy sins was slain:
His help therefore invoke, to Him betray
Thy secret faults, mourn weep, complain, and pray."]

(Note that Tasso here speaks only of heavenly Grace; Fairfax gives to the passage a more evangelical emphasis, by speaking of Christ's propitiatory sacrifice.)

Rinaldo can accomplish nothing until he has formerly confessed to the Hermit, and has received absolution — confirmed in his case by a miraculous sign from Heaven. Previously, he has received a marvellous suit of armour and shield from an old magician, who allegorically represents Moral Philosophy. This old man is, appropriately, a converted pagan. He directs the knights who are searching for Rinaldo to a mysterious damsel, at once old and young, who will guide them. The latter is Philosophy herself, who appears in this young-old form in Boethius' *Consolation.* This incident, of course, corresponds to Achilles' receiving new arms forged by Hephaistos. But here it suggests the Pauline Image of the Christian's armour of Righteousness. Rinaldo's moral conversion precedes his Confession and Absolution. The whole episode is a clear image of the Sacrament of Penance, as conceived by post-Tridentine theologians.

But it is not in the martial parts of his epic, but in the various love-stories that are interwoven with them, that the blending of Classical and Romantic material is to be most clearly discerned. It is in this that the true character of Tasso's genius, and the nature of the transformation which he effected, declare themselves. His men are merely stock heroic types; his women are highly individualized characters, whose treatment foreshadows that exploration of psychology which was to be effected by the great French and English novelists of the succeeding three centuries.

Tasso was a South Italian, born at Sorrento. In temperament he contrasts strongly with the essentially masculine character of such Northerners as Dante and Ariosto. His poetry is marked by a *morbidezza* which, at times, passes into morbidity. I have termed him the first Romantic. He was also the first of the considerable number of modern European poets a large part of whose life was spent under the shadow of insanity. I do not know whether there is any modern study, from the clinical point of view, of the recorded symptoms of Tasso's madness. It may have been a cyclic insanity, of the manic-depressive type, such as afflicted Cowper. But the violent megalomania of Tasso's outbursts — so paradoxical in a nature essentially gentle and modest — perhaps point to the later effects of that syphilis which was sweeping through the whole of Europe in Tasso's generation. Tasso's biography gives evidence of a continual tension between an intellectual desire for conformity, and an emotional nature hyper-sensitive and essentially unstable. When he first felt the onset of mental illness, he voluntary requested the Inquisitor to examine him on the orthodoxy of his faith — in much the same spirit that, today, one might submit oneself to the surveillance of a psychiatrist. This tension might be taken as symptomatic of the split in European culture which both the Reformation and the Counter-Reformation signalized. It has left its mark upon Tasso's poetry. On its Classical side it has, as we have seen, a clear design and explicit purpose. But its Romantic elements open the door to a world where passion, not reason, holds sway, and where the images are largely derived from deep, unconscious sources. The enchanted grove, outside the walls of Jerusalem, which it is Rinaldo's mission to destroy, is such an image. The Christians wish to cut down this grove, in order to obtain timber to build siege-engines — a prosaic reason enough, which has, in fact, its basis in the actual history of the siege. But to prevent this, in the poem, the magician Ismeno has filled it with a multitude of invisible evil spirits. When they enter it, the heroes are beset by illusions. The branch of a tree, when cut, drips blood — a traditional motif, derived from Virgil, which Dante had also adapted in his description of the Wood of the Suicides. A myrtle, struck with the axe, groans with a woman's voice. Rinaldo himself finally encounters a spirit in the form of Armida, from whose enchantments and love he had only recently succeeded in escaping. This grove is, in fact, a fragment of the great Forest of the Unconscious — Dante's *selva oscura*, Broceliande, the Woods of

Westermaine. Its nightmare atmosphere powerfully suggests the delusions which Tasso himself suffered during his bouts of madness.

The original cause of the Trojan War was the abduction of a woman. That of the wrath of Achilles was a quarrel over a woman. Odysseus, seeking to return to his wife, was repeatedly detained by women, both mortal and divine. The love of a woman was the chief obstacle which delayed Virgil's Aeneas in the accomplishment of his mission. The resistance of Turnus arose from a slight about a woman. Yet Romantic Love is unknown in Classical Epic — at least in the form in which we conceive it. Romantic Love forms the second main theme of Tasso's poem. He writes as the inheritor of that tradition which arose as a secular ideal in twelfth-century Provence, and which Dante had succeeded in integrating with Christian orthodoxy. But in Tasso's hands it undergoes a further refinement, approaching the sensibility which we find in the later Romantic movement of the nineteenth century. Furthermore, it acts as a major transforming factor upon the traditional Classic themes and incidents.

Two of Tasso's characters, Odoardo and Gildippe, are actually married lovers, *amanti e sposi* — a conception which seemed impossible to the Provençal poets, and even to Dante. For them, the relation of the lover to his lady was necessarily a clandestine and normally an adulterous one. The quasi-Platonic idealisation which it involved might altogether exclude the possibility of physical consummation, and actual marriage between two lovers automatically terminated their former relationship. The appearance of Odoardo and Gildippe is, I think, the first instance in literature of a fusion between the Romantic ideal and that of Christian marriage. Tasso in his letters, makes it clear that Odoardo (Edward) and Gildippe are an English couple. It may be merely a coincidence, but the idea of the synthesis between Romantic Love and Marriage was to be largely developed in English literature. We may trace it from Spenser, Shakespeare, and Milton, through the eighteenth-century novelists, to its final flowering in Patmore and Browning. In French literature, this synthesis never really took place. This fact, together with an apparent lack of knowledge or misreading of English literature largely distorts M. Denis de Rougemont's analysis of the Romantic ideal in his *Passion and Society*. It is to be noted that Odoardo and Gildippe, as well as being married lovers, are also comrades-in-arms. In one sense, they represent the heroic *male* lovers — Achilles and Patroclus, Nisus and Euryalus — who present the real prototype of Romantic Love in Classical literature.

In the episode of Olindo and Sofronia, Tasso foreshadows another development of later Romantic sensibility. Aladino, the infidel King of

Jerusalem, accuses the Christians within the walls of stealing an image of the Virgin, which had been removed to a pagan temple. Sofronia, a Christian virgin, though guiltless, confesses to this act, in order to save her fellow Christians from the king's wrath, and is sentenced to be burnt at the stake. But Olindo, her lover who had previously concealed his passion, himself confesses — though equally guiltless — in order to save her. But the two are bound, back to back, to the same stake, and are only released at the intercession of Clorinda. Before this happens, Olindo looks forward with rapture to sharing the last agony of his beloved, while she herself directs his thoughts to Heaven:

> Ed oh mia morte avventurosa appieno,
> Oh fortunati miei dolci martiri!
> S'impetrerò che giunto seno a seno
> L'anima mia nella tua bocca io spiri:
> E venendo tu meco a un tempo meno,
> In me foor mandi gli ultimi sospiri."
> Cosi dice piangendo: ella il ripiglia
> Soavamente, e in tai detti il consiglia:
>
> "Amico, altri pensieri, altri lamenti
> Per più alta cagione il tempo chiede:
> Ché non pensi a tue colpe, e non rammenti
> Qual Dio prometta ai buoni ampia mercede?
> Soffri in suo nome, e fian dolci i tormenti,
> E lieto aspira alla superna siede:
> Mira il Ciel com' è bello, e mire il Soie,
> Ch' a sé par che n'inviti e ne console."

> [*"Yet happy were my death, mine ending blest,*
> *My torments easy, full of sweet delight,*
> *If this I could obtain, that breast to breast*
> *Thy bosom may receive my yielded sprite:*
> *And thine with it in Heaven's pure clothing drest,*
> *Through clearest skies might take united flight."*
> *Thus he complained, whom gently she reproved,*
> *And sweetly spake him thus, that so her loved.*
>
> *"Far other plaints (dear friend) tears and laments*
> *The time, the place, and our estates require:*
> *Think on thy sins, which man's old foe presents*
> *Before that Judge that quits each soul its hire,*
> *For His name suffer, for no pain torments*
> *Him whose just prayers to His throne aspire:*
> *Behold the Heav'ns, thither thine eyesight bend,*
> *Thy looks, sighs, tears, for intercessors send."*]

Professor Mario Praz cites Olindo's speech as the first clear expression in literature of the "Romantic Agony"—the identification of pain and death with sexual consummation, which he regards as a major theme running through the literature of the nineteenth century. But Sofronia reproves her lover in the words of orthodox Christianity. The whole episode recalls the method of the later Baroque artists, who loved, as Miss Mahood in her *Poetry and Humanism* has pointed out, to concentrate on the dramatic moment of martyrdom or conversion, when depicting the saints. The story of Tasso's own undeclared love for Leonora D'Este probably belongs to the realm of literary legend. But tradition may perhaps be right in reading a strong element of subjective feeling into the eroticism of Olindo.

But it is the three figures of Clorinda, Erminia and Armida, who are drawn, as it were, at full length. All three heroines are on the pagan side, but are brought at last, to Christianity, through the love of a knight in the Christian ranks. Their stories may be taken as three exemplars of the working of Divine Grace, which is everywhere the real motive force of the poem. Clorinda was born of a Christian mother, who desired her baptism. But this is unknown to her until shortly before her death. She fights bravely for the infidel side, where she mistakenly supposes her allegiance to lie, but is instinctively moved by pity towards the Christian would-be martyrs, Sofronia and Olindo. Tancredi, who has fallen in love with her, unwittingly kills her. But, dying, she is given baptism at his hands, and is received into Heaven. Erminia, a princess of Antioch, moved by the clemency of Tancredi towards her when he captured that city, has fallen in love with him, though he himself loves Clorinda. Her love leads her, though naturally timid, to venture forth from the "infidel" fortress to seek him. She finds him, and nurses him devotedly, when he is severely wounded in his fatal combat with Clorinda. It is implied that he will finally accept her love, and that she, also, will receive baptism. The enchantress Armida, on the other hand, fights deliberately against the Christians. She succeeds in seducing Rinaldo from his duty, but, falling in love with him, carries him off to her magic island in the Atlantic. When he deserts her, her love turns to hatred. She tries to kill him in battle. But in the last resort, her old love is too much for her, and her hand falters. She is overcome, and finally she, too, is converted, and becomes Rinaldo's wife.

Clorinda and Erminia are closely associated. They represent two contrasting types of heroine—the one daring and independent, the other gentle and retiring—whom we frequently find, as companions, in later literature. Clorinda is an Amazon. She derives partly from Ariosto's

Bradamante, partly from Virgil's Camilla. Behind Camilla is the figure of Penthesileia, in the Greek cyclic poets. Penthesileia was the Queen of the Amazons who came to the assistance of Priam, and was killed, to his own grief, by Achilles. Ultimately this figure is mythological — the Asiatic Artemis, the virgin warrior-goddess. Penthesileia's death at the hand of Achilles may be taken to represent the suppression of the ancient religion of the Goddess by classical, patrilineal Greek culture. It is a tragedy; Achilles's grief cannot be assuaged, and it is mocked by Thersites. But the synthesis of Christianity, Humanism, and the Romantic Love ideal which is brought about by Tasso, makes it possible for the Artemis image once more to find an integral place. Tancredi no less tragically kills Ciorinda, but she can also receive, through the Sacrament of Baptism, Eternal Life at his hands. Her reception into Heaven is confirmed by a miraculous vision.

Erminia, on the other hand, has no classical prototype — except in the scene where she names the Christian champions, for Aladino's benefit, from the walls of Jerusalem. This is closely imitated from the scene in the *Iliad* where Helen names the Greek champions to Priam. She is drawn with great delicacy and psychological subtlety. The description of the conflict in her mind between her love for Tancredi and her natural timidity, anticipates the technique of the psychological novelist. She is a creation of pure sensibility — in a sense the most modernly conceived of all Tasso's characters.

But it is the story of Armida into which Tasso has poured the richness of his sensuous and passionate imagination. A number of mythological figures are fused in Armida, though all of them ultimately derive from the same archetype: the Eternal Feminine, the White Goddess, the Anima — what you will. The final redemption of Armida represents the imaginative redemption of this figure in the cultural synthesis formulated in Tasso's poem.

On the one hand, Armida derives from Ariosto's Alcina, and hence, from a long line of enchantresses and Queens of Elfland in Mediaeval romance, especially Morgan le Fay, who detained Arthur and Ogier in her magic island of Avalon, and who is, perhaps, the Irish goddess Morrigu ("Queen of Nightmares") whose love was spurned by Cu Chulain. But the goddess Calypso ("She who conceals") likewise detained Odysseus on a magic island, where he spurned her love, and was only released through divine intervention. It is largely on Homer's description of Ogygia that Tasso has based his account of Armida's island, which was translated by Spenser when he came to describe Acrasia's Bower of Bliss. Armida, as an enchantress, is both Calypso and Circe. Circe was interpreted by the allegorical exegesists of Homer as representing sensual passion, which transforms men into beasts. But Armida, in her very human love for Rinaldo, also represents Virgil's Dido — herself a complex figure, partly based on Apollonius Rhodius' Medea.

As we have seen, Dido personifies the city of Carthage, as the historical rival of Rome, and representative of Asiatic civilisation. She is, in fact, Elissa, the tutelary goddess and legendary founder of Carthage. Aeneas' imperial destiny involves the destruction of Dido, just as that of Rome involved the destruction of Carthage. Virgil's treatment of Dido's story is touched with the feeling of guilt arising out of the memory of the destruction of Carthage and the guilt of a much nearer memory — Augustus' destruction of Cleopatra, whose empire represented a coalition of Asiatic powers. Tasso, in describing Armida's flight from the pagan ranks after their final defeat, actually compares her in an elaborate simile, to Cleopatra at Actium. Dido is the feminine image of all those forces which Roman civilisation was compelled to suppress — above all, female romantic passion. But such is the power of these forces, that she nearly succeeds in shattering the framework of the poem, and making Aeneas forfeit the reader's sympathy. As Charles Williams, in *The Figure of Beatrice*, has pointed out, in the *Aeneid*, the image of the Feminine is suppressed for the sake of the image of the City. In the *Gerusalemme*, where the image of the City is likewise the chief end of the poem, Dido is, in effect, redeemed.

When, at the behest of the gods, Aeneas determines to abandon Dido, she reproaches him with passionate eloquence, and he has no answer. They will never meet again, except in the Shades, where Dido will scornfully turn from her former lover. Armida's reproach to Rinaldo, when he is going to leave her, is a close paraphrase of Dido's speech. But Rinaldo's words to her are gentle and courteous:

> Poi le risponde: "Armida, assai mi pesa
> Di te: si potess' io, come il farei,
> Del mal concetto ardor l'anima acessa
> Sgombrarti; odii non son, né sdegni i miei;
> Né vuo vendetta, né rammento offesa:
> Né serve tu, né tu nemica sei.
> Errasti, è vero, ê trapassasti i modi,
> Ora gli amori essercitando, or gli odj.

> "Ma che? son colpe umane, e colpe usate:
> Scuso la natia legge, il sesso e gli anni.
> Anch'io parse fallii: s'a me pietate
> Negar non vuo', non fia ch'io te condanni.

Fra le care memorie ed onorate
Mi sarai nelle gioje e negli affanni.
Sarò tuo cavalier, quanto concede
La guerra d'Asia, e con l'onor la Fede."

[*"Madam," quoth he, "for your distress I grieve,*
And would amend it, if I might or could;
From your wise heart that fond affection drive;
I cannot hate nor scorn you, though I would:
I seek no vengeance, wrongs I all forgive,
Nor you my servant, nor my foe I hold:
Truth is, you err'd, and your estate forgot;
Too great your hate was, and your love too hot.

"But those are common faults, and faults of kind,
Excus'd by Nature, by your sex and years;
I erred likewise; if I pardon find,
None can condemn you, that our trespass hears:
Your dear remembrance will I keep in mind,
In joys, in woes, in comforts, hopes and fears;
Call me your soldier and your knight, as far
As Christian faith permits, and Asia's war."]

Ultimately, as we have seen, Armida is to be converted and re-united to Rinaldo. When we read the speech just quoted, we realise what the creation of the tradition of Christian chivalry has achieved. Rinaldo, in fact, behaves like a gentleman, and Aeneas doesn't. But the distinction must not be taken as trivial. Virgil, the gentlest spirit of the ancient world, whom Mediaeval tradition regarded, perhaps rightly, as a prophet of the Incarnation, nevertheless ends his epic with a hero who refuses to forgive a fallen enemy. Tasso's *Gerusalemme* ends with the grace which converts, forgiveness, and reconciliation.

[1951]

■ Leopardi as Poetic Thinker

LEOPARDI WAS BORN in 1798, ten years later than Byron, six years later than Shelley, and three years later than Keats. The year in which he died, 1837, saw the death of Pushkin. This chronology will serve to place him in that general movement of European literature which we may term Romanticism in the broad sense of that word. The qualification is necessary because the word Romanticism is employed in relation to continental literatures, including the Italian, in a more specialized way, to indicate a type of sensibility which draws its inspiration from the Gothic, the exotic, and the extravagant. In this sense, Leopardi is not a Romantic. He is indeed a Classicist. His poetry seeks its models in those Greek and Roman authors of whom he possessed a profound and scholarly knowledge. But one has only to think of the work of Keats, and of much else in the English Romantic tradition, and of such poets as Hölderlin in Germany, to realize that a nostalgia for the clear light and the pure forms of the antique world could itself be a feature of Romanticism.

Characteristic of the whole movement was the poets' recognition of their alienation. As the nineteenth century dawned, this was borne in upon them by the new currents of political, philosophical, and scientific thought. Everywhere the old patterns of society were in the melting-pot, and long-established ideas were being challenged. The poets could no longer be certain of their role in society, nor sure of their audience. They were therefore forced to rely more and more on particular inspiration, fitful and transient though it might turn out to be, and less and less on exterior sanction and occasion. Since the traditional forms of religious belief seemed largely to have lost their significance, the poets constructed their own systems, taking their symbols from revived mythologies, or from their experience of erotic passion or of natural beauty. This found a fairly superficial expression in the self-dramatization of such a poet as Byron, a profounder one in Wordworth's pursuit of a solitary communion with nature, or Keats's contemplation of sensuous beauty. But Leopardi, perhaps more than any of his contemporaries, goes farthest in the exploration of his own alienation. It is this which makes him in some ways a more modern figure than they, a precursor of the existentialist thought of our own age.

All Leopardi's work presents at one and the same time both a remarkable unity and a curious duality. He is, as we have said, at once a Romantic and a Classicist. He is even, indeed, an anti-Romantic. There is both the lyrical poet of the *Canti* and the hard dry prose writer of the *Operette Morali*. Yet the poems of the former and the dialogues of the latter frequently deal with common themes and complement and comment upon one another. In his verse Leopardi often handles many of those subjects which preoccupied the Romantic poets in general. The English reader may particularly be struck by the number of times in which his poetry suggests that of Wordsworth. This may seem a paradox, since Wordsworth is one of the most joyful of poets, and Leopardi the saddest. Yet it is nevertheless the case. For example, "Memories" presents a close parallel to "Tintern Abbey" both in its theme and in its structure. In each poem a scene is contemplated for what it now is and also in terms of the poet's memory of it at an earlier period of his life. Wordsworth's poem reaches its final note of hope in his invocation to his sister Dorothy. She is still in communion with that natural beauty with which Wordsworth himself will lose touch. Leopardi's ends with his despairing lament for the lost Nerina. The one poem might almost be considered as an inversion or mirror-image of the other. Again, Leopardi's Sylvia and Wordsworth's Lucy are parallel figures, not only pathetic images of girls who died young but symbols of something more essential which the poet himself has lost for ever. "Il Risorgimento" examines the central Romantic dilemma of the poet's relation to his own inspiration. So also do Wordsworth's ode on "Intimations of Immortality" and Coleridge's "Dejection". Wordsworth and Leopardi were, as far as I know, entirely unaware of one another's existence. But the fact that two poets so utterly different in background and in temperament should so strikingly approach each other shows to what an extent common experience underlay the European poetry of their day.

The Greek affiliations of Leopardi's poetry bring it into relation with other widely current preoccupations of his age. He is more truly a Hellenist than Shelley or Keats. We should think rather of André Chénier in France and of Landor in England. The latter was resident in Italy during Leopardi's lifetime, and it is rather surprising that he nowhere in his writings refers to the Italian poet. For these two have more in common than their Hellenism and their employment of the dialogue form (with, in each case, a debt to Lucian). Both are aristocrats; both seem to have held a kind of Roman republicanism as their political ideal, and possessed a contempt for the mob, as well as for the more vaporous enthusiasms of their age. When Nietzsche singled out these two, with Heine and

Mérimée, as the four greatest prose writers of the nineteenth century, he divined in them more in common than their stylistic purity.

In his poem "To Spring" Leopardi laments the loss to modern man of that mythopoeic view of the world whereby the Greeks were able to humanize the natural scene, and to feel at home in the universe. Thus also Keats lamented, and Wordsworth, that he could not hope to hear old Triton blow his wreathed horn. Thus also Schiller in his famous ode "The Gods of Greece". But above all it was Hölderlin who was driven by the same nostalgia to seek to reconcile his Hellenistic neo-paganism with the Protestant Christianity of his upbringing, before he was driven into the abyss of insanity. At one period of his life Leopardi made some approach to a similar attempt at a synthesis. From an early age he had been in revolt against the grim and life-denying Catholic pietism of his mother. But in later years he drafted fragments of an ode to Christ, and to the Virgin, in which he sought to rehabilitate these images in terms of his own subjective and Romantic myth-making. But such a solution, if it might be a solution, was not for him. His universe remains, as for his own Brutus, one in which human anguish has not dimmed the stars.

For Leopardi is not only the child of the Romantic movement, but also of the Enlightenment. The *Operette Morali* are essentially a product of the rationalism of the eighteenth century. Like the prose of Schopenhauer, the coincidence of whose thought with Leopardi's has often been pointed out, they are in the tradition of the French moralists of the preceding age — La Rochefoucauld, for example. Behind this tradition stands the figure of Pascal. Leopardi's English disciple, James Thomson (the poet of *The City of Dreadful Night*), devoted an interesting essay to a comparison of the nineteenth-century Italian and the seventeenth-century Frenchman. Of Leopardi it might indeed be said, as Baudelaire said of Pascal, that he carried his gulf with him wherever he went. Both possessed that terrifying experience of the empty interstellar spaces which finds expression early in Leopardi with "The Infinite", one of his best-known poems. For a religious mind like Pascal's this experience may be a preliminary stage towards a mystical purgation. For a mind rendered incapable by temperament or upbringing of entering into such a state, it can only erect a backcloth of total despair against which the human drama is enacted. Moreover, Leopardi's universe is perhaps vaster and in a sense more terrifying than Pascal's. The universe of Newton had expanded into that of La Place, for whom God was an unnecessary hypothesis. Thus in "The Broom" Leopardi speaks not only of the stellar universe as we know it, but also of the galaxies which lie beyond it. This vision is only just beginning to be accommodated to the general educated consciousness in our own day. Even more remarkably, in his "Dialogue between Copernicus and the Sun" he anticipates, however playfully, what is in effect the modern theory of relativity.

These observations may serve to suggest that Leopardi's pessimism has a wider significance than has sometimes been recognized. It has too often been treated as a merely subjective romantic melancholy which had its roots in the pathetic circumstances of his life. Not, of course, that a consideration of these is irrelevant to an understanding of Leopardi's work. It does not require much acquaintance with modern psychology to see that the child's failure to love and to be loved by his mother led to the man's projecting that maternal figure upon an indifferent or even hostile nature. It is the image of this indifferent nature which manifests itself in the colossal figure, like an Easter Island statue, which confronts the wanderer in the "Dialogue between Nature and an Icelander". Sometimes, indeed, Leopardi does suggest that there is a Power behind the phenomena of the universe, but an actively malignant one. As well as the poems he planned to Christ and the Virgin he drafted one to Ahrimanes, the Power of Evil in the dualistic system of Zoroastrian religion. That it remained unwritten is significant. A Satanist no less than a Christian answer would for him have been an over-simplification. It is here only that Leopardi comes near to the Byronic type of Romanticism, which in general he held in low esteem.

The characteristic setting of Leopardi's poetry is landscape transfigured by moonlight. One may surmise that his weak eyes and the fear of that scorn to which his deformed figure exposed him, gave him a preference for nocturnal excursions. But the moon, throughout Leopardi's poetry, is a recurrent symbol for that beauty which so poignantly touches the darkness of human existence. This beauty is mutable and transient. In his early fragment, "The Dream", Leopardi imagines that the moon might fall from the sky; while in his last poem, said to have been composed upon his death-bed, the moon finally sets for him, leaving total darkness behind. So it is also with Nerina and Sylvia, idealized figures of young girls loved at a distance, whose early death symbolizes for Leopardi the passing of youth and hope. In a later poem, "On the Portrait of a Beautiful Lady, carved on her Sepulchral Monument", Leopardi momentarily seems to suggest a quasi-Platonic view — that mortal beauty is a ray cast by an eternal splendour. But the poem ends with a paradox and a question mark.

For Leopardi the perpetual condition of man's existence is *noia*. This is a difficult word to translate effectively. It may literally be rendered "boredom" or "tedium". But in Leopardi's writings it assumes the quality almost of a metaphysical absolute which these words scarcely suggest. The French *ennui*, its etymological equivalent, gives a better idea of its scope, and it can be related to the use of the word "spleen" by English writers of the eighteenth century, and also by Baudelaire. From this condition man is momentarily liberated by the exercise of his imagination and his intellect. Thereby he apprehends the ideas of beauty, of virtue, and of love. But these are seen in the end to be mere illusions. Sappho dies an outcast from beauty, and Brutus cursing virtue; while in the most terrible of his poems, "To Himself", Leopardi records the passing of love, the last illusion.

It is from the apprehension of these ideas, however, that Leopardi's poetry takes its life; the fact that they are seen to be illusions gives it its peculiar lyrical poignancy. In the prose *Operette Morali*, which Leopardi speaks of as if they were (what they scarcely can be said to be) systematic philosophy, he embarks on the task of liberating man by demolishing his delusions one by one. For Leopardi, the ultimate wisdom to be gleaned from experience is that men fully conscious of their condition — that they are in a universe without God, where neither Nature nor Destiny is on their side — may learn to be more humane, in the solidarity of suffering. This is the moral of "The Broom", his longest and most ambitious poem, where Mount Vesuvius stands as the symbol for the destructive potency in nature, and the insecurity of man's lot. In this poem Leopardi pours scorn upon the nascent optimistic philosophy of Progress. It so happened that the year in which Leopardi died ("as if unable to bear the prospect", as Ford Madox Ford put it) saw, in England, the opening of the Victorian era, in which this optimism was to be dominant. In another late poem, his "Palinodia", Leopardi ironically parodies Virgil's Messianic Eclogue in celebrating the new Golden Age which England and her machines are to bring about. Its equivalent in prose is to be found in the "Dialogue between Tristan and a Friend".

The duality and the paradox then remain. To some, Leopardi's aristocratic humanism will seem sterile and reactionary; but to others he will appear the most essentially modern and clear-sighted, as well as one of the greatest, of the poets of his time. It is too facile to dismiss his work, as it sometimes has been dismissed, as merely the product of a sick body and a sick mind. It is of the nature of poetic insight to transcend such things. In reading his poetry we cannot fail to be moved by the pathos of Leopardi the unloved hunchback. But the impression which finally remains is rather of the gentleness and dignity of spirit which shines through all his bitterness and scorn of life.

[1966]

IV

The Astrological Basis of Spenser's *Shephearde's Calender*

It was about twenty years ago, a little after it had been published, that I read Professor Alastair Fowler's book, *Spenser and the Numbers of Time*. This study is primarily concerned with Spenser's use of numerology in *The Faerie Queene*. Alastair Fowler also convincingly demonstrates that there is an astrological symbolism running through the poem as well. *The Faerie Queene* as we have it, consists of six books and a fragment of a seventh, the so-called Mutabilitie Cantos. This is only just short of a quarter of what Spenser had planned, that is to say the first part of twelve books, to be followed by a second part consisting of another twelve books, making twenty-four books in all.

Fowler, to my mind very convincingly, demonstrates that the extant books of *The Faerie Queene* correspond to the seven planets, not in the order of their apparent distance from the earth in the Ptolemaic system but in the way in which they are related to the seven days of the week — a system which probably goes back to Babylonian times.

Book I, the Legende of Holinesse, corresponds to the Sun. It is full of solar symbolism; and the Red Cross Knight, who is St. George, the hero of this book, in some sense lives out the life of Christ, the Sun of Righteousness; while Una, who represents Truth or the True Church (in Spenser's view the reformed church) is the woman of Revelations, clothed with the Sun. She is also accompanied and protected by a lion. The Sun is, of course, the planetary ruler of the zodiacal sign Leo.

The second book, whose subject is temperance, is ruled by the Moon which acts as a mediating influence. The third book, the Legend of Chastity, has for its heroine Britomart whose name Spenser interprets as "the martial Britoness". She is therefore a Martian figure, Mars being the ruler of the third day of the week; but as a virgin warrior she also has characteristics of Pallas Athene, who, according to the system of Manilius, is the ruler of the sign Aries, more usually assigned to Mars.

[John Heath-Stubbs wishes to acknowledge the assistance of Annabell Kitson in the writing of this essay.]

The ruler of the fourth book is Mercury whose sign is Gemini. The subject of this book is friendship, and Fowler shows how the twins of Gemini are represented in this book by a number of dualities of friends. The book also closes with the revelation that Venus is in fact hermaphrodite, sexual love and friendship being ultimately the same. Hermaphroditus was the son of Mercury and Venus.

The fifth book is the Legende of Justice and corresponds to Jupiter. Artegall, the hero, has adventures which largely correspond to those of Hercules, Jupiter's son. The sixth book, Courtesy, is pastoral in character and very largely amatory so it naturally corresponds to Venus.

In the fragment of a seventh book of the Mutabilitie Cantos, the Titan Mutabilitie challenges the order of Jove, maintaining that everything lies under her sway. The reply that is given to her is that although things seem to change they move cyclically and eventually return to their original place. The fragment ends with a vision of the eternal sabbath. Saturn, the ruler of Saturday, rules the sabbath. Fowler also shows that Spenser was familiar with Ptolemy's star catalogue, and that the number of the characters in each episode corresponds to the number of stars in the zodiacal constellation appropriate to the book.

There is a difficulty, it seems to me, in fitting this convincing scheme into a system of twelve and, finally, of twenty-four books. I asked Professor Fowler about this and he told me that he was confident that this could be managed, using the very complex multiplication of spheres which later Ptolemaic astronomy — that of Spenser's time — demanded. I suggested to him that if his interpretation were right it would be theoretically possible to predict the subjects and scheme of the completed poem. I hope I am not betraying a confidence if I say that he informed me that he had made such a predictive scheme and had deposited it in the Bodleian Library, not to be opened until and unless lost books of The Faerie Queene should come to light. He believed it might be possible that some lost material might be amongst the Essex papers.

Helena Shire in her Preface to Spenser postulates a scheme similar to Fowler's except that she sees Venus as primarily the ruler of the third and fourth books, though joined to the influence of Mars and Mercury respectively. Frances Yates in The Occult Philosophy in the Elizabethan Age gives another scheme which takes account of the Venetian, Francesco Giorgi, and his "planetary-angelic-sephirotic" formulations which were influential in Elizabethan Neoplatonist circles (see especially her chapters 4 and 9).

THE SHEPHEARDE'S CALENDER

My reading of Alastair Fowler's book prompted me to wonder whether a similar scheme was not to be found in Spenser's earlier poem *The Shephearde's Calender*, published in 1579. There are two explicit astrological references in this poem in the August and November eclogues, but they are puzzling and will be considered later. Spenser has an astrological scheme in this poem and each of the twelve eclogues, corresponding to the twelve months of the year, contain references to the planetary rulers of the appropriate signs of the zodiac. In Helena Shire's *A Preface to Spenser* (1978), the woodcuts illustrating each month are reproduced, with the appropriate sign shown in the heavens.

First of all I should explain that the nature of this poem is a series of pastoral poems or eclogues. Pastoral poetry originated with the Greek poet, Theocritus, native of Sicily, who worked in Alexandria in the later part of the third century B.C. The majority of Theocritus' idylls are idealised scenes from the life of the shepherds in Sicily. (Sicily had been settled by immigrants from Arcadia and it is for this reason that the word "arcadian" has become synonymous with pastoral innocence.) Though idealised they also contain a strong realistic element. Later workers in this genre progressively moved it further from reality towards the portrayal of a purely imaginary and artificial world. An element of allegory entered in, especially with Virgil, whose eclogues had references to the political events of his own day, particularly to the death and deification by his successor, Augustus, of Julius Caesar. The form never wholly died out during the Middle Ages and was revived by the humanists of the Renaissance. Petrarch (1304–74) introduced into his eclogues an element of ecclesiastical satire, attacking the corruptions of the church of his day. This was a perfectly natural thing for a Christian writer of pastoral poetry to do, since both Old and New Testaments are full of pastoral imagery. Petrarch's poetry was written in Latin; so was Mantuan's, also an ecclesiastical satirist. Mantuan (1448–1516) was the favourite poet of Holofernes, the pedantic schoolmaster in *Love's Labour's Lost*. He was very widely read in Spenser's time, a standard schoolbook for Elizabethan boys and an influence on the poet. Spenser's English predecessors as pastoralists were Alexander Barclay (1475–1552) and Barnabye Googe (1540–94).

Spenser knew and used the Greek pastoral poets as well as Virgil, Mantuan, and the sixteenth-century French poet, Clément Mareau; but he claims as his English predecessors Chaucer, whom he called Tityrus, and

William Langland, "the shepherd who the ploughman played awhile". He also took the name of Colin Clout, by which he designates himself in his poems, from another English predecessor, John Skelton.

Nevertheless Spenser's poems are highly original. F.W. Bateson, in his *English Poetry: A Critical Introduction*, compares the importance of their publication with that of the *Lyrical Ballads* by Wordsworth and Coleridge in 1798, and T.S. Eliot's *Prufrock and Other Observations* in 1917. They signalled the beginning of the great flowering of Renaissance poetry in England as much as Wordsworth's and T.S. Eliot's initiated the periods of Romantic and Modernist poetry.

The Shephearde's Calender is accompanied by a commentary by "E.K.". Who E.K. was is a matter of controversy: some have believed him to be simply Spenser himself, perhaps Edmundus Calendarius, but others have supposed him to be a friend and colleague, perhaps Edward Kirk, which I am inclined to believe. It seems to me that E.K.'s point of view is not always the same as that of Spenser — for instance, he is a more extreme Calvinist than Spenser is. It would also appear, if I am right, that E.K. misunderstood some of Spenser's astrological references.

A novel feature of this poem is the assigning of the twelve eclogues to the twelve months of the year. The poem's title is taken from a handbook for shepherds translated from the French. Helena Shire describes it as follows:

> This was 'an old book', familiar to men of Renaissance Europe in print in many languages, in English *The Kalendar and compost of Shepherds, le compost et kalendrier des bons bergiers*. It was ... a handbook for everyman 'the shepherd', bringing together all he needed to know for his physical, moral and spiritual wellbeing. 'It gave a regime of diet for the season, a tree of the virtues and vices (with penalties) ... it taught him to find his way by the stars and showed in diagrams how his body was constituted and conditioned by celestial powers of planet or zodiac sign.'

Another original feature of Spenser's poem is the welding of some of the individual eclogues together by an ongoing story. This story has to do with the three-cornered relationship between Colin (Spenser himself), Hobbinol (his close friend, Gabriel Harvey, Cambridge scholar and Protestant pamphleteer) and Rosalind, who represents Machabyas Chylde, later to be Spenser's first wife. This three-cornered relationship, involving passionate friendship between men in tension with the love of a woman or sometimes two women, was to become a recurring theme in Elizabethan literature. We find variations of this, for example in Lyly's *Alexander and Campaspe* (1584), and in Shakespeare's *The Two Gentlemen of Verona* and *The Merchant of Venice*. Shakespeare's sonnets are highly original and doubtless contain an autobiographical element, but it is against this convention, I am convinced, that we ought first of all to read them before treating them as historical documents and endeavouring to identify the persons involved, as A.L. Rowse among others has attempted to do; his methodology seems to me to be extraordinarily naive in this respect.

THE TWELVE ECLOGUES OF THE SHEPHEARDE'S CALENDER

I shall now consider the twelve eclogues of *The Shephearde's Calender*, beginning with the January one and attempting to show that each of them has references to the relevant zodiacal sign and its ruling planet.

In January the Sun enters Aquarius, whose ruling planet is Saturn, the bringer of melancholy and old age. Here we have Colin as the lover afflicted with the lover's melancholy, which springs from the cold influence of Saturn and apparently affects not only Colin but all his flock.

> Such rage as winters reigneth in my heart
> My life-bloud friesing with unkindly cold;
> Such stormy stouures do breede my balefull smart,
> As if my yeare were wast and woxen old;
> > And yet, alas! but now my spring begonne,
> > And yet, alas! it is already donne.
>
> Edmund Spenser, *The Shephearde's Calender*,
> Januarie Eclogue, stanza 5

It will be noted that Colin seems also afflicted with old age, though he is in fact young.

The February eclogue is mostly taken up with the fable of the oak and the briar, which the old shepherd, Thenot, tells to the young shepherd, Cuddy, as a warning to him not to despise old age. The fable is attributed to Tityrus — that is to say to Chaucer — and is meant to be in Chaucerian style. The oak is the tree of Jupiter and the Sun enters the sign of Jupiter in Pisces. However, the oak here stands for old age, as does the speaker of the fable; and the briar has the brashness of youth. So the oak has Saturnian as well as Jovian associations. According to Lilly, all trees that are prickly belong to Mars, which would include the briar. This makes a link with the following Mars-ruled sign.

The March eclogue is closely modelled on a Greek original by Bion, one of the earliest followers of Theocritus, but it is transferred to a very English setting. Two boys, Willy and Thomalin, go beating the bushes which are as yet leafless, in search of birds; instead of a bird they disturb Cupid, who wounds one of them with his arrow. There are various mythological accounts of the parentage of Cupid, but that most commonly given him makes him the son of Mars and Venus. The sun enters Aries, whose ruler is Mars, in March and here we have Cupid the son of Mars, "all in arms".

In April the Sun enters Taurus, whose ruler is Venus. The April eclogue therefore continues and enlarges the love theme of Colin and his wooing of Rosalind. But Colin here is the youthful poet, not the afflicted melancholy lover of the January eclogue. His lyrics culminate in a song in praise of Eliza who is, of course, none other than Queen Elizabeth I. The song is one of the best and most successful of Spenser's lyrics. The Virgin Queen was never identified with Venus but with the Moon, Cynthia. The moon is in fact exalted in Taurus. The rose and the lilly, both flowers dedicated to Venus, are here associated with Eliza, the rose being the red and white Tudor rose and the lilly, or fleur-de-lys, representing the English sovereign's continuing claim to the throne of France.

In May, the Sun enters the sign of Gemini, whose ruler is Mercury. Spenser's May eclogue takes the form of a débat between two shepherds, Piers and Palinode. The occasion of their dispute is the May-day games which Piers — who takes his name from Piers Plowman — condemns and Palinode is prepared to tolerate. E.K. takes Piers to represent the reformed clergy and Palinode the popish clergy. But as I have already indicated, I think that E.K.'s point of view is slightly different from Spenser's, and that they should rather be identified with a Puritan and a moderate Anglican point of view respectively. The use of the débat form here suggests the duality of the twins. As in the fourth book of *The Faerie Queene*, this eclogue concludes with another fable, told by Piers. It is the story of the wolf and the kid, evidently a folk tale, with affinities with two well-known stories. One is that of the Three Little Pigs and the other the episode in Snow White when the evil queen disguises herself as a pedlar and tries to poison Snow White. It is a tale of trickery and theft, appropriate to Mercury, the patron of thieves.

In the June eclogue the love scene, Colin's wooing of Rosalind, continues, but as the Sun enters Cancer Colin suspects Rosalind of infidelity and his chaste passion for his friend Hobbinol now takes precedence over his erotic passion for her.

Hobbinol invites Colin to leave the hills, that is to say, Lancashire, for the dales or Cambridge, a watery spot which one may take to be ruled by the watery influences of the moon. There is a specific reference to the moon goddess in the following lines:

> But friendly Faeries, met with many Graces
> And lightfoote nymphes, can chace the lingring Night

With Heydeguyes, and trimly trodden traces,
Whilst sisters nyne, which dwell on Parnasse hight,
Doe make them musick for their more delight:
And Pan himselfe, to kisse their crystall faces
Will pype and daunce when Phoebe shineth bright:
Such pierless pleasures have we in these places.

The Shephearde's Calender, June Eclogue

The fairies are also associated with the Moon and moonlight. Titania, their queen in Shakespeare's *A Midsummer Night's Dream*, takes her name from a title of the moon goddess, who, according to Hesiod, was a daughter of the Titan, Hyperion. Keats knew this when he wrote in "Ode to a Nightingale": "And haply the Queen-Moon is on her throne, / Cluster'd around by all her starry fays."

In the July eclogue we come upon the first of Spenser's explicitly astrological references and at the same time on a puzzle.

And now the Sonne hath reared up
His fyerie-footed teme
Making his way between the Cuppe
And Golden Diademe:
The rampant Lyon hunts he fast,
With dogs of noysome breath
Whose balefull barking bringes in hast
Pyne, plagues, and dreery death.

The Shephearde's Calender, July Eclogue

Part of this is perfectly clear: in July the Sun enters the sign of Leo, and this constellation is accompanied by the two constellations of Canis Major and Canis Minor, with their principal stars, Syrius and Procaion. Syrius rises with the sun at this time of the year and these so-called Dog Days were traditionally supposed to bring fever and plagues and particularly rabies among dogs. But the references to the "Cuppe" and the "Diademe" are very puzzling. These can only be the constellations Crater and Corona Borealis.

The Cuppe and Diademe, be two signes in the Firmament, through which the Sonne maketh his course in the moneth of July.

Lion, Thys is poetically spoken, as if the Sunne did hunt a lion with one dogge. The meaning whereof is, that in July the sonne is in Leo. At which time the Dogge starre, which is called Syrius, or canicula, reigneth with immoderate heate, causing pestilence, drougth, and many diseases.

The Shephearde's Calender, July Eclogue, gloss by E.K.

Now the first of these statements appears simply to be wrong. The constellations of Crater and Corona Borealis are nowhere near the sign of Leo. Crater is a southern constellation and Corona Borealis, the Northern Crown, is a northern one. The eclogue itself is a debate between the shepherd, Thomalin, and the proud goatherd, Morrell, who sits at the top of a high hill. Morrell has been identified with Robert Aylmer, who had been among the Protestant exiles of Queen Mary's reign, was now the Bishop of London, and was regarded as a "proud prelate" and a suppressor of Catholic recusants and Puritans alike. The poem is a piece of rhetoric of a traditional kind, debating the virtues of high and low, valley and hill; Morrell cites various sacred hills, among which are included Latmos, on which the sun was supposed to rise.

> Morrell:
> Besyde, as Holy fathers sayne,
> There is a hyllye place
> Where Titan ryseth from the mayne
> To renne hys dayly race
>
> *The Shephearde's Calender*, July Eclogue

The poem concludes with an attack on the pride of the Roman clergy in particular. The theme of this poem is therefore primarily pride and height. If we think of the year as beginning in January, the transition from June to July gives us the central point of the sequence. Professor Fowler has shown in *Silent Poetry* that the mathematical centre of a poem written during the Renaissance period is liable to give us an image of the sun or of royalty, since the Sun is in the centre of the heavens and Christ, the Sun of Righteousness, was crucified in the centre of the earth. Thus the mid-point of *Paradise Lost* gives us the image of the Messiah and his chariot overwhelming the hosts of Satan. The mid-point of Gray's "Elegy Written in a Country Churchyard" is an image of inverted royalty: "Some Cromwell, guiltless of his country's blood." To these I would add among others Collins' "Ode on the Poetical Character", where the mid-point of the poem has the image of the "bright youth of day", that is Apollo.

Therefore, although we are past midsummer's day, I think that Spenser wanted us to think here of the Sun riding at its highest point, shining as it were in its pride and therefore as nearly as possible equidistant between north and south, that is to say between the southern constellation of the Crater and the northern one of Corona Borealis.

Professor Fowler, in *Conceitful Thought*, suggests the following solution to the problem:

A difficult passage: though Corona Borealis and Crater straddle the sun's ecliptic path, neither was in the July sign, Leo. (Crater was in Virgo, Corona in Libra.) Spenser follows an astrological schematic tradition such as Manilius' or Firmicus Maternus', giving paranatellonta or constellations that rise or set with the signs. Thus Hyginus *Poet. astron.* 3.4 connects Corona's setting with Leo's rising. According to Firmicus 8.10 and 8.11 Corona rises in 5° of Virgo, the sign to which precession had moved Leo by Spenser's time. Corona had moved too; but concerning extrazodiacal constellations Firmicus had the authority of literary tradition: c.f. the Sala dei Venti programme, in which Corona was still connected with Virgo . . . Spenser's 'calendar for every year' may even assume a poetical astronomy with constellations occupying their ancient positions.

The August eclogue follows Theocritus in giving us a singing game which is here converted into an English rhyme-capping game. The Sun enters Virgo in August and the constellation Virgo was often identified with Astraea, the goddess of Justice, who left the earth at the end of the Golden Age. Elizabeth was very frequently identified with Astraea and her birthday was in this sign. The planetary ruler here is Mercury and this I think may be the clue to Spenser's poem; the singing contest is in fact a contest of eloquence, of which art Mercury was the patron, and the presence of Astraea may represent the justice of arbitration. The September eclogue consists of a dialogue between Hobbinol and Diggon Davy. Ian Maclean in "Spenser's Shephearde's Calender" in *A Study in Elizabethan Allegory* identifies the principal speaker in this poem, Diggon Davy, with Richard Davies, Bishop of St David's, a prelate of whom Spenser and Harvey approved for his support of the "prophesyings" — free Bible-reading sessions of which the established authorities tended to be suspicious. A large part of this eclogue is taken up with an attack on the pride and corruption of the Roman clergy. It is a little difficult to connect this eclogue with the sign of Libra, whose ruler is Venus. I can only suggest that we should concentrate here not on the image of the planetary ruler, but on that of the sign itself, the scales. They may represent God's justice and in particular His judgement on a corrupt church. In *Paradise Lost* — and Milton was Spenser's greatest disciple — the sign of Libra is used as a symbol of God's justice when God hangs the sign in the heavens to put an end to the incipient conflict between the archangel Gabriel and Satan when the two encounter one another in Eden.

In October the Sun enters the Martian sign of Scorpio. This eclogue deals with "the perfecte paterne of a Poete". But there is particular emphasis on his ambition to essay poetry of a higher kind, epic or tragic:

Cuddie:
> O if my temples were distain'd with wine,
> And girt in girlonds of wild Yvie twine,
> How I could reare the Muse on stately stage,
> And teach her tread aloft in bus-kin fine,
> With queint Bellona in her equipage!
>
> *The Shephearde's Calender*, October Eclogue

Bellona, the goddess of war, was the sister or wife of Mars. We are to think here particularly of epic poetry, though the "stately stage" and the "buskins" point rather to tragedy. But epic and tragedy were essentially considered to be the same genre, differing only in that the one was narrative in form, the other dramatic. Since the time of Virgil it had become a tradition that the poet should start out with the humble form of pastoral poetry before passing on to the epic. Petrarch's eclogues had preceded his Latin epic, *Africa*. Spenser was to follow *The Shephearde's Calender* with his epic, *The Faerie Queene*. The tradition continues more or less with Spenser's successors. Milton's earlier poems up to and including "Lycidas" are all roughly pastoral in character. Pope represents himself as inheriting his pipe from Colin (Spenser). He certainly wished to proceed to an epic poem, though his projected "Brutus" was never written. Blake's *Poetical Sketches* and his *Songs of Innocence*, and Wordsworth's *Lyrical Ballads* may in some sense be considered as pastoral essays preceding an epic ambition. Many of Tennyson's early poems show the influence of Theocritus, but his own epic was in fact to be a series of idylls — the *Idylls of the King* — rather than an epic in the full classical or Renaissance sense of the word. The last of the poets in this tradition was W.B. Yeats, who tells us that his earliest work was a play in which he endeavoured to combine the styles of his two favourite poets, Spenser and Shelley. Fragments of this play survive as "The Song of the Happy Shepherd" and "The Sad Shepherd", the two poems with which his *Collected Works* opens. Epic, at any rate up to Milton's time, dealt with "wars, hitherto the only argument heroic deemed". Therefore Mars, or Bellona, the ruler of the sign of Scorpio, is naturally its patron.

In the November eclogue we come upon another explicitly astrological reference, and again at first sight it would appear to be incorrect. Spenser writes:

> Colin: Thenot, now nis the time of merimake,
> Nor Pan to herye, nor with love to playe;
> Syke myrth in May is meetest for to Make,
> Or summer shade, under the cocket hay.

> But now sadde Winter welked hath the day,
> And Phoebus, weary of his yerely taske,
> Ystabled hath his steedes in lowlye laye,
> And taken up his ynne in Fishes haske.
>
> *The Shephearde's Calender*, November Eclogue

E.K. adds the gloss, "the sunne reigneth, that is, in the sign Pisces all November: a haske is a wicker pad, wherein they use to carry fish".

E.K. is quite clearly wrong here, but was Spenser? The November eclogue is mostly taken up with an elegy for a lady called Dido. She has been variously identified, but E.K. says that her name is a secret. At first I thought it possible that Spenser had written this elegy earlier and incorporated it when he came to write *The Shephearde's Calender* because he wished to include an elegy in this eclogue since November is the month liturgically associated with the dead. The lady, I thought, might actually have died in February; Spenser had not noticed the reference to Pisces; for during November the sun moves into Sagittarius. But Scorpio would have coincided with the first days of November which would have included All Saints' Day (1 November) and All Souls' Day (2 November). That Spenser, in spite of his Puritan leanings at this time, was conscious of the ecclesiastical calendar, is borne out I think by Alexander's essay on Spenser's *Amoretti* in *Silent Poetry*, edited by Alastair Fowler. Dunlop points out that this series of sonnets is linked to the church's lectionary, as witness the most celebrated, "Sonett for Easter Day". So Spenser wishes to associate his elegy for Dido with these festivals.

We now come to the last of Spenser's eclogues, that for December. The Sun now enters the sign of Capricorn, whose ruler is Saturn. This links up with the first eclogue, the one for January also ruled by Saturn. In both of them we see Colin oppressed by lover's melancholy, and with a sense of old age. In the December eclogue he seems actually to have become old in bidding farewell to youthful pastoral poetry. The December eclogue in some ways anticipates Wordsworth's *Prelude* in giving, though in miniature, the growth of a poet's mind. It is noteworthy that two significant episodes in Wordsworth's poem, the robbing of the raven's nest and the plundering of the nut tree (although I have no doubt they were actual events in Wordsworth's youth), seem to be literary echoes of Spenser's poem. Spenser writes:

> How often have I scaled the craggie Oke,
> All to dislodge the Raven of her nest?
> How have I wearied with many a stroke
> The stately Walnut-tree, the while the rest

> Under the tree fell all for nuts at strife?
> For ylike to me was libertee and lyfe.
> *The Shephearde's Calender*, December Eclogue

For Spenser, in fact, is the great founder of a tradition of mainly Protestant visionary poetry which runs through Milton to Blake, Wordsworth and onwards to Yeats. It is also noteworthy that in this eclogue he refers to his own astronomical studies:

> I learned als the signes of heaven to ken,
> How Phoebe fayles, where Venus sittes, and when.

(The next stanza tells us that Spenser had also studied the tides, the "power of herbs, both which can hurt and ease", and soothsaying based on the flight of birds.)

The study of astronomy which included astrology was part of the quadrivium, so anyone who had been at university would have some knowledge of it; and to understand almost any poetry from the Middle Ages to the seventeenth century some knowledge of it is essential.

My own knowledge of astrology is very sketchy, and I have no objective belief in it; but I hope that the foregoing may have shown that such studies were very much integral to Spenser's work not only in *The Faerie Queene* but also in *The Shephearde's Calender*.

[1989]